CW00410202

# EVERYTHING
## YOU WANT TO
## KNOW ABOUT
# JESUS

## Other Books by Peter Downey and Ben Shaw

*Everything You Want to Know about the Bible*

# EVERYTHING
## YOU WANT TO
# KNOW ABOUT
# JESUS

WELL...MAYBE NOT EVERYTHING BUT ENOUGH TO GET YOU STARTED

# PETER DOWNEY & BEN SHAW

ZONDERVAN®

ZONDERVAN.com/
AUTHORTRACKER
*follow your favorite authors*

*Everything You Want to Know about Jesus*
Copyright © 2007 by Ozdad, a division of Sons of Thunder Press

Requests for information should be addressed to:

Zondervan, *Grand Rapids, Michigan* 49530

---

**Library of Congress Cataloging-in-Publication Data**

Downey, Peter, 1964 –
    Everything you want to know about Jesus : well . . . maybe not everything but enough to get you started / Peter Downey
and Ben Shaw.
        p.  cm.
    Includes bibliographical references.
    ISBN-10: 0-310-27337-4
    ISBN-13: 978-0-310-27337-0
    1. Jesus Christ — Person and offices.  I. Shaw, Ben (Ben James), 1968 –  II. Title.
BT203.D69 2007
232 — dc22                                                                                            2007011019

---

All Scripture quotations, unless otherwise indicated, are taken from the *Holy Bible, Today's New International Version*™. TNIV®.
Copyright © 2001, 2005 by International Bible Society. Used by permission of Zondervan. All rights reserved.

Scripture quotations marked NIV are taken from the *Holy Bible, New International Version*®. NIV®. Copyright © 1973, 1978, 1984 by
International Bible Society. Used by permission of Zondervan Publishing House. All rights reserved.

All rights reserved. No part of this publication may be reproduced, stored in a retrieval system, or transmitted in any form or by
any means — electronic, mechanical, photocopy, recording, or any other — except for brief quotations in printed reviews, without
the prior permission of the publisher.

*Interior design by Tracey Walker*

*Printed in the United States of America*

---

07 08 09 10 11 12 13 • 10 9 8 7 6 5 4 3 2 1

# CONTENTS

## STUFF AT THE FRONT

Foreword . . . . . . . . . . . . . . . . . . . . . . . . . . . . . . . . . . . . . . . 11

About the Authors . . . . . . . . . . . . . . . . . . . . . . . . . . . . . . 13
*Ben and Pete* **who?**

About This Book . . . . . . . . . . . . . . . . . . . . . . . . . . . . . . . . 17
*Will the real Jesus please stand up?*

Thanks To . . . . . . . . . . . . . . . . . . . . . . . . . . . . . . . . . . . . . . 21

## Part 1
## FIRST THINGS FIRST

1. If History Had a Fulcrum . . . . . . . . . . . . . . . . . . . . . 25
   *Introducing the Son of God*

2. Yeshua Ben Yosef ... Who? . . . . . . . . . . . . . . . . . . . 31
   *What's in a name?*

3. Strange Days Indeed . . . . . . . . . . . . . . . . . . . . . . . . . 37
   *Life in Jesus' day*

## Part 2
## WAITING FOR THE KING

4. I'm Just a Girl . . . . . . . . . . . . . . . . . . . . . . . . . . . . . . . 45
   *Introducing Jesus' mother*

5. "Honey, You Better Sit Down" . . . . . . . . . . . . . . . . . 51
   *Mary shares her news*

6. No Crib for a Bed . . . . . . . . . . . . . . . . . . . . . . . . . . . . 55
   *The birth of Jesus*

7. Angels, Shepherds and Evil Dictators . . . . . . . . . . . 59
   *People hear the good news*

## Part 3
## MAN WITH A MISSION

8. Rebel with a Cause . . . . . . . . . . . . . . . . . . . . . . . . 69
   *The start of Jesus' ministry*

9. Follow Me . . . . . . . . . . . . . . . . . . . . . . . . . . . . . . 73
   *Jesus puts his team together*

10. New Sensation . . . . . . . . . . . . . . . . . . . . . . . . . . 79
    *Jesus makes an impact*

11. Square Peg, Round Hole . . . . . . . . . . . . . . . . . . 85
    *Jesus' new way of looking at things*

12. Mustard Seeds and Lost Coins . . . . . . . . . . . . . . 89
    *Jesus uses parables*

## Part 4
## NOT OF THIS WORLD

13. The Return of the King . . . . . . . . . . . . . . . . . . . 101
    *The arrival of God's kingdom*

14. Wine, Storms and a Handful o' Fish . . . . . . . . . 107
    *Jesus did amazing things*

15. Be Healed . . . . . . . . . . . . . . . . . . . . . . . . . . . . . 115
    *Jesus' power over life*

16. Getting Tough with Evil . . . . . . . . . . . . . . . . . . 123
    *Jesus' power over the dark side*

## Part 5
## FOR MY FINAL ACT

17. Public Enemy Number One . . . . . . . . . . . . . . . . 131
    *Jesus' enemies gather*

18. Into the Eye of the Storm . . . . . . . . . . . . . . . . . 141
    *Jesus arrives in Jerusalem*

19. So Long, Farewell, Amen . . . . . . . . . . . . . . . . . . 147
    *Jesus' last evening with his friends*

20. Will the Jury Please Stand? . . . . . . . . . . . . . . . . 155
    *The trial of Jesus*

21. Long Walk to Golgotha . . . . . . . . . . . . . . . . . . . . . . . . . . . . . 163
     *The execution is carried out*

22. The Killing Tree . . . . . . . . . . . . . . . . . . . . . . . . . . . . . . . . . 167
     *Jesus dies*

23. Dead Man Walking . . . . . . . . . . . . . . . . . . . . . . . . . . . . . . . . 173
     *Jesus comes back*

## Part 6
## CHILDREN OF THE REVOLUTION

24. Upon This Rock . . . . . . . . . . . . . . . . . . . . . . . . . . . . . . . . . . 185
     *What happened next?*

25. So What? . . . . . . . . . . . . . . . . . . . . . . . . . . . . . . . . . . . . . . . 197
     *Following Jesus today*

## STUFF AT THE BACK

How Do We Know? . . . . . . . . . . . . . . . . . . . . . . . . . . . . . . . . 207
     *Jesus in antiquity*

What People Say about Jesus . . . . . . . . . . . . . . . . . . . . . . . . . 217

# STUFF AT THE FRONT

I grew up in church—mostly a good kid and all. Went to Sunday school every week from the day I left the nursery. So I heard my share of Bible stories; heard my share of Jesus stories.

One of my favorites is the story of Jesus walking on the water. I can still picture—I mean, really, I have the picture in my mind right now—the flannelgraph images of Jesus hovercrafting in his pretty blue robe across a glassy bit o' blue. (Flannelgraph, by the way, was the archetypal Sunday-school teaching technology back in the day: little die-cut foreground figures—people, boats, the occasional tree—with a felt backing that quickly and neatly stuck to flannel backgrounds with various nondescript Bibleland topographies. My mother-in-law still possesses one of the world's most complete collections of mint-condition flannelgraph paraphernalia. Seriously, her stuff should become the main attraction in a Sunday-school museum someday.)

Back to the hovercrafting Jesus . . .

In my frozen mental image, Jesus is white and nicely coiffed (seriously, when we reinvented Jesus as white, I'm surprised no one thought to reinvent his hair into a more churchy level of appropriateness—maybe a nice TV-evangelist combover). And he's scooching (seriously, *hovercrafting* is the best word I can think of) in the middle of day across an idyllically calm body of water. Sometimes, in my childhood image, he has one hand raised halfway, about chest high, in either a sort of blessing or a casual wave. ("Hey, dudes, relax; it's me.")

I'm sure that by the time I reached my teens, I knew this flannel-backed image of Jesus walking on the water wasn't quite accurate. But there it simmered, percolating in my spiritual subconscious.

I'm sure that, during my time at a Christian college and graduate school, I at *least* knew that Jesus wasn't white, would have walked rather than hovercrafting, and a few other tweaks. But I didn't let that spoil my childhood picture.

I'm even sure that after years of being a youth pastor and telling this story, I knew that there were more inaccuracies—like the status of the water. (I clearly remember a retreat speaker I'd hired doing the single worst rap I'd ever heard in my life about how the boat was buffeted by the waves: *b-b-b-buffeted . . . b-b-b-buffeted.*)

But I allowed my childhood image to exist, encased in psychic Plexiglas in the museum of my mind.

I remember—the experience more than the time and place—finally realizing, well into adulthood and professional Christianing, that the text clearly says the whole water-walking thing took place in the middle of the night (on a stormy night, at that). Of course, that would make a boring flannelgraph, since you wouldn't be able to see anything. And the water: it wasn't smooth and flat. These expert sailors—the disciples—couldn't get the boat back to land because a massive wind storm had come up and the waves were so pickin' big they were smashing the boat away from shore (*b-b-b-buffeted*). *This* is the water Jesus walked on.

So much for hovercrafting. Now I have to picture the real, dark-skinned, Middle Eastern Jesus climbing his way through the peaks and troughs of a wild sea storm. His clothing would have been drenched from spray. His hair would have been blown all over the place. (Where's a good hair-tie when you need one?) Now the scene looks more like a pitch-black episode of extreme bouldering (on water!), or like an X Games rollerblading competition at night, with Jesus grinding down the "rail" of one wave, hopping to the next, and dropping down into a trough to set up for his next trick.

Crash! The psychic Plexiglas around my childhood image is finally smashed. And now I can begin the reconstructive task of observing the *real* Jesus.

On a much bigger scale, and with lots more stories, this is what Ben and Pete accomplish in this book: smashing the psychic Plexiglas encasing all of our false images and ideas of Jesus. It's a noble work of deconstruction and reconstruction. Some might even say reimagining.

And whether your thoughts and pictures of Jesus are from childhood or from some other phase of your life, whether you have lots of ideas about Jesus or only what you've heard through hearsay, we all have some seriously jacked-up ideas about who Jesus was and is, and what he did and does. Pete and Ben are ready with their hammers. They'll lead you on a casual, blunt, and even whimsical road rally through ... well ... everything you need to know about Jesus. (Well, you know ... read the subtitle.)

—MARK OESTREICHER
PRESIDENT, YOUTH SPECIALTIES

It's important when reading a book such as this to know a bit about the authors. But the names Peter Downey and Ben Shaw probably mean very little to you.

If you typed our names into a search engine, you would immediately be in trouble because there are more than one Peter Downey and Ben Shaw in the world.

So for the record, the Ben Shaw who wrote this book is not Ben Shaw the painter, Ben Shaw the baseballer, Ben Shaw the professor, Ben Shaw the conceptual mime artist nor, obviously, Ben Shaw who went to the gallows for murder. Nor is he Ben Shaw the spokesman for the Church of Scientology. Similarly, Peter Downey is not an Arizonian professor of computer science, a Canadian forest ranger, a stand-up comedian nor the guy with a criminal record for smashing car windscreens with a bat.

So to business ... who are Peter Downey and Ben Shaw?

Ben was born in Vancouver, spent most of his life in Sydney and currently is living in London. Peter was born in London, spent most of his life in Sydney and has never even thought about going to Vancouver.

Their paths crossed for the first time in the mid-eighties in the backstage room of a rock gig, and they've been good friends ever since. Ben was playing in a band called In the Silence and Pete in a band called Priority Paid. For the next six or seven years, they played many concerts and festivals together and even journeyed across the Tasman Sea a couple of times to perform at large Christian music festivals in New Zealand. Little did they know as they sat next to each other aboard a 747 at thirty-five thousand feet that twenty years later they would be writing books together.

## Pete

... started going to church when he was sixteen, primarily as a way to meet girls. But what he learned about Jesus at church and from the Bible changed his life. Pete came to realise then that living Jesus' way made good sense. In colloquial terms, he "became a Christian". Over the next years, he found himself supervising Sunday school and youth groups, leading on summer missions and camps, playing in the aforementioned pretty-boy eighties Christian rock group and preaching. He went on to do bachelor and master's degrees, eventually becoming a doctor, although he is quick to let people know he is a doctor of education, not of medicine, because he lives in constant fear that at the theatre someone will call out, "Is there a doctor in the house?" and then he'll be expected to perform an emergency appendectomy right there in the aisle with nothing but nail clippers and safety pins. He has been a senior English teacher for over twenty years and currently is deputy principal of a large Christian school in Sydney, Australia.

Pete is married and has three teenage daughters. He has written three best-selling parenting and marriage books, as well as for a range of journals, magazines and papers. He enjoys playing guitar,* swimming, camping, spicy food, the beach, books and movies.

* And air guitar! I've seen him!          – Ben

### Ben

… grew up in the harbourside suburb of Mosman in Sydney and, like Pete, didn't start going to church 'til his mid-teens after learning about Jesus at school. His teacher at the time invited the whole class over to her home for "scones and Bible study". They, of course, went for the scones! But after hearing Jesus' story, he and a number of his mates became Christians. Shortly thereafter, they formed a rock band, not deterred by the fact that they couldn't play their instruments or read music. But they learnt a few chords, took some lessons and went on to make it their full-time careers for over five years. When the band folded, Ben started work for a church before getting his degree from Moore Theological College. He developed a keen interest in early Judeo-Christian and New Testament history and went on to pursue this at Macquarie University. Today Ben works as a curate at Emmanuel Church Wimbledon in London, and he continues to speak in schools, universities and churches. His Bible overview course (The Bible in Three Hours) has been run in Australia, Hong Kong, England and Ireland. He is married to Karen, and they have a dog named Bear. He still manages to play competitive cricket and soccer but enjoys just about any sport … and writing books with Pete.

** Ben wanted to do a complete history of the great Australian Christian rock bands of the eighties, but I talked him out of it.          – Pete

Pete and Ben's attempt to conquer the publishing universe began five years ago when they partnered to write *Everything You Want to Know about the Bible: Well … Maybe Not Everything but Enough to Get You Started*, which was published by Zondervan. And the rest, as they say, is history. That book was barely off the presses before they cast their minds to their next project.**

The choice was simple. One of the frustrations of writing their Bible book was that its key figure, Jesus, got only a few brief chapters. In sixteen pages, they had to summarise the life and teachings of the most important person in history. And they weren't happy about it. So the book you are holding is the result.

Happy now?

Good.

Turn the page and let's get started. No time to delay. Hi ho Silver! Tally ho! Stand and deliver! Awaaaay!

The internet provides a dizzying array of images of Jesus – cartoons, paintings, sculptures, mosaics, drawings, stained glass and stills from movies. It soon becomes apparent that Jesus exists in our cultural consciousness in many different guises.

In some depictions, Jesus is a smiling baby with blue eyes, a mop of blonde hair and a candlelike aura emanating from his head. He is lying serenely in a bed of straw in a picturesque nativity tableaux, surrounded by friendly barnyard animals who, to all intents and purposes, look like they are humming a jolly tune together.

But this is in stark contrast to the next image: a painting of a shirtless Jesus as a muscular Superman with a rippling six pack,* bulging pecs and highly cut biceps.

Some depictions of Jesus are more serene: Sitting quietly in a lush garden surrounded by vines and flowers (and, more often than not, a group of clean-cut young children of various nationalities dressed in little suits and party dresses), he is a soft-handed, milky-skinned metrosexual with rosy cheeks. Bathed in a shaft of light, he stares longingly and pensively up into the clouds as if trying to compose a line of poetry.

Some pictures show him as a ruggedly handsome poster boy. He is a tall and charismatic man with broad shoulders, piercing eyes, square jaw, perfect teeth and a purposeful expression.

This is quite a contrast to traditional Byzantine art, which presents Jesus as a glum, insipid, feeble husk of a man with drawn cheeks, a sour expression and weepy lost-puppy eyes. More often than not he has a fishbowl aura and is sitting on a throne. He is wearing a crown and a robe and holds up one hand regally as if he is pointing out something interesting he has just spotted on the ceiling.

Then there are the more bizarre depictions: Jesus as a giant intergalactic head looking down over earth, crying his tears through the atmosphere . . . a Jesus whose heart is visible through his chest . . . the ceramic figurine depicting a WASP Jesus playing with a little boy on a bike and a little girl on rollerblades . . . Jesus as a Lego figurine . . . Jesus playing a duet with Elvis . . . Jesus as a mysterious ink blot or image on a piece of burnt toast. The list goes on.

Far from being seen as a real person, Jesus exists in our modern collective psyche as a stylised caricature. We have sanitised him in pious jargon, wrapped him in religious baggage and framed him in stained glass. Like a

> * Hey, you mean just like me? — Pete
>
> In your dreams, buddy! — Ben

> It soon becomes apparent that Jesus exists in our cultural consciousness in many different guises.

We have sanitised Jesus in pious jargon, wrapped him in religious baggage and framed him in stained glass.

ship adrift on the ocean, he has floated through the centuries picking up the barnacles of religion along the way so that now, Jesus is like a sort of religious cardboard cutout who swans across the biblical landscape dispensing greeting-card advice, goody-goody epigrams and Christian sound bites. He has ceased to be a real person.

Many people have only a bitsy, patchwork-quilt knowledge of Jesus, an amalgam of ideas loosely remembered from Sunday school stories and Christmas pageants. They have constructed their picture of Jesus in the same way a child might create a collage face out of magazine cutouts. They've grabbed a bit from here and a bit from there and slapped them together to create … hey presto … Jesus! They've seen Christmas cards showing gentle baby Jesus. They remember a snippet of a children's prayer in which he is "meek and mild". They remember some of the songs from *Jesus Christ Superstar* and *Godspell*. Oh … don't forget that scene in *Life of Brian* in which he stood in the background lecturing people about "the blessed cheesemakers". There is a vague string of anecdotes and half-remembered stories: something about him walking on water, turning water into wine, healing a blind man, smashing up tables in a fit of rage … and they just watched the DVD of *The Passion of the Christ*.

Just about everyone, it seems, has an opinion about Jesus. Some say that he was a moralist, a great orator and teacher, or a revolutionary, a prophet, a healer; some say he was a magician or sorcerer, while others are happy to categorise him as just a good bloke[*] but nothing more. Then there are others who would argue that he was deeply misunderstood, that the Jesus who is portrayed by mainstream Christianity is an amalgam of history and tradition and is in fact not the real Jesus of the first century at all. There are even those who say he is just a myth, a fictitious product, in the same ballpark as Santa, the tooth fairy, Alice in Wonderland or Frodo Baggins. Actor and director Mel Gibson summed it up well when he said, "Growing up as a kid, [the story of Jesus] had always been sanitised and not real, like a fairy tale. It sort of struck me that it really happened, the Word of God tells you it happened, and it's backed up by every kind of historical detail."[1]

When we (Ben and Pete) were growing up, we had our own ideas about who Jesus is. Ben never went to church and so first learnt about Jesus through Easter movies and the occasional lesson at school. For him Jesus was just a nice blue-eyed, blonde-haired hippy who spoke about love and picked flowers. He existed in history but was pretty irrelevant to anyone in today's world … or so he thought.

As a kid, Pete went to Sunday school, where he spent most of his time colouring in worksheets of Jesus performing miracles. Jesus, therefore, was a sev-

*Aussie talk for "man" or "ordinary guy".

---

1. Ken Duncan, *The Passion: Lessons from the Life of Christ* (Wamberal: Ken Duncan Panographs, 2004), 70.

enties peace activist with a Cheshire cat grin, a groovy headband and – for some reason – always one thumb up and a winking eye as if he were saying, "Hey, dude … leprosy be gone, man! Wow! Check me out! Keep on truckin'. Yeah!"

If we are to sharpen our understanding of Jesus, we need to leave our preconceptions at the door and start from scratch.

And that's why we wrote this book. It's our humble (albeit somewhat presumptuous) attempt to look at Jesus with fresh eyes. We are under no delusions about the limitations of our book. It is not "the definitive work" on Jesus – it's laughable to think it even comes close. But hopefully it plays its part. In addition, we acknowledge the literary theory that says that, to a degree, all interpretation is perspective-bound. This book is a product of the lives and times of the authors, and we can *never* fully detach ourselves from the cultural filter through which we understand the world.

Of course, it's one thing to have such grandiose intentions, but it's another to actually do it. We discussed a number of different approaches but in the end received our inspiration from the humble cow.

*Huh?*

When you go to the butcher and look up on the wall, there's a poster of a cow in profile, divided up like an old Soviet map into its constituent meaty parts. These dislocated cow bits do not exist in isolation. Like pieces of a jigsaw, they are individual units. But it is only when they join together that their purpose is revealed and the whole picture is formed. In our bovine analogy, while we may understand the shank, tenderloin, rib eye, flank, chuck, rib, plate, brisket and short loin to be separate parts, it is only when they are together that you achieve a unity of cowness. *

What we are trying to say is that while we have kept to a rough chronology, we have also tried to focus on individual themes and movements in Jesus' life and ministry. But each of these in isolation gives us only a part of the overall picture they form when they come together to give us an understanding of who Jesus is and what he did.

The short of it is that the book is in six main parts:

**Part 1 ("First Things First")** sets the scene for us before we begin.

**Part 2 ("Waiting for the King")** looks at what was going on around the time Jesus was born.

**Part 3 ("Man with a Mission")** takes us through the adult life and ministry of Jesus.

**Part 4 ("Not of This World")** explores the miraculous things that Jesus did.

**Part 5 ("For My Final Act")** looks at the end of Jesus' life as he was convicted and executed, and then as he returned from death to life.

> If we are to sharpen our understanding of Jesus, we need to leave our preconceptions at the door and start from scratch.

> * I'm confused. Is the jigsaw a picture of a cow?
> – Ben

**Part 6 ("Children of the Revolution")** explores what happened after Jesus, including what it means to follow him today.

Of course, more books have been written about Jesus than about any other person or topic in history. Every single word of the Gospels and everything Jesus ever said and did has already been picked apart, turned inside out, chewed over, translated, examined, dissected, twisted, stretched, regurgitated, interpreted, pasteurised and buried in compost. There are innumerable doctoral dissertations, lecture series, sermons, articles, podcasts, concordances and entire wings of libraries filled with books about Jesus that are so big they would break bones in your foot if you dropped one on it. Many of these writings dive into the depths of Jesus' life. This book, on the other hand, is an overview, more like a rock skimming across the surface of this most important figure of world history.

This is not an academic treatise. We are not interested in radical interpretations, theological debates, controversial issues or creating our own zany theories (ie: Jesus was a travelling circus performer from Italy with seven wives). This is not that kind of book.[*]

When Pete was at Uni, he had a mate[**] who crammed for a history exam not by reading the required text but by reading a set of crib notes. Now, crib notes are a good springboard into a topic, but they are certainly no substitute for the real deal, as Pete's friend discovered when he got his marks back.[***] (The five bullet points he memorised did little to help him prepare for an extended argument relating to reasons for the decline of the Roman Empire!) This book is an introduction to Jesus and in no way is to be considered a replacement for actually reading the original writings about him in the books of Matthew, Mark, Luke and John in the Bible.

This book is simply a springboard from which to dive headfirst into the life of Jesus. We hope it will help you gain an understanding of Jesus and who he is and what he said and what he did. We hope you will get an understanding of his place in history and in the culture of his time. We hope you will get a broader picture of Jesus so that you can read about him with more understanding. And most of all, we hope that Jesus' life and message will change your life.

Hopefully you will come to see that Jesus is not just a baby in a manger or a po-faced sanctimonious preacher spouting desktop-calendar wisdom. And hopefully you will see that even two thousand years later in this hectic age of instant communication, MP3 players, MTV, high divorce rates, multinational corporations, reality TV, terrorism, globalisation, the international space station, global warming and dial-a-pizza, he is someone who is relevant and powerful today. No other person in human history even comes close to him.

So enough of this banter. Let's get on with it. Let's look at Jesus: who he is, what he said, what he did, what it all means anyway. Let's look at everything you want to know about Jesus. Well … maybe not everything, but enough to get you started.

* And also, we are pretty lazy.      – Ben

** Aussie talk for "friend".

*** Fess up, Pete. It was you, wasn't it?      – Ben

No, it most certainly was not me. Well, not really. I mean … yes.      – Pete

The Academy Awards is an annual spectacular recognizing actors and production crews for their contributions to the film industry. There are many high points in the evening, such as movie montages and tributes, theme songs performed by legendary musicians, the tension of finding out who won what and, for some viewers, what the stars are wearing.

But the low point of each night must surely be the uncontrollable ramblings of exuberant award-winners as they machine-gun through seemingly endless lists of thank-yous, the names of whom are meaningless to the billions of us watching. They may as well be reading out the ingredients from a cereal box.

So at the risk of sounding hypocritical … this is where we thank the people we want to thank, even though their names will mean little to you. Appreciate your reading this, but feel free to turn the page and move on. No, really.

## Pete

I want to thank my wife, Meredith, and my three kids, Rachael, Georgia and Matilda, for their patience, perseverance and constant supplies of hot chocolate and raisin toast when I locked myself in the study with the laptop. Thanks to my parents for (a) making me go to church as a teenager and (b) engendering in me a love of writing. Thanks to all the friends who have journeyed with me over the years through countless Bible studies and services, and of course to the Bible teachers, pastors, ministers, speakers, authors, scholars and leaders who have led, and continue to lead, the way off the main Bible highways and into the rough terrain. Thanks to my third-class teacher, Mrs Dunstan, who said I should be a writer (It was me who put salt in the fish tank. Sorry about what happened to Milton.), everyone in Australia (I love youse all), Richie for buying my first concordance and, of course, Ron. And world peace. And I want to thank Ben too. It's great having a writing partner who can watch my six and steer me back on course when my theological compass and historical sextant are miscalibrated.*

## Ben

It's been a pleasure writing a book with Pete once again, although this one was written on both sides of the globe. Such are the marvels of modern technology. Thanks, Pete, for inspiring writing, good laughs and hundreds of

* Pete, you can't actually miscalibrate a compass, but thanks all the same.
 – Ben

See what I mean? Fantastic! – Pete

emails. Thanks also to Jeremy and Lois Smith, Rhun and Shirley Gruffydd, Don Clarke and Nathan Norrie for encouraging prayers and general support. Thanks to Jonathan Fletcher and all at Emmanuel Church Wimbledon for employing me and putting up with my sermons, some of which have found their way into this book. A special thanks to my wife, who has brought me many cups of tea and who tirelessly supports me. I couldn't have done it without her.

Ben and Pete want to thank the Zondervan team: Stan Gundry for signing the contract and Katya Covrett for keeping her hands on the wheel. Thanks to Brian Phipps (developmental editor), Mike Cook (marketing director), Mark Sheeres and Melissa Elenbaas (interior design) and Ron Huizinga (cover design) for their editorial, design and marketing brilliance in making us sound smarter and look better than we really are.

## Part 1

# FIRST THINGS FIRST

Try this quick quiz.

*Who is this man?*

His mother, Mary, gave birth to him one day, a day much like any other day. He was born into a nondescript family, lived an ordinary life, went to the local school, and everybody thought he was an average guy. No one took much notice of him as a boy, but when he was a bit older, he came up with some ideas that would change the face of the world forever. It was the dawning of a new era, of a new way of looking at things.

News about this spread like wildfire, and today, years later, people in every corner of the globe know of him and his ideas. An enormous institution – one of the world's most powerful, influential and wealthy – has grown up around him and spread into nearly every city and country of the globe. It has expanded and diversified to incorporate community projects, health and education. His book has been translated into multiple languages and has been published in more than sixty countries. Many parts of modern life – from aspects of our home life to the way we conduct business – are directly influenced by his ideas. He is divisive: some people consider him a saviour while others turn their backs and curse his name.

*Who is this man?*

Well … odds are on you said Jesus. That would be perfectly reasonable considering you are, after all, holding a book about Jesus.

But *(insert "I'm sorry, you're wrong" hooter-type ding-dong FX here)* … it's not Jesus.*

The person described is … Bill Gates, founder of Microsoft.

Now, we have nothing against Mr Gates. He is one of the most powerful, wealthy, philanthropic and influential men in history. However, despite the amazing way he has changed modern life, his impact is chicken feed when compared with the person this book is about.

That's right *(cue curtain, segue drumroll and anthemic stirring entrance FX)* … Jesus.

Jesus is the most significant and influential person ever to walk the earth. Ever.

Nobody has had more of an impact on people's lives and on shaping human history. If history had a fulcrum, Jesus is it.

It's easy to read the previous sentences and shrug them off as meaningless religious babble. We've become numb to the hyperbole often used when

> \* That's like that joke: The Sunday school teacher asks a kid what has four legs and a tail and is covered in hair.    – Pete
>
> And the boy replies, "I know the answer must be God or Jesus, but it sure sounds like a dog!" – Ben

> Nobody has had more of an impact on people's lives and on shaping human history. If history had a fulcrum, Jesus is it.

* According to Guinness World Records, the Bible has sold over five billion copies since 1815.
** Seen by over five billion people in over two hundred countries and translated into over eight hundred languages and dialects.
*** Even though he was more likely born around 4 BC.

discussing Jesus. But let's just pause for a moment and think about this. Fast-forward to the twenty-first century, and the ripples and shadows of his life are still emanating through our daily existence.

Jesus is arguably the most talked about figure in history. There are more books written about him than about any other person who has ever lived. The Library of Congress in Washington, D.C., is widely regarded as the largest library in the world. It has around 530 miles of shelves containing more than 29 million catalogued books in over 400 languages. But out of all those books there are more books on Jesus than on any other person. And add to that: he is the main character of the most widely printed, translated and read book in the history of publishing – the Bible.*

In the arts, Jesus is unparalleled. From Handel to U2, he appears as the inspiration or within the lyrics of thousands of songs in just about every genre. There have been more movies about Jesus than about James Bond and Luke Skywalker put together. In fact the most watched film in cinematic history is the 1979 movie simply titled *Jesus*.** And walk into just about any national art gallery in the world and you'll find paintings of him there.

He has the biggest birthday party of anyone who has ever lived: the commemoration of his birth still remains the biggest annual celebration around the globe. Even our Western calendars – our very concept of time in terms of years – hinge on his birth.***

One third of the world's population today – that's about two billion people in Africa, Asia, the Middle East, Europe and the Americas – declare themselves to be his followers[1] and to base their lives on his teachings. As such, he is the cornerstone of the world's biggest religion.

His influence is behind the building of countless schools, cathedrals and orphanages. His followers have lead the way on a global and historical scale in shaping our planet: in providing literacy and education for the masses, hospitals, aged care, the abolition of slavery, women's rights, exploration, science, charities, lobby groups and welfare organizations. His teachings have influenced our history and our laws. So entrenched is he in our culture that his name has – unfortunately – become a curse word used by people who hit their thumb with a hammer.

And ultimately, his teachings directly influence the thoughts and actions – the very way of life – of billions of people around the world every day. He inspires those who follow him to live in sync with the way God wants ... to serve others and to live *right,* to live the way we are supposed to. Jesus clears away the muck that clogs up our lives and restores us into a right relationship with God.

Yep, from Julius Caesar to George Washington, from Albert Einstein to Bill Gates, from Mozart to Bono, from Joan of Arc to Mother Teresa, no one else comes close to Jesus of Nazareth.

---

1. Guinness World Records.

Not bad for a guy who didn't go to Uni, never  
didn't even venture more than a few hundred kilo.  
his birth.

Jesus was born to young parents in a backwater o.  
Empire two thousand years ago. He probably spent his fi.  
suing the trade of his "earthly" father in building cabinets a.  
We don't know much about his early life. We know the story  
birth and one event from his childhood (which we'll get to la.  
about it. All the stories about his teachings and travels in the Bib.  
just one action-packed three-year period after he turned thirty. 1.  
that he started wandering around speaking incredible words and doi.  
ing things. He changed people's lives and upset the establishment. 1  
things, did things and claimed things about himself that were controve.  
shocking … supposedly blasphemous.

Jesus – the carpenter's son, the boy next door – was not a trained the.  
logian or a high priest in the temple. Yet he astounded everyone with his  
words, knowledge, wisdom and authority. Everywhere he went, people gath-  
ered to hear the amazing thoughts, innovative ideas and life-changing teach-  
ings that came out of his mouth. People flocked to see him. These were no  
polite visits of a small and well-mannered delegation. The scenes surround-  
ing Jesus were more reminiscent of what we see today when a victorious  
sporting team or an international rock star comes to town. Jesus obviously  
had *something* special – charisma, power, authority, appeal. He gave people  
hope, assurance, dignity, peace, direction and contentment, but more than  
that, he offered one thing that is unique in human history. Jesus claimed  
something very special about himself. He claimed that he was no ordinary  
human being but was in fact the Son of God who lived among us so that  
people could be in relationship with God. He claimed that because of him,  
people could get right with God and that *he* was the doorway to life after  
death.

This is a pretty big claim, and in some respects, words are cheap. But  
Jesus went on to prove himself. After being tried for blasphemy and con-  
victed, he was executed by crucifixion by soldiers of the Roman Empire. He  
displayed his power and authority in doing something that no one had ever  
done before or has done since. He came back from death, not as a spooky,  
Star Warsy, flickering, ghostly image but in real flesh and blood.

News of this man exploded throughout the world like a bushfire, across  
borders, beyond governments and ultimately through the centuries. People  
began changing their lives according to his teachings. They began to read  
the reports about him and to meet together. Buildings were erected where his  
followers could meet. These church buildings are now to be found in pretty  
well every corner of the planet.

News of this  
man exploded  
throughout the  
world of this

…d the  
…every day.

...st, Jesus was a Jew. You probably already know this deep down, but ...s easy sometimes to forget this simple fact, kind of like how we sometimes forget that the Bible wasn't written originally in English. Because Jesus is the central and iconic figure of the Christian faith, it's easy to slip into the trap of thinking that he was somehow "badged", that he was an Anglican or a Catholic or a Pentecostal (or indeed that he was even white!), or that he was "born again", or that he was widely familiar with the doctrines and liturgies of the faith – Christianity – that have grown up around and after him. Not so. Jesus never set foot in a Christian church or sang "Amazing Grace." The cross symbol that has come to represent the Christian faith was in his days a terrifying tool of execution.

Jesus' earthly father – Joseph – came from a long line of Jewish ancestors (whom you can read about in Matthew chapter 1), and as such, Jesus was raised as a devout Jewish man in a Jewish community. When he was eight days old, Jesus was circumcised in accordance with Jewish custom. His parents took him to Jerusalem, where they sacrificed two birds by way of dedicating him to the God of the Israelites. They returned annually to the temple in Jerusalem, where they celebrated the Feast of the Passover. He would have attended the synagogue school for a few years and there learned to read the sacred writings of the Law and the Prophets. In fact, not only did he learn to read, but it is likely he would have memorised much of the Law (the first five books of the Old Testament) and studied how to interpret and apply it. His clothing and manner and rituals were all in accordance with the religion and way of life of the Jews of the time. In the synagogue, he would have read the scrolls in their original language – Hebrew – but when he ventured out into the streets and talked with builders and farmers and fishermen, his everyday language was the local dialect, Aramaic.

Which segues nicely into our second point.

During the Australia-Croatia game of the 2006 World Cup, as one of the Australian players took to the field, the TV commentator announced, "And here's Josh Kennedy, who many people say looks like Jesus." Which sums up pretty well the way many of us see Jesus. He (and Kennedy) is a tall, ruggedly handsome, athletic, white Anglo-Saxon Protestant with a long face, piercing eyes, rock star – style hair and a close-cropped beard. This image is reinforced by handsome actors (such as Jim Caviezel or the ridiculously Nordic Max von Sydow) playing him in movies and by Warner Sallman's 1941 painting *Head of Christ*, which has been reproduced over 500 million times.

The fact is that none of the original reports describe what Jesus looked like, so any artistic, cinematic or stained-glass depiction of him is pure fantasy. It is reasonable to assume that he probably had a beard and moustache

... the ...like a ...ushfire, across borders, beyond governments and ultimately through the centuries.

in the style of young men of the time. Archaeological evidence suggests that the average man then was a bantamweight of just over five feet tall. It is also fair to assume that given the harsh Mediterranean climate and his outdoor lifestyle, together with his years of work in the building trade in an era before power tools, he would not have been a pasty ashen Bohemian as he is often portrayed in pictures. In fact, he would probably have been a rather muscular, sinewy nugget of a bloke, dark skinned and tough as old boots.

It is important to remember this humanness of Jesus. Despite the extraordinary claims made about him later (we'll get to those soon), he was in all respects an ordinary human being. He went to school, ate and drank, laughed, slept, worked hard, had friends and probably swam in the river. While the Bible records his important words of teaching and wisdom, it is important to remember that he also would have engaged in everyday banter relating to food, the weather and the building trade. He didn't walk around glowing, and he didn't float centimetres off the road. To most of the people who met him during his first thirty years, he was just plain-old Jesus, the bloke from Nazareth. And even after he started doing amazing things, there were still a lot of people (including members of his own family) who regarded him as such and rejected his claims.

But to many people who met him later – and to people who have learned about him over the past two thousand years – he was and is a lot more than plain-old Jesus. He was the infinitely more majestic Jesus Christ, the saviour of the world.

This name actually tells us a lot about Jesus – who he was and what he was about. But that's a big topic in itself, so we'll leave it for the next chapter.

The lights go down and the movie begins. It is a sci-fi epic set in the twenty-second century on a space station orbiting the moons of Jupiter. A nervous scientist comes around the darkened corridor and is faced with a giant, slobbering monster alien, all teeth and claws. He opens his mouth and screams, "Jesus Christ!"

Hmm. Interesting.

Putting aside the issue of the inappropriate use of Jesus' name, here's the thing. Although we colloquially know him as Jesus Christ, this was not actually his name. His mother, for example, when calling him to wash up for dinner, did not yell out, "Jesus Christ, you come in here right now!"

During his life, people referred to Jesus in many ways. These actually tell us a lot about who Jesus was and how people saw him. So let's go sideways for a moment and look at the various names and titles by which Jesus was known.

### Jesus

Most names have a meaning. Our names – Peter and Benjamin – come, respectively, from the ancient Greek word Petra (which means "rock") and the ancient Hebrew name that was originally Benyamin (meaning "son of right hand"). However, we got our names not because Peter looked like a brick when he was born* nor because Ben's mum played right-handed guitar, but because our parents simply liked the sound of them.

> * Although, Pete was a pretty heavy baby!  – Ben

In Jesus' day, things were different. Like most children of the era, Jesus wasn't given his name just because it was the flavour of the month in Bethlehem, or because Joseph and Mary thought it sounded better than Dan or Adam. Rather, it was given to him because of the meaning of that name. It wasn't even Joseph and Mary's idea to call their son Jesus. They were both told separately by a messenger from God that this baby was going to be unique and have a special role in God's plan for all mankind.[1] The name **Jesus** is highly significant. This is clearly seen in the angel's announcement to Joseph: "She will give birth to a son, and you are to give him the name Jesus, because he will save his people from their sins."[2]

His actual Hebrew name was **Yeshua,** which means "God saves" (or more literally, "Yahweh is salvation"). This was the name that his mother

---

1. Luke 1.
2. Matthew 1:21.

and father and friends would have used as he was growing up. Because the family lived in a time when Greek was still a dominant language of business, when Yeshua was dealing with tradesmen and merchants – and later, with the officials of the Roman government – he would have been known by his Greek name: **Iesous.** (The name that we use for Jesus is actually a modern Anglicised version of this Greek name. Yeshua himself never heard his name pronounced as we say it: "GEE-zuhs".)[*]

It is also interesting to note that Jesus was quite a common name – like Ben or Pete today – and at the time there were many blokes around named Jesus.

### Jesus: Son of Joe

As we said, many people mistakenly believe that Christ was Jesus' surname. Actually, surnames as we know them did not gain popularity for well over a thousand years after Jesus' death. To make things easier in expanding local and national populations, families adopted surnames to help them sort out one John from another. The adopted names came from a number of different sources; for example, based on the father's occupation (Smith, Miller, Cook, Baker, Zappa, Painter, Butcher, Taylor, Carpenter, Plummer, Hunter, Shearer) or some family attribute (Small, Wise, Burns, Gross, Butt, Armstrong, Wallbanger, Pratt, Longbottom, Savage, Slaughter).

In many cultures, a quick way of referring to a person was in relation to one's father's name. So for example, "David son of Jack" became "David Jackson" and "Ian son of Jeffery" became "Ian Jefferson". Throughout history, pretty well all cultures and language groups developed their own patriarchal identifiers, which can be seen in the Gaelic *O'*Grady, the Scottish *Mac*Donald, the Italian *De*Luca, the Scandinavian Johann*sen*, the Norman *Fitz*william or the Russian Ivan*ov*.

Jesus would have also been identified by his family line. In Jesus' time, they did not use O' or Mac or Fitz but rather used the prefix Ben or Bar to refer to being a "son of". So **Jesus son of Joseph** would have been known colloquially in his region as Yeshua Bar Yosef or Yeshua Ben Yosef.[**] (Interestingly, there is another Jesus in the Bible, and in his case we also see this type of family identification used. When the crowds scream out for the release of the insurrectionist Barabbas,[3] they are likely calling out for Jesus son of Abbas and, in doing so, are condemning Jesus son of Joseph.)[***]

### Jesus of Nazareth

Another way of identifying a person referred to where their family originated or lived (Ford, Hill, Milani, Wood, West, York, Lane). Jesus was also referred to by the place where he lived. The writers of the Bible record that

[*] Other languages, for example, refer to him differently: Jesu Christi (German), Jézus Krisztusnak (Hungarian), Ihu Karaiti (Maori), Yesu Kristo (Swahili).
[***] Our educated guess is that this is probably true, and this is the way Barabbas is described in many Bible versions, although the earliest manuscripts of Matthew just have "Barabbas" and not "Jesus Barabbas".

[**] I just thought of something, Ben. If you lived in Jesus' time and your dad was also called Ben, you would be known as Ben Ben Ben.          – Pete

You need to get out more.
          – Ben

---

3. Matthew 27:17.

people often referred to him as **Jesus of Nazareth.** Interestingly, Nazareth wasn't a high-profile place and was considered something of a second-rate town.*

## Jesus the Christ

Christ was not a surname but a title, like the terms king or president. The Israelite people had been waiting for the arrival of their **Messiah** – a highly loaded term which basically means "anointed one". The Greek word for this was **Christos,** from which we get Christ.

Many people don't know that way before Jesus came on the scene, the kings of Israel were also called messiah because they ruled the people as God's specially chosen "anointed ones". So for example, King David** was called a messiah. In fact, when a new king came to the throne, an elaborate coronation ceremony took place during which expensive oil was poured over his head and body. This symbolized his anointing by God. He was then seen by all to be God's human representative to rule his people.

However, the prophets of the Old Testament predicted that there would be a day when the supreme Messiah would come. A king of kings. One like no other. One who would be God's true representative on earth and rule on his behalf. The writers of the New Testament claim that Jesus of Nazareth was this predicted Messiah. Hence he would have originally been called **Jesus the Christ** or **Jesus the Messiah,** but over time that was simply shortened to **Jesus Christ.**

## Lord

People who met and talked with Jesus often referred to him as **Lord** or **the Lord Jesus Christ.** Our English word *lord* is the translation of the Greek word **kyrios,** which was used in a number of ways in the first century. For example, it could mean "sir" or "master" as a sign of respect and to convey a certain sense of status. So the owner of a vineyard or an owner of slaves or an official ruler could be referred to as a lord. When Christians originally began calling Jesus Lord, it was probably more in this sense of the word.

However, the term lord also had a sense of divinity attached to it.*** Roman Emperors were sometimes called lord in this context, because they claimed to be partly divine. Likewise, in both the Old and New Testaments, God himself was referred to as *the* Lord. And as time progressed, Christians increasingly used the title Lord for Jesus in this sense.

## The Son of God

One of the most important titles for Jesus was **the Son of God.** In fact, the opening line of the Gospel of Mark is, "The beginning of the gospel

* In fact, John records that Nathanael's initial response to hearing about Jesus was to quip, "Nazareth! Can anything good come from there?" (1:46).
** Whom we read about in 1 and 2 Samuel and who lived about a thousand years before Jesus.
*** So, for example, in the early Greek translation of the Old Testament – the Septuagint (LXX) – kyrios is used for the Hebrew proper name for God.

about Jesus Christ, the Son of God,"[4] as if to say the rest of Jesus' story is all about understanding this title.

This tells us that Jesus was unique. Although the Israelites in the Old Testament were called sons of God or children of God, Jesus was the one and only true Son of God. In the words of one of the most famous verses in the Bible, "For God so loved the world that he gave *his one and only Son*, that whoever believes in him shall not perish but have eternal life."[5]

And it also tells us that Jesus was divine. He was God personified, a human version or representation of God: the God-man. When asked by one of his disciples to show them God the Father, Jesus said, "Anyone who has seen me has seen the Father."[6] Likewise, the apostle Paul said, "The Son is the image of the invisible God."[7]

It is also worth noting that it was this term that became one of the sticking points at the trial that led to Jesus' crucifixion. That Jesus and his followers claimed he was the Son of God was considered absolutely blasphemous, and it provided one of the main reasons the Jewish authorities thought that he should be executed.

## Son of Man

Jesus frequently referred to himself as the **Son of Man,** preferring it to other titles. But for us today, it's one of his most puzzling titles. Isn't every son technically a son of man? Bible scholars have written essays and doctoral theses the size of phone books on this unusual term.

Interestingly, while something of a cryptic title to us, it was not so strange to Jesus and many of the people of his time. The title Son of Man is used over ninety times in the Old Testament books of Ezekiel and Daniel. Jesus and the people he was speaking to would have been familiar with the writings of these prophets and the use of this title. So in referring to himself as Son of Man, Jesus was deliberately making a connection in the minds of the listeners between himself and their existing knowledge and familiarity with the title.

And what was that knowledge? In the book of Daniel, the writer describes a vision in which one "like a son of man" is given authority, glory and sovereign power; all peoples, nations and men of every language worshiped him. His dominion is forever and it will never disappear. He will rule over a kingdom that will never be destroyed.[8]

---

4. Mark 1:1 NIV.
5. John 3:16, emphasis added.
6. John 14:8–9.
7. Colossians 1:15.
8. Daniel 7:13–14.

Jesus is in effect declaring that this is him. In calling himself the Son of Man, Jesus is saying to his listeners that *he* is the one, that *he* will rule as a mighty leader whose kingdom will never end.

However, Jesus infuses the term with additional meaning. When Jesus refers to himself as the Son of Man, it is often in the context of his prophetic teaching about his suffering and death. It seems that for Jesus,[*] the Son of Man is also a divinely appointed human who suffers and serves the world by dying. This double meaning of both a ruler and a suffering servant seems to be the meaning behind the title the Son of Man when Jesus uses it about himself.

## Emmanuel

When Pete was a kid, he had a Christmas record with a hymn on it that began, "Oh come, oh come Emmanuel and ransom captive I-hi-hisrael." This led to many years of confusion as Pete grew up wondering who this Mexican guy Manuel was, why Israel had been kidnapped and what it all had to do with Christmas anyway.[**]

[**] Mate, you are a drongo! (friendly Aussie talk for a buffoon or idiot)
– Ben

In fact, **Emmanuel** is a highly significant name given to Jesus that means "God with us". Jesus is literally God amongst us. Or – if you want to get technical – God *incarnate*. Some years ago, Joan Osborne had a hit with the song, "What If God Was One of Us?" The writers of the Bible claim that there are no what ifs, that in the form of Jesus, God did indeed become one of us.

## Teacher

Jesus' friends – including his twelve closest companions – and enemies referred to him as **Teacher** or **Rabboni.** Now, for some of us, that might have some very negative connotations. We might picture Jesus pointing to a blackboard and handing out assignments and saying, "There'll be a test this Friday on Parables 1–7." But this was a highly esteemed title.

Only the best of the best students and scholars got to be a rabbi, after a lifetime of study and after apprenticing themselves to a rabbi for many years. Rabbis taught others and interpreted the writings of the Law and the Prophets. They argued and debated and discussed with other rabbis about how to interpret and apply the law.

Referring to Jesus as Rabbi was to pay him the highest honour. It was an indicator of the esteem in which he was held by many people.

So there you have it.

Jesus of Nazareth, the son of Joseph, the Christ, Rabbi, Emmanuel, Son of Man, Son of God … all different ways of expressing Jesus' identity.

So let's settle in and let our historical microscope drift back two thousand years and zoom in on a patch of land on the eastern shore of the Mediterranean. While life in those days bore some similarities with our own lives, in so many ways it was a time totally unlike our own. In fact, they were strange days indeed.

When Pete was a kid, one of his favourite possessions was an old Viewmaster. He had a pile of exciting reels like "Batman Saves the Day", "Thunderbirds Are Go!" and "Ornithology for Beginners!" (It was Pete's insane jealously of his friend Kevin's Viewmaster with Sound that lead to the rapid end of their friendship, but that's sidetracking.)*

And then one Christmas his aunt gave Pete a reel of "Tour of the Holy Land". (You can imagine how exciting this was for a twelve-year-old boy.) It contained a range of pictures of places mentioned in the Bible, like "Mount of Olives, Looking West", "Fishing Boats on a Lake", "The Jaffa Gate", "Shepherds Tending Their Flocks", "Women Drawing Water from Well" and "Men in Traditional Dress". **Yee-hah.**

While the slides were useful in providing a sense of the serene rural splendour of the time (and maybe the sounds of the time too, if you had a Viewmaster with Sound like Ben and Kevin, that boasting little poser who ... oh, sorry), they didn't provide any real sense of what daily life was like for the people of that era.

So what was life like in the time of Jesus?

> * Hey, I had a Viewmaster with Sound! – Ben
>
> Oh yeah? Well, I hate you. – Pete

## The Roman Empire

Jesus lived in the first century AD in a small town called Nazareth in Judea, a province of what was then the superpower of the world – the Roman Empire. In Jesus' day, the Roman Empire extended as far west as what is now known as Spain, south to the top of Northern Africa, north to Asia Minor and modern Germany, and as far east as Judea, where Jesus lived. The population of the entire empire numbered somewhere between 50 and 60 million people, and its capital was the city of Rome, with a population of between 750,000 and 1 million people.

The supreme ruler of the empire was the emperor. The Gospel of Luke tells us that Jesus was born during the reign of Emperor Augustus. Augustus died when Jesus was in his late teens (AD 14), and the new emperor was Tiberius (Augustus' adopted son), who ruled the Roman Empire until after Jesus' death and resurrection. When Jesus held up a coin and asked whose head was pictured on it,[1] it was Tiberius' portrait.

---

1. Matthew 22:18–21.

Although at this time the world was largely dominated by the Romans, it was still heavily influenced by the Greeks. Greek thought and culture (Hellenism) penetrated much of the Roman Empire in areas such as philosophy, religion, recreation, language and art. So Jesus lived in what historians term the Greco-Roman world.

There were dozens of languages used throughout the Roman Empire, so many people were multilingual. But the two main languages were Latin and Greek. Although Jesus would have been familiar with these languages and used them from time to time, his primary languages were Aramaic and Hebrew. The traditional language of the Jews was Hebrew, but by Jesus' day Hebrew was a dying language used mainly only in religious contexts and discussions. It seems that most of Jesus' teaching, particularly around Galilee, was done in Aramaic.

### Similar to Us

We often think of the "ancient world" as being primitive or uncivilised. Not so. Life in the ancient world in Jesus' day was in many ways similar to ours. There were highly developed legal, communication, financial and tax systems. There were laws and punishments for breaking the laws. There were towns and cities, trade routes, hotels, schools and forms of universities. People played organized sport and games, and went to gymnasiums, clubs, libraries, theatres, bars and restaurants. They celebrated birthdays, sporting victories and marriages and participated in religious festivals and holidays. There were sophisticated public works, such as ports, roads, canals, stadiums, buildings, statues, sanitation systems and palaces.

People wore undergarments, footwear, hats, makeup and some women even wore athletic garments that looked like bikinis.* There were carpenters, sailors, lawyers, musicians, tax officers, fabric makers, scholars, artists, doctors, chefs, governors, plumbers, soldiers, architects, farmers, merchants, importers, tailors and engineers. They had governments, armies, battles, weapons and wars. People fell in love, had sex, raised families, worked hard, enjoyed friendships and wanted good lives, just like we do. They had weddings and funerals, and art, music and poetry. Kids went to school, played games, climbed trees, learned a trade. They enjoyed good wine and food like vegetables, eggs, fruits, cheese, chicken and fish seasoned with herbs and spices. Women ground flour, baked bread and spun wool. They marvelled at a pretty sunset and as farmers were grateful for good rain. They earned wages, banked money and even paid superannuation. And they were concerned with life after death. You might say that the ancient world was not so ancient.

### Different from Us

Obviously, however, there were many differences. There were, of course, no mobile phones, televisions, cars, planes, MTV, space shuttles or comput-

We often think of the "ancient world" as being primitive or uncivilised. Not so.

* Regarding this whole "bikini" thing, I want to say for the record that I do not believe that the ancient Romans had bikinis.        – Pete

No, seriously, they did. Technically, the bikini was invented by some French guy in the 1940s and named after an atoll in the Marshall Islands where atom bombs were tested, but Roman women did have these two-piece athletic outfits that were essentially bikinis.   – Ben

Hmm.                – Pete

ers. No iPods, microwave ovens, Xboxes or websites. No one had heard of Albert Einstein or William Shakespeare or Joan of Arc or Walt Disney, or seen a painting by Michelangelo, or listened to the Beatles or seen a movie. No one had tasted a Mars Bar, popcorn or Coca Cola. What is the stuff of everyday history to us – the Crusades, the invention of the printing press, the World Wars, the *Titanic*, the international space station, open-heart surgery, the fall of communism – was unimaginable to them, the same as our trying to contemplate what life will be like in the year AD 4000.

There was a high level of superstition throughout the ancient world. Religious rites and practices were a part of just about everyone's way of life. There were numerous cults, myths and philosophies and hundreds of different belief systems. The official religion of the empire was the Roman cult, which worshiped the emperor as a kind of god. Most religions of the day had priests and priestesses who performed all sorts of ceremonies and animal sacrifices in temples. Just about all other religions – except that of the Jews – were polytheistic (meaning they believed in not one God but many). Furthermore, there was an underlying belief that if you pleased the gods, you would prosper materially, your crops would grow and you'd have victory in war. Displease the gods, however, and you'd be cursed with ill health, a bad crop or death.

Another major difference was that this was a largely verbal and oral society. Unlike today, when the written word – newspapers, books, magazines, SMS, internet, email – is a large part of everyday life, and when it is assumed that everyone is literate, only about one in five people in Jesus' day could read and write. The number of literate people was considerably higher amongst some groups like the Jews, since just about every Jewish boy was taught to read. But the average person living in the first century was illiterate.

It was also a brutal time in which to live. Slavery was a common part of everyday life; as many as one third of the people living in the Roman Empire were slaves of some sort. Not all slaves had it bad. Many were treated very well by their masters, and some were even treated like family.

In some respects, life was cheap and death was an everyday occurrence. Medicine was in its infancy. The intricate workings of the human body were still very much a mystery. It was not uncommon for women and babies to die during pregnancy or childbirth. Likewise, wounds, infections, diseases and common illnesses that are treated today with tablets, injections or an operation could easily be fatal back then. So the average life expectancy in the ancient world was around the mid-thirties.

Thousands of people went to see gladiators fight each other to a violent and gruesome death with the same casualness as we would go to the theatre or basketball or a movie. And there was no such thing as a conscience in relation to animal welfare. The Romans, particularly, used animals in incredible

It was also a brutal time in which to live.

numbers for sport against each other. At the inauguration of the Colosseum in Rome in the first century, as many as nine thousand animals were killed in "games" against each other.[2]

In Jesus' day, public execution was common and swift. You could be thrown not just to the lions but to a whole range of animals, such as bears, tigers, dogs, bulls and even alligators. Or you could fight it out with one of the local gladiators, who could be armed with a range of weapons, including spears, swords or whips. Added to this, there were stonings, beatings and whippings. You could even be sawn in half. And of course, there was the slowest and most savage of all executions – crucifixion. About seventy years before Jesus was born, a visitor to Rome approached the city on a road lined on both sides with six thousand crucified rebels.[*] The ancient world through which Jesus walked was not for the fainthearted.

### Judaism

Jesus was born into a Jewish family living in ancient Palestine. He was born in Bethlehem but grew up in the town of Nazareth, a small farming village west of the Sea of Galilee that had a population of probably no more than a few hundred people. It was mostly, if not exclusively, Jewish. Larger cities like Jerusalem had a much greater mix of cultures, people and languages, including Romans and Greeks. In outer towns and villages such as Nazareth, the houses and dwellings were simple, functional structures of wood, mud-brick and stone, with dirt floors and flat roofs. Community life revolved around the marketplace, the crops, the well and the synagogue.

Traditions, the law and history were very important to the Jews. A deeply religious people, they celebrated the Sabbath day each week, as well as annual feasts such as the Passover. Rules relating to sacrifices, God's commandments and religious purity were very important to them.

Their sacred texts were what we call the Old Testament – the first thirty-nine books of the Bible. They regarded these inspired words of God as a record of their people's history as well as a testimony to their unique place as the chosen people of God.

### Waiting for a Hero: The Expectation of a Messiah

It's very important to understand the political and religious climate in which Jesus lived and preached.

History (and our nightly news) is littered with examples of one country or superpower invading and occupying another country. Typically, there is a military invasion followed by the establishment of a government and – more often than not – the imposition or infiltration of foreign rules, culture, language, religion, currency. (Think of the European invasions of the Americas

> Traditions, the law and history were very important to the Jews.

* When Marcus Lucinius Crassus crushed a slave rebellion and crucified the rebels along the Appian Way between Rome and Capua.

2. Ronald Auguet, *Cruelty and Civilization: The Roman Games* (London: Routledge, 1994), 107.

and Australia, the Chinese in Tibet, Indonesians in Timor, the English in India, the Spaniards in Mexico, even the American occupation of Iraq.) And then you have a fragile balance between a superior military force that has moved in and taken control of a disgruntled population that, more often than not, would prefer things back the way they were, thank you very much for asking.

We are all too familiar with scenes on the nightly news of civil unrest from these hot spots; pictures of youths throwing rocks and Molotov cocktails at police, chanting crowds, arrests, placards, shots being exchanged, military reprisals, city streets lined with bodies and burning debris.

Jesus lived in a similarly tumultuous situation.

About seven hundred years before Jesus was born, Assyrian forces marched into Israel and occupied the country. That was just the start of hundreds of years of oppression by a succession of foreign powers. The Assyrian forces were ousted by Babylon. Alexander the Great then conquered the region and the Greeks ruled for hundreds of years until the incredible might of the Roman Empire spread throughout the world.

So by the time Jesus was born, generations of Jewish people had grown up under foreign rule. The Jews were broken, persecuted and humiliated. Their land was a battlefield, a slave nation to foreign forces, soldiers and rulers. They suffered exile, the dismantling of their culture and the burden of heavy taxes to these foreigners.

As such, most Jews of the first century believed that the real enemy of God's people was the Roman Empire, which now ruled Palestine and occupied the holy city of Jerusalem. And the worst thing about that was not the high taxation, or the foreign laws, or the brutality of oppression; the worst thing was that the Romans were pagans. They were enemies of God. They erected their statues in the temple and put their symbols of power all over Jerusalem. This was disgraceful and insulting to the Jews, a continual thorn in their side. They were desperately looking forward to, and waiting for, someone to lead them out of their oppression and save them from the occupying Romans.

We are familiar in our entertainment culture with the idea of waiting for a hero. In the popular Bruce Willis film *The Fifth Element*, spiritual leaders had been waiting for hundreds of years for the predicted arrival of a saviour to lead civilisation out of its dark days. A similar theme emerges in *The Matrix* trilogy, in which people looked for the arrival of the one – Neo – who would rise up and save them from their enslavement. Even *The Lord of the Rings* has its king whom everyone is waiting for to lead the people to victory against the powers of darkness.

This is nothing new. For centuries before Jesus, Jewish spiritual leaders had foretold that one would be born who would save the people and lead

> So by the time Jesus was born, generations of Jewish people had grown up under foreign rule.

** Or a Terminator like Arnold's T-800!    – Pete

Sure, Pete, whatever you say.    – Ben

them in a revolution that would cast off pagan Roman rule. They were looking for a dramatic, highly visible, military-style event that would overthrow the Roman forces, judge corrupt leaders, and restore God's true people to their former glory. They declared it would be a time when God would put to right a world that seemed out of control. There was a tremendous sense of expectation and wonder among the Jewish people about who this would be and when this triumphant event would take place.*

The prophets of the Old Testament promised the arrival of such a hero who would bring about this great event and be powerful and mighty in physical and political ways. They referred to him with the Hebrew word for "anointed one" – simply, **Messiah.** The Jewish people of Jesus' time longed for this Messiah to come, hoping that he would take up his sword, inspire and organize the people to take to the streets, to defeat the Romans and make Israel the most powerful nation on earth under the Messiah's leadership. They were looking for a revolutionary like William Wallace or a gladiator like Maximus Decimus Meridius.**

The prophets promised that this Messiah would be recognized by the great things he would do. They spoke in terms of God's giving this figure his Spirit; he would bring good news, justice and freedom for God's people.

Every so often, a young man emerged and led a rebellion against the Roman forces. Every time, the people must have wondered, *Could he be the one we have been waiting for? The one promised to us? Are we to be saved? Is this it?*

And so, there were clashes in the streets, bands of renegades hiding in the mountains, battles and skirmishes outside city walls. Armouries were raided. Death was commonplace. In the decades before Jesus was born, revolts in Palestine were common and men were killed or executed in the hundreds of thousands. So politically, it was quite an unstable region.

Despite continual oppression and failed rebellions, many people still clung to the hope that someone would rise up to save them. And while all eyes were turned perhaps to the most likely sources of leadership – wealthy families, influential rabbis, the leaders of renegade bands – something happened in the most unlikely of places. An announcement came, direct from God, that the Messiah, at last, was on his way.

But the announcement was delivered not in a palace or synagogue but to a teenage girl in a small village.

## Part 2

# WAITING FOR THE KING

# Chapter 4

# I'M JUST A GIRL
## Introducing Jesus' mother

In the opening scene of the Douglas Adams novel and film *The Hitch-hiker's Guide to the Galaxy*, the main character, Arthur Dent, receives a visit from an old friend who has some interesting news. His friend Ford tells him that he is not really from Guildford but is an alien from a small planet near Betelgeuse and that in just a few minutes the world is going to blow up.

Having such a pronouncement dropped into his lap like that is so gob-smackingly breathtakingly enormous that Arthur cannot really even come to terms with what Ford is talking about. The news is just too big for his brain to comprehend.

Two thousand years ago in a little village near the Mediterranean Sea, a similarly mind-numbing message was delivered. Nazareth was a town of little consequence up in the Galilean hills. It wasn't the centre of anything, and it wasn't a place where anyone important lived. It wasn't the hub of economy, and it wasn't on a trade route. It was, in fact, something of an out-of-the-way second-rate town with a small population.

In a house in this village lived a young woman. She was pledged to be married to a local tradesman and was probably preparing for her upcoming wedding. Life was normal and on course. But although she didn't know it yet, she was about to receive a visitor with news that would turn the rest of her life – and indeed the rest of world history – on its head.

Her name was Mary.

Again, the internet provides us with a panoply of images of Jesus' mother. Mary has achieved a saintly and holy status in some parts of the church, and this is certainly reflected in sculpture and art over the years. Mary is a serene, noble, virginal and finely manicured woman dressed in elegant robes. She seems to perpetually exist in one of two meditative poses: either as a loving mother looking peacefully down at the infant cradled in her arms or as a Joan of Arc – type character bathed in sunlight with arms outstretched and gazing yearningly up to heaven, obviously accompanied by choirs of angels singing in exultation. You would expect nothing less of the mother of the Son of God.

The reality of Mary's pregnancy was perhaps more earthy.

In that era, young women did not enjoy the same freedoms and lifestyle that they do today. For example, they did not choose their marriage partners. They were very sheltered and in most cases were not even allowed to speak

> Although she didn't know it yet, she was about to receive a visitor with news that would turn the rest of her life – and indeed the rest of world history – on its head.

* There were a lot of rules about marriage. Did you know that according to the law, a recently married man was free from military service or any other duty for one year, so he could create a happy home for his wife (Deuteronomy 24:5)?

— Ben

Huh! And my paternity leave was only a day!

— Pete

to men outside of the family. If venturing outside — only in the company of a guardian — they had to wear a veil to cover their face. It was the girl's parents who chose a partner and arranged the marriage after she was about thirteen. It was more of an economic arrangement than the fulfilment of any modern notion of romantic love. There was no courtship or dating as we know it. Some women may have even met their marriage partner only for the first time on their wedding day. Given the size of Mary's village, however, that's unlikely in her case.

It appears that Mary's parents had pledged their daughter to marry a local tradesman, a good and righteous man called Joseph. It is likely, according to custom,* that he would have paid a sum of money to her parents by way of compensating them for the loss of their daughter to him. There is no evidence to suggest her age, although speculation based on custom suggests that she may have been in her mid-teens at the time of her engagement to Joseph.

Mary was perhaps looking forward to her wedding. On that day, she would be beautifully dressed and ornamented (for a rural peasant girl), ready to marry her husband. Joseph would come through the village with his companions to collect her, generally making a lot of racket. Then there would be a noisy procession back to a wedding canopy. There was little of the ceremony and hoo-ha that we have today. Basically the wedding contract was read out and agreed upon.

Like today, it was a very special event to which many guests came, wine flowed, food was consumed, vows were exchanged, blessings were given and prayers were offered. Celebrations could last for many days, even a week or longer. For the Jewish person especially, a marriage was the sacred binding of two people under God. It was as much a spiritual occasion as it was a legal one.

And that was it. From there, it was on to the wedding chamber.

Modern Western culture dictates that the first days of a newlywed couple's life — especially their first night together — are a private and secret affair. Not so back then. In that culture, the bride's virginity was of critical importance. It was expected that the bride and groom would consummate their wedding on that first night, and the wedding celebration would not take place until after the bride and groom had joined together sexually.

The groom's best man would wait outside the wedding chamber for a sign from the groom confirming that his new bride was in fact a virgin. The physical evidence of this was bloodstains on the wedding sheets, which would be kept by the bride's parents as evidence should the groom ever decide later to accuse her of sexual immorality.[1]

If the bride was a virgin, then the wedding celebration would take place. However, if she was found not to be a virgin, the groom could denounce her

1. Deuteronomy 22:13–19.

and the marriage would be nullified.* This brought much shame, disgrace and humiliation to the bride's entire family. In fact, the woman could be punished by being dragged to the doorstep of her father's house and there stoned to death by the men of the town.[2] Promiscuity of any kind was not tolerated.

This is all important background to understand the context in which Mary was about to find herself.

On several occasions in the Bible, God chose a particular person to perform a particular task. For example, Moses chosen to lead his people out of Egypt, Noah chosen to build an ark and Jonah chosen to preach to the city of Nineveh. However, on this occasion, a young woman in a nondescript village found favour in God's eyes to perform the most important task of all. (The Bible actually details a number of miraculous births. For example, Abraham and Sarah [Abram and Sari] gave birth to Isaac when they were both very old.[3]** Samuel was born to a barren mother.[4] Even Moses' birth story[5] has an element of the miraculous about it. But these were all preparation for the greatest and most miraculous birth of all.)

Mary was visited by a messenger from God who appeared to her with greetings and a message. It's easy to assume that Mary was totally fine with this visit, as if the sudden appearance of an angel were an everyday occurrence for her. In a classic example of understatement, however, we read that "Mary was greatly troubled at his words."[6] *As one would be!* But if she was troubled by his greeting, she must have been bowled over by what he had to say next.

Imagine the scene: The messenger told Mary not to be afraid. She had been chosen by God to conceive and give birth to a son to be called Jesus, who would grow up to be the saviour everyone was waiting for. His kingdom and throne would have no end.[7]

Stony silence.

*Say what?*

Mary – probably still struggling with this unexpected declaration – quickly identified the flaw in the announcement. *She was a virgin! She had not been with a man! How could this birth come about?*

The messenger told her that she would conceive by the Spirit of God ... God – the creator of all life – would place a life in her womb.

Again, stony silence.

---

2. Deuteronomy 22:20–21.
3. Genesis 17 and 21:1–7.
4. 1 Samuel 1–2.
5. Exodus 1–2.
6. Luke 1:29.
7. Luke 1:30–33.

** Apparently the oldest woman in the modern era to give birth is a retired Romanian professor, who gave birth at age sixty-six.          – Pete

Thanks for that. I am going to lose sleep over this tonight.          – Ben

* In some societies today, the "proof of virginity" is still practiced. Women can still be stoned to death for being unfaithful to their husbands.

> The messenger told her that she would conceive by the Spirit of God ... God – the creator of all life – would place a life in her womb.

* Some of the strict rules and codes relating to marriage are spelled out in the Old Testament book of Deuteronomy (22:13 – 30).

The Bible records that rather than running into the street and screaming her lungs out (as would be quite tempting, one would imagine), Mary declared that she was God's servant and would do whatever was asked of her. And with that, the messenger left. Mary's declaration is a great credit to her strength of character and a reflection of her piety and sense of obedience. Although she was young, we see not a fragile flighty girl but a determined young woman. God obviously chose carefully.

One can only imagine what thoughts scrambled in Mary's mind in those first hours as she fought to comprehend the unfolding implications of this message. Maybe she rubbed her eyes and shook her head comically as if to check that her brain was working as normal.

A natural reaction would be to ask, *Why me?* Surely the saviour would be born to a princess in a royal palace, attended by guards and advisers and priests, with visitations of the world's most powerful people. She was just an unmarried teenage peasant girl in a backwater town! ***Ridiculous!***

Then there would be the realisation of the magnitude of the responsibility that she – Mary of Nazareth – had been chosen to bear. It's hard enough raising kids without having the extra expectation of raising the nation's saviour!

Mary probably also wrestled with the normal thoughts that accompany any woman's pregnancy. Perhaps a concern about her body's changes, the joy of bearing a child, the natural worries of pregnancy and questions about the birth itself. And perhaps underlying these dawned a quickly rising fear of being inexplicably pregnant in a society in which promiscuous women were publicly executed. While it was all right for the messenger to come out with grandiose statements about immaculate conception, Mary may have wondered if the elders of the village would be quite as understanding.

Then, of course, there was the matter of her family and her future husband. While Mary knew that her pregnancy was miraculous, to everyone else, she would just be a young pregnant woman in a society in which such things were unacceptable.* Joseph wouldn't even need to wait for the wedding night to accuse her of infidelity. The growing bump on her stomach would be a highly visible source of shame for her family. And it probably dawned on her that she could kiss her wedding goodbye. There would be no procession, no banquet, no celebration for her.

Whatever her doubts and fears, the fact that she had encountered an angel with a personal message from God would have inspired her to trust that everything would be okay.

So here we have Mary juggling opposing thoughts: on the one hand, the joyous knowledge of being specially chosen by God to bear the Messiah, and on the other hand, the harsher realities of being engaged and pregnant. Hindsight and the Gospels allow us the knowledge of how the story pans out.

But to unmarried and pregnant Mary by herself on that day, the future might not have seemed so clear. She was alone and in something of a bind.

There was, however, one person who might understand her situation.

In a nearby town in the hill country of Judea lived Mary's cousin. An older woman, Elizabeth was six months pregnant herself. Mary perhaps knew that Elizabeth's pregnancy was also miraculous. Elizabeth, of all people, would understand and would make a good ally.

And so as we conclude this part of her story, we find Mary packing her things and hurrying out of town to visit Elizabeth. There, she does indeed receive a warm welcome. When Mary arrives, Elizabeth's baby kicks and wriggles in her womb, a miraculous and otherworldly indication of the spiritual link between these two unborn males – John and Jesus. Elizabeth declares that Mary and her child are both blessed, and she considers herself favoured to be visited by the mother of her Lord. "Blessed is she who has believed that the Lord would fulfill his promises to her!" she says.[8] What a relief it must have been to Mary to receive such a blessing from a friendly relative in whom she could confide. Rather than hostility and accusation, she instead received support and confirmation of what she already knew.

Mary stayed with her cousin for three months. But that is only just the beginning of her story.

---

8. Luke 1:41–45.

> While Mary knew that her pregnancy was miraculous, to everyone else, she would just be a young pregnant woman in a society in which such things were unacceptable.

# Chapter 5

# "HONEY, YOU BETTER SIT DOWN"
## Mary shares her news

I t was a rainy day one March when Peter's wife, Meredith, picked him up from work and declared that she had some news. It would be an understatement to say that Peter was less than prepared to hear her announcement. *She was pregnant! They were going to be parents!* **He was going to be a dad!**

There was a pause, accented by an orb of tumbleweed that rolled past. Somewhere on the breeze, a solitary cricket chirped. Then Pete's knees buckled and he stumbled about like a mumbling zombie, his face a picture of bug-eyed terror and slack-jawed fear. He gave his wife a clumsy hug and attempted to say some deeply momentous words about love and family and the circle of life.* After he had caught his breath, he started to feel quite chuffed about the whole idea and settled down to feeling warm and fuzzy. With great excitement, they began to share the news with relatives and friends, who were all equally overjoyed. There was much celebration, backslapping and champagne.

It was perhaps not quite such a rosy scenario for Mary and Joseph all those years ago.

We do not know exactly when this took place, but at some point – perhaps after her three months away in a neighbouring town – Mary probably shared her news with her parents. One can only imagine their horror as she told them her "news" and their incredulity at their daughter's implausible story of divine messengers and immaculate conception. It was perhaps her father's duty then, with heavy shoulders, to inform Joseph that his bride-to-be was pregnant and that the wedding would no doubt be off. Instead of flowers and champagne and backslaps, the whole thing reeked of shame, humiliation and dishonour. In a village of only a few hundred, the news would spread fast, and it would be ugly.

Joseph must have been upset and hurt at the news. His bride-to-be was pregnant. So he had a choice to make.

Certainly he could have publicly denounced Mary and caused a scandal for her family – or worse. Old Testament law dictated that if a man slept with a virgin pledged to be married, both the man and the woman were to be taken to the town's gates and there be stoned to death.[1]

However, the Bible says that "because Joseph her husband was a righteous man and did not want to expose her to public disgrace, he had in mind

> \* Ah yes. One can only hope this great story from the vault of Pete's life is leading somewhere.
> – Ben
>
> All will be revealed in time, my impatient young Padawan.    – Pete

> Joseph must have been upset and hurt at the news. His bride-to-be was pregnant. So he had a choice to make.

---

1. Deuteronomy 22:23–24.

"Because Joseph her husband was a righteous man and did not want to expose her to public disgrace, he had in mind to divorce her quietly."

to divorce her quietly."[2] Here we see a man who is righteous in following the Old Testament laws of divorce, but who at the same time is humble and compassionate in not wanting to make a scene for the woman who would have been his wife.

While he was considering this, Joseph had a dream in which a heavenly messenger told him not to be afraid to take Mary as his wife, because what was conceived in her was from God.[3] The angel said that she would give birth to a son to be named Jesus and that he would save his people from their sins.

When Joseph awoke, he must have felt some relief at the realisation that not only had his wife been faithful all along but that the two of them had the enormous privilege of being chosen by God for this important task. What thoughts must have coursed through Joseph's mind as he contemplated the responsibility of being the earthly father to the Son of God?

Joseph took Mary home as his wife. Given the circumstances, it is unlikely that there would have been the expected procession and a banquet. More likely, Joseph would have turned up at Mary's house and taken her back to his house to marry her.

We, who are so familiar with this story, tend to take this in our stride, as if Joseph and Mary were two perfectly self-actualized individuals who coped just fine with their tumultuous situation, who weren't bothered by the whispers behind hands as they passed and who had no qualms at all about divine messengers delivering news that they were to raise the most important person in history.

One can only imagine them alone, talking about their excitement, doubts and fears – as any couple would do – and looking at Mary's expanding body and wondering what the future would hold. No doubt the memory and message of God's messengers was prominent in their minds as they contemplated the fact that their son was something special.

The months ticked by as the miracle of God's Son on earth unfolded inside his mother. A spark of life spontaneously appeared in Mary's fallopian tube. The chromosomes and uniquely God-man genes had already blueprinted the growth of this child and its physical characteristics. The nucleus split and split again exponentially. This microscopic dot – technically termed a *blastocyst* – spent three or so days bobbing down into the uterus looking for a good spot to embed itself. This embryo then developed a spinal chord and the beginnings of a head. Then came the brain, nerves, muscles, intestines and blood vessels, the embryo all the time drawing nourishment from its mother. The heart began to beat, the lens, cornea and iris of the eyes developed. Fingers sprouted out. Over the coming months, the foetus grew, float-

---

2. Matthew 1:19.
3. Matthew 1:20–21.

ing in warm salty fluid in a sac inside his mother's body. He began to suck his thumb, kick, stretch, move. And then on a given day, the final grain of sand fell through the hour glass and it was time for the baby to be born. The Son of God was about to enter the world.

But sometime in the lead-up to this momentous event, Joseph got some news – news that led the two parents to embark on a journey to a town in the south, a town called Bethlehem.

The months ticked by as the miracle of God's Son on earth unfolded inside his mother.

Jesus' birth is the most widely celebrated annual global event … a time of turkeys, chestnuts roasting on an open fire (apparently), fir trees, goodwill to all, and Bing Crosby.

If you've ever been to a preschool Christmas concert, you already know the drill. The nativity scene unfolds like this: Cue Joseph leading his wife on a donkey. Joseph has a large walking cane, while his wife clutches a doll with blonde hair. Cue assortment of barnyard animals (all kids who didn't get a lead role, dressed as sheep, cows and donkeys, and one kid who turned up dressed as a zebra). Cue angels (rosy-cheeked girls in ballet dresses with fairy wings from the dress-up box). Sing "Hark the Herald Angels Sing". Bring on the shepherds (the rowdy boys in dressing gowns with large shepherd's canes). Sing "While Shepherds Watched Their Flocks by Night". Cue the three wise men, each clutching elaborate presents for the newborn king. Sing "We Three Kings".* Big finale of "The Twelve Days of Christmas", and then Santa arrives to hand out presents and everyone heads off for coffee and mince pies.**

Years of watching nativity scenes and Christmas television specials have blurred the lines of reality into cliche. We have this picture in our heads of a particularly ill-timed trip as Joseph decides to take Mary on the four-day journey just as she is hitting the end of the ninth month of her labour. As they roll into town – Joseph leading Mary on a donkey – night falls and Mary goes into labour, so she stands out in the street, wincing with contractions, while Joseph runs up and down banging on doors trying to find somewhere to stay, only to have doors slammed on him by gruff innkeepers saying things like, "Full up inside. There's no room at the inn!" So in desperation they go round the back to the barn and – *then we kind of skip a bit because no Christmas card or nativity scene ever actually covers the birth itself* – suddenly they have a glowing child, whom they put in a manger. Minutes later, a bunch of shepherds and three kings on camels bearing gifts turn up, and they all bow in reverence before the manger. The light from the makeshift cot is so bright that it shoots out the doors and windows in harshly defined beams. Somewhere in the background, angels are singing. Some people even throw in a little drummer boy, who turns up banging his drum, just for good measure. (Like that's exactly what a woman wants to hear just after she's given birth!)

The whole event has a homely and tranquil feel to it, a serenity which leaves you with a warm glow on the inside and a desire to consume turkey

> * Hey! I was a wise man in a play once. I rode in on a horse with wheels.
> – Ben
>
> Not now, Ben, not now!
> – Pete

** Aussie talk for traditional Australian Christmas fare: moist fruit mince in a light tart, dusted with icing sugar.

Years of watching
nativity scenes
and Christmas
television specials
have blurred the
lines of reality
into cliche.

and figgy pudding. Jesus' Christmas card – style birth has a certain rural splendour, an earthy majesty to it. It is important, however, to separate what we know from the Bible and cultural norms from what we know because we have been to Christmas pageants.

Luke's account of Jesus' birth tells us that Caesar Augustus had decreed that a census of the Roman world should take place.[1] This required all men to return to their place of birth to register.[2] Joseph's hometown was Bethlehem, a small town of no more than a few thousand people, seventy-five miles to the south of Nazareth.

The Bible says that Joseph did go to Bethlehem and that he took Mary and that "while they were there, the time came for the baby to be born."[3] The fact is that no one really knows if Joseph and Mary were in Bethlehem for a week or a month before Jesus was born. Being poor, they would have walked the journey rather than rode a donkey, as is sometimes assumed. Any parent who has lived through the final weeks of pregnancy knows only a foolish couple would embark on a journey of several days just as the woman was reaching her full term.

The classic Christmas-card picture of Jesus being born in a wooden stable out the back of an inn with a "No Vacancies" sign on it may have some merit to it. But such an assumption largely comes from the fact that his first cot was a manger – an animal's feeding trough. Another possibility is that Joseph and Mary may in fact have found a shepherd's cave on the outskirts of town in which to set up their camp and have their child. This outdoor living was not so strange given that the four-day journey from Nazareth to Bethlehem would have meant sleeping out under the stars anyway. There were no conveniently placed hotels for backpackers back then.

There is a far more likely scenario about this "first Christmas". Given that Bethlehem was Joseph's hometown, it is highly likely he would have had a number of relatives there. Although there were no proper private lodgings for them (with the upper room of the house filled with other family visitors in town for the census),* they would have stayed somewhere in makeshift accommodations with Joseph's relatives. Houses in ancient Bethlehem were often cut into the side of a hill and had a courtyard area and a central room for cooking and a cistern for water, and rooms off this central space. Houses also had a lower-ground cave dug out and annexed to the house, where the family's animals sheltered. It is perhaps here that makeshift accommodation was set up to give Mary privacy during her birth. She would have been attended by other women of the family, and Joseph would not have been present.

* There is no mention of an innkeeper in the Bible, and the traditional use of the ancient Greek word that we translate as "inn" could also be translated as "guest room" or "upper room".

1. Luke 2:1.
2. Luke 2:3.
3. Luke 2:4–7.

Our relatively modern Christmas carols have also romanticized the story so that we are led to believe that the night was silent and that all was calm and all was bright. However, it was unlikely that the night was silent. There would have been the sounds of community and town living … the voices of men talking, children playing, travellers moving around the town, perhaps some Roman soldiers walking outside, animals crying on the nearby hillside. There would have been the smells of animals and fire and torches and cooking.

While many people hold a picture of a serene Jesus who is so noble at this stage of his life that "no crying he makes", it's important to remember that Jesus was born just like everyone else.* He did not emerge regally as a clean radiant bundle with a meditative Son of God expression on his face. There was blood and fluids and sweat and contractions and pain. Jesus was born covered in vernix and blood. The women attending the mother and child helped clean him up and cleared his throat of placental fluids. They delivered the placenta and cut his umbilical cord and placed him on Mary's breast. They helped to clean the new mother, perhaps with a purifying bath, although technically she remained ritually unclean for seven days.[4] They prepared an improvised cot for the baby, cleaning out an animal's feeding trough – a manger – and lining it with straw.**

Regardless of all these "it could have been like this" scenarios, the main point is that the most important event in history took place two thousand years ago in a very modest setting in a small town in an insignificant region of the Roman Empire. This is so amazing that it almost defies comprehension. The dimensions of time and space and heaven and earth crossed over and all came spiralling to a single point watched by God himself and armies of unknown spiritual beings. And in the epicentre, we find a husband and his young wife and newborn son.

The Son of God was now on earth.

---

4. Leviticus 12.

* That's because "the little Lord Jesus, lots of crying he makes, just like any other newborn" doesn't scan quite as well in the song.   – Pete

Oh, I don't know. I think it's kinda catchy.   – Ben

** Jesus' date of birth is, in most countries, traditionally celebrated on December 25. The exact date of Jesus' birth, however, is uncertain. Some historians, for example, believe it was more likely in April or May.

# Chapter 7

# ANGELS, SHEPHERDS AND EVIL DICTATORS
## People hear the good news

A birth is a time of great celebration, of new beginnings and looking to the future. It's an *event*. People sit up and take notice. When each of Peter and Meredith's children were born, it didn't take long for the phone and email networks to kick into gear and for the news to spread in ever-widening circles of gossip. There was a flurry of cards and flowers and even a helium balloon or two. A notice appeared in the church newsletter. And then there were the visitations. Friends and relatives came out of the woodwork to visit mother and child in hospital to see for themselves. They came in droves to offer best wishes, ask gratuitous questions, bring booties and bibs, talk in ridiculous coochy-woo baby voices and generally overstay their welcome. There were congratulatory handshakes, cuddles, backslaps, kisses and photographs.

Though there was little pomp and ceremony in Jesus' lowly birth, it certainly didn't go unnoticed. In the spiritual plane, eyes imperceptible to man were cast toward this spot on the planet. And in the physical world too there were a number of people who were confronted by this birth, each with their own reactions. In the countryside and local area, some people heard the news: the Messiah had been born.

Let's have a look at the different encounters.

### Angels and Shepherds (Luke 2:8 – 20)

On the outskirts of town were a bunch of shepherds who were protecting their livestock from thieves and predators. They were on guard, probably chatting and telling stories and jokes about sheep* to keep themselves awake around the warmth of the fire.

Suddenly there was a bit of a commotion – some movement, noise, light – and "an angel of the Lord appeared to them, and the glory of the Lord shone around them." Like everyone else in the Bible who meets an angel, their reaction was natural: pure and unadulterated fear. Maybe they cowered on the ground, maybe they yelled and swung their shepherd's staves at the visitor, maybe they ran for it … we don't know. But we do know that "they were terrified."

The angel told them not to be afraid and that he had good news. He declared that on that very day in Bethlehem, the Messiah had been born. Not only that, but he told them the child was wrapped in cloths and lying in a manger. And then came the grand finale. To pack a punch, the Bible says a

> In the countryside and local area, some people heard the news: the Messiah had been born.

> * Hey Ben, what do you get if you cross a sheep with a kangaroo? – Pete
>
> What?                – Ben
>
> A woolly jumper!    – Pete

great company of spiritual beings appeared with the angel and praised God, declaring, "Glory to God in the highest heaven, and on earth peace to those on whom his favor rests."

Can you imagine the scene on that dark hillside all those years ago as a bunch of lowly shepherds witnessed such a mind-boggling display?

This was the most amazing thing to ever happen to these men. The Messiah had been born right in their own backyard! Excited, they scrambled into town, where a frenzied search led them to the place where the new parents and their son were staying. We can only imagine the comical scene as Joseph was confronted by a bunch of smelly herdsmen who asked to be admitted to see the newborn. In shuffle the shepherds, eyes wide and mouths open, to see for themselves the Messiah who would save their nation. After they had seen him, they left and excitedly spread the word amongst the people about what had happened. And everyone was amazed. The shepherds returned, glorifying and praising God for everything they had heard and seen that day.

No doubt Joseph and Mary remembered their angelic messengers all those months ago. Now for the first time, other people had received a message about their son. Their private knowledge was now public. Mary contemplated what the shepherds said to her and treasured everything that happened to her.

### Simeon and Anna (Luke 2:21–38)

In the days following Jesus' birth, Joseph, Mary and Jesus took part in a number of traditional Jewish ceremonies.

For seven days after childbirth, a Jewish woman was considered ceremonially unclean.[1] During this time, the baby did not officially have a name. But then on the eighth day, the parents would participate in a ceremony to formally name the baby and, if a boy, to circumcise him. Circumcision was a significant symbol within Jewish society, and it was considered an important sign of a young man's identity as part of the Israelite nation and God's chosen people.[2]

So on the eighth day, Jesus was named and circumcised – probably by the local rabbi in Bethlehem. In accordance with the angel's direction, they gave him the name Jesus.

Joseph and Mary stayed in Bethlehem, and just over a month later (when Mary had waited the required time before going to the temple), it was time for two other important ceremonies. For these, Joseph and Mary walked six miles north to the city of Jerusalem. They made their way through the busy streets and markets to the temple, a vast and majestic structure and the centrepiece of Jewish life.

---

1. Leviticus 12:1–2.
2. Genesis 17:1–14; Leviticus 12:3.

> In shuffle the shepherds, eyes wide and mouths open, to see for themselves the Messiah who would save their nation.

First, Mary participated in a cleansing ceremony as a way of ritually purifying her from the bleeding of childbirth, as required in the law.[3] At one of the gates of the temple, she purchased two birds to be given to a priest for sacrifice.

Second, according to the law, the firstborn male in any Israelite family was to be ceremonially "given" to God.[4] With some similarity to a modern infant baptism, the baby Jesus was given to a priest, who said some words and dedicated him.

And it was there in the courts of the temple, while Joseph and Mary were in the midst of these rituals, that they were approached by two strangers.

The first was Simeon, a Jerusalem local described as righteous and devout. A man finely in tune with God's voice, Simeon believed that the Messiah would come in his lifetime, and that he would not die until he had seen the Messiah with his own eyes. And after all that waiting, that day had come at last.

Over the previous weeks, Simeon may have heard the exciting rumour going around: Just a few miles down the road, some shepherds claimed to have had an angelic visitation. Not only that, they had actually visited the Messiah themselves. Perhaps Simeon knew that the family would be coming to the temple for the rituals. So when he saw Jesus, he knew his wait was over. He took the baby in his arms and praised God, declaring that his eyes had at last seen the means of salvation and that this child would be a light to many. Joseph and Mary marvelled at Simeon's words, the moment perhaps made more poignant in that they stood there in the shadow of the temple, the most important edifice in the religious life of the nation.

But Simeon had not finished. He blessed them and then had a further – in some ways more sombre – message for the young mother. He said to her, "This child is destined to cause the falling and rising of many in Israel, and to be a sign that will be spoken against, so that the thoughts of many hearts will be revealed." With these words, Simeon pointed to the impact that this baby would have on the nation and to the fact that he would change lives and cause people to take sides. Mary must have been chilled, though, to hear his conclusion: "And a sword will pierce your own soul too."[5] Perhaps over the years, Mary thought back on this encounter and wondered what it all meant. She had about thirty years to wait before these words would echo horribly in her ears, as she endured a mother's anguish at seeing her son mocked, ridiculed, arrested and executed.

At that time, they must have been surprised to see another enthusiastic stranger. Anna was a prophetess, an elderly widow who virtually lived at the

> Simeon took the baby in his arms and praised God, declaring that his eyes had at last seen the means of salvation and that this child would be a light to many.

---

3. Leviticus 12.
4. Exodus 13:1–2, 12.
5. Luke 2:34–35.

temple, where she prayed and fasted. She approached them at that moment and began to give thanks to God that the Messiah had been born. Not only that, but like the shepherds before her, she began to spread the word about the child to all of the visitors, pilgrims, travellers and locals who had been looking forward to the long-awaited salvation of the nation.

After Joseph and Mary had completed all the rituals required by the law, they returned to Nazareth. They had been away long enough, with their extended stay in Bethlehem as well as the visit to Jerusalem. It was time to go home.*

As they travelled north over several days, this time with a baby son, perhaps they discussed the events of the past months … the angelic messengers, the miraculous pregnancy, cousin Elizabeth's remarkable reaction, the journey to Bethlehem, the makeshift cot and the visits from a bunch of shepherds and the old man and old woman at the temple. If they had any doubts before, they were well aware by now that something big was unfolding around them.

But not all who heard the news about the Messiah were pleased.

### The Magi and Herod (Matthew 2:1–18)

One of the most well-known icons of Christmas-card imagery is that of three kings on camels silhouetted under an inky sky as they cross a vast Arabian desert. Generally there is an enormous star in the corner that is twinkling in a way that … um, well … is twinkling in a way that stars do only on cards.

Other cards show three kings, resplendent in their royal garb, kneeling before a baby in a manger, and in front of them, three jewel-encrusted golden gift boxes containing royal gifts.

It's a nice image, but it's not very accurate.

Here's what we do know.

A group of magi came from the East to pay tribute to the Messiah.** There may have been three of them, but given the nature of their journey and who they were, a larger group is more likely. They were not kings but magi or, traditionally, wise men. However, these wise men were more than clever guys who knew lots of stuff and went around posing riddles. The magi were the supreme and esteemed priestly caste from the Persian Empire to the east. They had an official and scholarly function within society, and they performed duties in relation to advising rulers. They interpreted dreams and visions, performed rituals and had a particular focus on things celestial. In a curious mix of astrology and early astronomy, they sought to make sense of life and the world through the patterns and shapes of the stars, comets, sun and moon.

So here we have a sect of priests in a distant country whose very bread and butter is watching the stars and interpreting prophecy. Several hundred

* Admittedly, working out the exact chronology of these events is a bit of a nightmare. The accounts of Luke and Matthew are hard to marry at times because one describes a journey to Jerusalem and Nazareth while the other narrates an urgent escape to Egypt. Just in what order some of these events took place is hard to determine, but we just have to live with that.

** The traditional names of the three magi are Casper, Melchior and Balthazar, although these names are not cited in the Bible. Men like the magi were around for hundreds of years before Jesus. In the first five chapters of the book of Daniel, for example, we read that Daniel was placed in charge of the wise men of Babylon — the magicians, enchanters, astrologers and diviners.

A group of magi came from the East to pay tribute to the Messiah.

years before Jesus was born, many Israelites were exiled to the East. It is likely that their knowledge of scriptural prophecies relating to the coming king-Messiah had survived through the years and was still alive and well in this distant land. The magi knew that one would be born who would be king of the Jews. And then one night, somebody spotted a star, a portent that something was happening. They interpreted this as a sign of the fulfilment of the ancient prophecy, and promptly dispatched a convoy to travel the trade route to the main Jewish city of Jerusalem to pay homage to this king.

The "yonder star" that they "follow" is sometimes presented as a glowing orb darting around like Tinkerbell, leading them this way and that along their journey. In other images, the star even shines a crisp shaft of light like the search beam from an alien spacecraft right down onto the manger, providing a homing beacon for the distant travellers. Such representations come from the imaginations of the designers of Christmas cards, and the reality was perhaps somewhat more mundane.

So these magi set off from home bound for the Jewish capital. Given their status in society, together with the fact that they obviously had some wealth, their convoy would have been sizeable, involving many men and camels. They would have had servants for protection as well as workers to look after the animals, set up camp, cook and stay on guard against desert brigands.

In contrast to the often noble and elegant image we have of this purposeful band of travellers crossing a rather pleasant rustic landscape, T. S. Eliot's famous poem "The Journey of the Magi" poses an image of a long and arduous journey for these travellers. In the poem, his magi encounter sharp cold weather in the dead of a desert winter. The camels are exhausted and stubborn, while the camel men curse and grumble and complain about the lack of women and liquor. The cities are hostile, the towns unfriendly and the village lodgings are dirty and overpriced. While their night fires go out and they struggle with the lack of shelter, voices of doubt ring in their ears and they think back on their pleasant life in the summer palaces they left behind.

But eventually they arrived in Jerusalem. And this is where things get tricky.

Herod was an ambitious and cruel politician, a puppet ruler who had been placed in power over Judea by the Roman ruler Mark Antony forty years before. Herod, however, was not Jewish, and many Jews hated his rule and the sacrilegious Roman and Greek influences he tried to impose on his kingdom. His kingship was marked by an incredibly brutal dictatorship that saw the annihilation of any person or group who threatened his power. He had several members of his own family killed, including his wife, uncle and many of his in-laws. He drowned his wife's brother because he was becoming too popular with the Jewish people. His wife was understandably incensed, and this led to a rift in their relationship and eventually to her execution as well. He murdered teachers and students who tried to remove a Roman symbol from the temple. After Herod had two of his own sons executed, Emperor Augustus quipped that it would be preferable to be Herod's pig than his son. He even arranged that many of Jerusalem's important citizens would be executed on the day he died, to ensure a sombre and mournful mood in the city. This is all important background to bear in mind as the convoy of travellers from the East roll into the city.

As important international guests, the magi were granted an audience with the ruler, Herod, whom they asked, "Where is the one who has been born king of the Jews?"

You probably could have cut the air with a knife. Here was Herod, the ambitious and jealous ruler who could not tolerate any kind of challenge to his rule, being asked where the **new king** was? The people of Jerusalem were also greatly troubled at this pronouncement, perhaps realising what murderous rampages and purges would soon follow.

Immediately wanting to locate and execute this new king, Herod consulted the Jewish priests and rabbis, who quoted the prophecies to him[6] that Bethlehem would be the birthplace of the leader of Israel. So Herod sent the visitors on their way, trying to deceive them into reporting back to him with the new king's location so that he too, supposedly, could pay homage. His intentions, of course, were less than honourable.

The magi did find the child with his mother, Mary.* They paid honour to him by bowing down and worshiping him. They presented him with gifts of gold, frankincense and myrrh.** At last their long quest was over and it was time to depart for home. However, they were troubled by dreams about Herod and, with such a warning, decided not to report back to him but to travel home via an alternative route.

Joseph must have been thrilled to receive such a delegation come to pay honour to his son. And the gifts they brought were beyond any wealth he had seen before. But for the second time, Joseph had a dream, this time a troubling one. An angel appeared to him and warned that his son was in danger. Herod was after him, and it wouldn't take his spies and officials long to track down where the visitors had been. The humble carpenter's family became public enemy number one. He woke and immediately grabbed Mary, his son and some provisions and headed off into the night. On the run, so to speak, they needed to get a long way away out of Herod's grasp. So they turned their feet south toward Egypt.

It didn't take Herod long to realise that the magi had pulled a swifty on him. His response was fast and brutal. If he couldn't locate and kill the usurper to his throne, he would destroy *all* potential new kings. He was tak-

*This event was probably some time after the birth, even many months. It was not on the same night, as is so often depicted in Christmas-card scenes.

** What are frankincense and myrrh anyway?
– Pete

Glad you asked. They are resins from dried tree sap. They were very valuable and were used as the main ingredient in perfumes, incense and embalming ointment.
– Ben

6. Micah 5:2.

ing no chances. So he despatched Roman soldiers to Bethlehem, where they massacred all the male children under the age of two. While this is a horrific act, especially to us today, it wasn't that unusual in a country under the heavy hand of a murderous ruler.

Joseph and Mary stayed in Egypt while the situation remained dangerous for them back at home. We know nothing of their life there, although it's possible that Joseph secured work to have a steady income. Alternatively, they may have used some of the gifts from the magi to finance the journey and to provide food and lodging in this foreign country.

When Herod died, Joseph returned with his family to Nazareth.

### Jesus as a Boy (Luke 2:41–52)

Apart from these early stories, we know nothing of Jesus' upbringing, with the exception of one event that took place twelve years later.

According to custom, Joseph and Mary undertook an annual journey to Jerusalem to celebrate the Feast of the Passover. (This was an important part of Jewish history and life, which we will come back to later.) Pilgrims from all over the country travelled to Jerusalem for this festival. The roads in and out would be crowded with caravans of travelling groups made up of friends, neighbours and family, while Jerusalem itself would be packed.

After the celebration concluded, Joseph and Mary, along with their large contingent of extended family, friends and other Nazarene locals, began the long journey back home.

The popular film *Home Alone** begins with a large extended family heading off for a Christmas vacation interstate. There are uncles and aunts, cousins, nieces and nephews and sons and daughters everywhere. As they are running late, there is a frenzied departure as all the various people pile randomly into a fleet of minivans to rush them to the airport, where they all sprint for the plane and get on board just in time. It is only a while later when the plane is in full flight that one of the mothers sits bolt upright and screams out, "Kevin!" In the large group and in the rush, her young son Kevin had been left home alone.

Mary and Joseph found themselves in a similar predicament on the return journey from the feast. It was after a day's travel that Mary sat up and screamed out, "Jesus!" In the midst of this large travelling community, Jesus had been left behind. Joseph and Mary no doubt went through one of those "I thought he was with you!" "No, I thought he was with you!" conversations. A quick search revealed that twelve-year-old Jesus was not in their party. He had indeed been left *In Jerusalem Alone*.

They rushed back to the city and searched the streets and lodgings and markets for him, but to no avail. For three days they searched, and on the third day, they found him in the crowded courts of the temple, the

> The magi did find the child with his mother, Mary. They paid honour to him by bowing down and worshiping him.

> * Hey Pete, did you know that according to several largely unreliable internet sources, *Home Alone* is ranked somewhere in the top three highest-grossing comedies ever? – Ben
>
> Well no, Ben, I didn't. Thanks for sharing. – Pete

This twelve-year-old boy obviously had a profound wisdom and learning beyond his years.

same courts where they had encountered Simeon and Anna all those years before.

There he was, sitting among the teachers, engaging them in animated conversation, listening to them and asking them questions. And everyone who heard him was amazed at his understanding. This twelve-year-old boy obviously had a profound wisdom and learning beyond his years.

Mary's somewhat humorous response is familiar to any parent who has felt the simultaneous relief and anger at finding a lost child in a crowded shopping mall: "Son, where have you been? How could you do this to us? Don't you know your dad and I have been worried sick! It's festival time! What do you think you are doing?"

Jesus' response is interesting. He says, "Why were you searching for me? . . . Didn't you know I had to be in my Father's house?"[7]

It appears that at this young age, Jesus already had a strong sense of his otherworldly identity. His home was in the house of his Father, God – the temple.

Despite their encounters with angels a decade ago, and their knowledge of their son's miraculous conception, birth and mission, Mary and Joseph did not understand what he was talking about. Perhaps they were too angry to be bothered with his cryptic response. No doubt their conversation would have been interesting as they sought to catch up to their party on the road over the next two days.

But then the Bible falls to silence about the life of Jesus.

He returned to Nazareth and lived the life of a Jewish male, observing the sacred rites and festivals and participating in the life of the synagogue. He grew up in a community, following the seasons, activities and rituals of rural village life. Given the miraculous nature of his birth and how news about it spread, perhaps over the years he was followed by sideways glances and the whispers of rumours. He also grew up in a family with its own relationships and domestic routines. His parents had other children – a daughter and some sons.* But we do not hear about Joseph again, so it's possible that he died during this period.

* Imagine being the brother of the Son of God!
– Pete

You could never win a fight!
– Ben

All we have to go on is Luke's summation: "And as Jesus grew up, he increased in wisdom and in favor with God and people."[8] These were formative years for Jesus, through which he must have grown into a sense of preparation for his mission ahead.

About eighteen years pass by before we hear about Jesus again.

It was then that Jesus, now a young man of about thirty years of age, would embark on his mission.

And that is when all ~~hell~~ heaven broke loose.

---

7. Luke 2:49–50.
8. Luke 2:52.

## Part 3

# MAN WITH A MISSION

The rocket ship breaks into the earth's atmosphere. It streaks down through the sky before ploughing across a field in a fiery ball. A married couple passing by pull their car over and go to investigate, only to discover that there is a baby inside the wreckage. Jonathan and Martha Kent rescue the child from the inferno, taking him back to their farm outside of Smallville. They adopt the boy and christen him Clark.

It doesn't take them long to realise that their baby is somewhat unique. Clark has special and incredible powers. He is faster than a speeding bullet, more powerful than a locomotive and able to leap tall buildings in a single bound. As the boy grows up, however, they hide these powers from the rest of the world. To everyone outside, Clark is a normal boy – simply the Kent kid. He does his farm chores and attends the local high school. His nickname is Specs. Only his parents know just how unique and special their son is. They know that at some point in the future, Clark's real identity will have to emerge in the public arena, and it will be something the world has not seen before. And of course, one day, this happens. Like a butterfly emerging from his superhero cocoon, Superman soon comes face to face with the world in all his red and blue splendour.*

Like the Kents, it must have been strange for Joseph and Mary watching their son grow up as an ordinary boy in their small village, at the same time aware that he was unique and special, that he was the Messiah. To everyone else, he was just one of Joseph and Mary's boys, along with his younger sister and brothers** – James, Joseph, Judas and Simon. He played with other kids and his siblings, went to school and synagogue, did his chores, learned a trade.

For the large part – aside from a few people at the time of his birth and those who had caught the rumours – only his parents and his mother's cousin seemed to know just how unique and special their son was. They knew that at some point in the future, their son's real identity would have to emerge in the public arena, and it would be something the world had not seen before. One can only imagine their conversations and expectations as they pondered what the future held for him and, indeed, for them. They would have remembered the strange events of years ago – the visitations and news from God's messengers – *but what did it mean?* When would he "become" the Messiah? What would happen? They knew something was going to happen. It was just a matter of when.

> \* Today's trivia is: Clark Kent's middle name is … Joseph! — Pete
>
> Mate, you have too much time on your hands. — Ben

** Some Christians believe that these were not really Mary's children, as they say that she remained a perpetual virgin throughout her life.

> In Jesus' time,
> the role of being
> a teacher of the
> Jewish religion
> and law – a
> rabbi – was
> highly esteemed
> and respected.

There comes a time in every superhero's life when they reach a crossroads and actually take a decisive step to reveal their true identity to the public.

Jesus did something like this when he was about thirty years old.[*]

And the world would never be the same.

In Jesus' time, the role of being a teacher of the Jewish religion and law – a rabbi – was highly esteemed and respected. Rabbis were important teachers and interpreters of the Jewish scriptures. If you wanted to be a rabbi, you had to not only be pretty smart and literate but also devote many years to study.

From the age of six, children were taught by rabbis, and they memorised what we know as the first five books of the Bible – the Torah. Most male children finished their schooling at that point and went off to learn a trade. The more able and devoted students, however, continued memorising the rest of their scriptures so that by about the age of fourteen, they knew much of what we know as the Old Testament off by heart. They also learned the robust art of questioning and answering and discussing and wrestling with what they were reading. Only the best pupils made it through, and at this stage – as young men – they would apprentice themselves to a particular rabbi and become one of his disciples. They would devote themselves to that rabbi, follow him, learn from him and try to imitate him. While all rabbis shared some core beliefs, they also had their own ways of interpreting certain verses or passages, so to apprentice yourself to a certain rabbi was to sign up, in effect, to be like him and teach his way of looking at things. After many years of devoted following, the apprentice could become ordained and at age thirty become a rabbi himself, travelling, teaching and having his own followers.

Similarly, it was when Jesus turned thirty that he also began his public work of travelling, teaching and drawing to himself a group of disciples.

Jesus headed out of town to visit his relative John, who was the same age. John lived in the bush[**] and was a bit of a wild man with a reputation for preaching about the kingdom of God. He moved around the country near the Jordan River, and many people travelled to hear what this new prophet had to say about God and the times to come. There was obviously a lot of religious excitement at the time and a fervour of expectation waiting for the Messiah. Many people thought that perhaps John might be the Messiah who would lead them in revolt against their oppressors. He was quite outspoken, and we know that he put a few noses out of joint by making disparaging remarks about the establishment and by being critical of the religious and political leaders of the time.[***] He was no soft preacher – he was blunt with tax collectors and soldiers and the crowds who flocked to hear him. He taught that people should turn away from their wrongdoings – from harsh words, corruption, selfishness, hypocrisy, violence and deceit. He baptised people

* It's hard to say exactly at what age Jesus began his ministry, but the consensus is that it was when he was about thirty years of age.
** Aussie talk for "wilderness".
*** In fact, it was his criticism of the son of Herod's marriage practices that soon led to his imprisonment and execution.

(by dunking them in the river) as a show of their desire to make a new start and get their lives in order with God.

While John was baptising, Jesus turned up among the crowd and was baptised too. However, this particular baptism was unlike any other because of its powerful supernatural component. The gospel writers record that God's Spirit came upon Jesus in a physically visible way – described for us as being like a dove – and that God himself declared Jesus as his Son.[1] His baptism was, therefore, like an ordination as he embarked on three years of ministry that would shape the world and change human history.

Jesus didn't go straight home, however. After he was baptised, he walked into the desert region of the lower Jordan Valley, a thirty kilometre stretch between the Jerusalem plateau and the Dead Sea. During this time, he was obviously contemplating the days ahead. It was also something of a trial as he wrestled with his dual nature as both God and man and resisted the temptation to let it all go.

When Jesus got back to town, he went to the local synagogue just as he would have done each week. However, this would turn out to be a very different occasion for those present. When the time came for the scriptures (the Old Testament) to be read, Jesus was appointed the reader. He had no doubt done this many times before, but this time would be very different.

When the scroll for the reading was passed to him, he chose and read out a passage written six hundred years before by a bloke called Isaiah. The words spoke about the Messiah: a person with God's Spirit who was chosen and sent to tell the good news, to free people and perform miracles.

All okay so far. But then it came time to speak. To the total surprise of all present, many of whom had probably known Jesus all of his life, Jesus suddenly declared that *he* was the one; *he* was the king that God had appointed; *he* was the one who would free people and who would bring sight to the blind.

One can only imagine the awkward silence, the heads snapping up, the jaws dropping, the orb of tumbleweed blowing across the room.

The crowd's reaction? They didn't believe it. They *couldn't* believe it. They knew Jesus' dad, they knew his mum and they had known Jesus since he was a kid. How could he be the one? *The carpenter's son!* ***Ridiculous!***

To get back to our Superman analogy, to the rest of the world – his friends, relatives, neighbours, colleagues – he is just an ordinary person. He lives in a house, has a job, goes to the shops and, more often than not, leads something of a mundane, uneventful, even boring existence. It is incomprehensible to everyone else that there is another side to him, a hidden identity which is incredible and powerful, that he goes around saving people and performing incredible feats. Not in their wildest dreams would anyone

---

1. Matthew 3:13–17; Mark 1:9–11; Luke 3:21–22.

* Pete, I've never heard of Mr Asparagus. Doesn't sound like much of a superhero to me.     – Ben

He is my own creation from a story I wrote when I was fourteen. Didn't really work, though.
     – Pete

** Aussie talk for "things quickly getting turned around and going wrong".

imagine quiet student Peter Parker as Spider-Man, clumsy Clark Kent as Superman, suave industrialist Bruce Wayne as Batman or tiny Jake Lamb as Mr Asparagus.* The idea is ludicrous! Can you imagine the scene if Peter Parker stood up in his school assembly and said, "Listen up, everyone, I have an announcement to make. I just wanted to let you know that … I am … um, well … Spider-Man." There would be perhaps a moment of gob-smacked silence, followed quickly by howls of laughter, yells of derision and a range of unflattering comments. No doubt he would soon find himself booted out the door.

It's easy for us looking back on Jesus' story to see him only through a historical lens as "Jesus Christ, Saviour", the Son of God who performed miracles, healed and taught people, and came back to life after death.

But it's important for us to remember that to his friends and neighbours in a small farming community, he was just one of the many young Jewish men growing up in the village and leading something of a mundane, uneventful, even boring existence: playing, learning, doing chores, going to school, growing up, working, eating, sleeping, travelling, paying taxes and going to the synagogue.

But then he came out with it: **"I am the Messiah!"**

His statement was confrontational. The crowd had to decide what they thought of his claim. Either he was the Son of God, the Messiah … or he was Joseph and Mary's boy – the bloke from up the road.

The crowd didn't choose the Son of God option. They didn't suddenly drop to their knees in reverence of the awaited king. Instead, the whole thing went pear shaped** and the crowd turned ugly. Their shock quickly turned to anger at such heresy, such blasphemy. They were so incensed that they dragged Jesus out of town and tried to throw him off a cliff. But Jesus escaped, turned his back on the town and headed down the road to the nearby town of Capernaum.

He was cast out of his hometown, branded as a blasphemer and rebel. It was hardly what you would call a highly dynamic or successful start to public ministry.

Over the coming days, weeks, months, years, he would go on to preach, teach, meet with the people and cause a sensation wherever he went. News spread about this man who claimed to be God's king; the Promised One who was going to bring in the good times of God's future kingdom. Jesus had lit the fuse. He was a rebel with a cause.

# Chapter 9

# FOLLOW ME
## Jesus puts his team together

One of the problems with reading the Bible is that it's difficult to read familiar stories with fresh eyes. Pete, for example, has always struggled with the whole description of events surrounding the calling of Jesus' twelve disciples. He attributes this in large part to one particular morning when he was a little kid at a Sunday school concert during which children performed skits from the Bible. The curtains opened to reveal a bunch of kids draped in towels and sheets and other hastily appropriated linen of the "clothing in ancient Bible times" variety. Some were holding a net while a couple of others had fishing rods, and they were talking about fishing and their boats and comparing their catches, all the time miming casting their rods and reeling in what could only have been giant marlin.

Enter stage left a tall boy in whitish dressing gown, sandals and for some inexplicable reason carrying a swag* and a giant walking staff. He walks to centre stage, faces the audience and declares in a reedy voice, "Come, follow me, and I will make you fishers of men."

He then turns and exits stage right. In total silence, the dozen or so other kids on stage throw their nets and rods and bags on the ground and march off after him in a trance.

It just all seemed so weird, like some bad science-fiction film in which zombies with their arms outstretched follow after their creator, mumbling, "Yhess ... mahs-ter ..." What would cause these men, who had lives and families and businesses, to down tools and suddenly head off with this stranger? Imagine your reaction if someone waltzed into your school or workplace and said, "Come, follow me." Surely, your reaction would be, "Um, thanks, but I'm a bit busy right now ..."

The first thing we have to understand is that the religion and faith of the Jews were not some sideline optional extras. Their ancient writings and teachings about God, various laws and history were the very bedrock of their society, which explains why rabbis were so esteemed and why their disciples devoted their lives to apprenticing under them. After many years, the disciple could himself become a rabbi and gather his own group of disciples. And so, the line of that rabbi, so to speak, was passed on to the next generation. (This whole concept has been appropriated in the Star Wars films, in which disciples learn the ways of the Force by apprenticing themselves to a master.)**

* Aussie talk for a sleeping mat and bag, rolled up and carried over the shoulder.

** That's right, like how Qui-Gon Jinn passes his ways on to Obi-Wan, who then apprentices Anakin Skywalker. But when Anakin apprentices himself to the evil emperor, he ... – Pete

Ahem ... Pete, let's stay on track, shall we? – Ben

It was a great honour to become the disciple of a rabbi. While many might aspire to be a rabbi, the path was long and arduous, and only the most astute, hardworking, dedicated and intelligent disciples would finish their apprenticeship. There is a scene in the great film *Men of Honour* in which a group of fresh navy cadets are berated by their master chief. He tells them that from their large group of hopefuls, only one quarter will finish their training. And then from that group, only three will make it to retirement as a navy diver. Only the elite will make it through. It was the same with the process of becoming a rabbi.

The main point is that Jesus' gathering a group of disciples to him was not some sort of one-off anomaly. It was a standard and accepted practice of everyday life in the Judean culture. There were lots of rabbis and lots of disciples around. John the Baptist, for example, had his own group of disciples (some of whom became disciples of Jesus). Similarly, Matthew reports that on one occasion, the disciples of a group of Pharisees were sent to trap Jesus by asking him weighted questions about the paying of taxes to Rome.[1] To us, the idea of people deciding to follow and dedicate their lives to some teacher is quite foreign, but at the time of Jesus, it was not.

Another point to make is that while the biblical narrative is quite abrupt in its delivery, it is unlikely that it was quite as inexplicably sudden as is implied. Pete always assumed that Jesus suddenly popped up from behind a bush and twelve men who had known him only for five seconds immediately fell under some mysterious spell and followed him like he was the Pied Piper.

Jesus' disciples were not limited to the famous group of twelve that we so often hear about. Jesus had many more disciples. Luke records that one morning Jesus "called his disciples to him and chose twelve of them, whom he also designated apostles".[2] In other words, the Twelve were a specific subgroup, chosen and sanctioned by Jesus from within the larger group of disciples as his – for want of better words – executive team. We also see this wider body of disciples later on when Jesus selects and sends out about seventy of them to travel around the towns of Judea preaching and healing.[3] But things weren't always rosy amongst Jesus' disciples. After he preached a message in the synagogue in Capernaum,[4] many of Jesus' disciples began to grumble and question his teachings. So affronted were they that John records that "from this time many of his disciples turned back and no longer followed him."* ** So we see that the core group of twelve existed within the framework of a much larger group of followers.

> * Just like how Anakin Skywalker also turned his back ...        – Pete
>
> Stop it, Pete. You're scaring the readers.        – Ben
>
> Stabilize your rear deflectors! Watch for enemy fighters!        – Pete

** It was at this point that Jesus asked his closest disciples, "You do not want to leave too, do you?" (John 6:67).

---

1. Matthew 22:15–22.
2. Luke 6:13.
3. Luke 10.
4. John 6:25–66.

And while the writers imply that Jesus had a certain level of – call it what you will – appeal, power and charisma, it is unlikely that Jesus was unknown to his disciples when they began following him. Jesus' public ministry had already started before he began calling people to follow him. He had something of a public kickoff when the popular prophet John baptised him. Luke records how after Jesus caused a stir at his own synagogue, he travelled to Capernaum, where he began to preach and teach. Jesus healed a man in the synagogue and "all the people were amazed."[5] Jesus then went on to heal more people and preach in the synagogues and gain popularity, and it is at this point – "one day as Jesus was standing by the Lake of Gennesaret," as Luke puts it, "the people were crowding around him and listening to the word of God"[6] – that Jesus called his first disciples. So it wasn't quite as out of the blue as Pete's old Sunday school play implied. The two sets of fisherman brothers – Simon Peter and Andrew, and James and John – had seen and heard about Jesus, and when the chance came to become disciples of this new and amazing rabbi, they jumped at it. Other disciples came later. Matthew (Levi), for example, seems to have joined Jesus quite late in the piece after Jesus had already established a following. And it was much later again, after many travels and preaching and healings, that Jesus called his wider body of disciples to him and from them chose and commissioned the Twelve as his closest companions.

Jesus' disciples were not limited to the famous group of twelve that we so often hear about.

But one question remains: Even if this new rabbi did turn up and say, "Follow me!" *why did they?* They were not schoolboys on the lookout for a rabbi to apprentice themselves to. Peter was married. Others had well-paying jobs or their own businesses. *So why did they go?* Well, as young Jewish men who had known nothing but life in the shadow of Roman occupation, they were only too aware of the expectation that a Messiah was soon to appear to save their nation. The hope of their entire country's past, present and future lay on the shoulders of this Messiah. And here he was, right in front of them. (This expectation is illustrated nicely when after encountering Jesus, "Philip found Nathanael and told him, 'We have found the one Moses wrote about in the Law, and about whom the prophets also wrote – Jesus of Nazareth.' ")[7] In short, they were being offered a chance to hook up with the most important man in their nation's history. This was an honour that any young Jewish man would jump at. To illustrate, Ben is a guitarist and a U2 fan, so imagine if when he was eighteen, he had front-row seats at a U2 concert, and then at the end of the show, the guitarist, Edge, jumped down from the stage and said, "Hey, Ben, right? Listen, I want you to come on tour with me, follow me around, live with me, jam with the guys ... you know, hang out together

5. Luke 4:36.
6. Luke 5:1–11.
7. John 1:43–51.

* Actually, Pete, I dunno if
I would go.          – Ben

Oh Ben, you so would!
You are so deluded!
                    – Pete

for the next few years. I can teach you some stuff, and it'll be a blast … so, c'mon, follow me." Do you think for a minute Ben would say, "Um, actually, no thanks, I've got to do my chores and I have a project due for school"?*

So from his followers, Jesus chose twelve men who became his close companions and support team. They were his pupils – his ***disciples.*** And what an eclectic bunch they were. There were the two sets of fisherman brothers – Simon Peter and Andrew (previously followers of John the Baptist), and James and John – Philip and his friend Nathanael (Bar – *son of* – tholomew), Matthew (Levi) the tax collector, Thomas (Didymus), James (son of Alphaeus), Thaddaeus, and Simon the Zealot (a member of a militant revolutionary group, who in all likelihood was not too happy about having Matthew – a Roman-sympathising tax collector – in the group). Despite their diversity, all of the men had one thing in common. They were all from Galilee in the north. All of the men, that is, except for one: Judas Iscariot. Judas's surname is a derivation of the Hebrew *ish Kerioth*, meaning he was a man of the city of Kerioth in southern Judea. Some scholars suggest that he was a sicarii – a member of an armed sect of Zealot freedom fighters who worked subversively to cause trouble for the Romans.

On one level, Jesus' disciples had a practical function. They acted as his constant travelling companions and support team, looking after the logistics of his ministry. They are often seen to be in Jesus' immediate presence, dining with him and others, protecting him from crowds or organizing transport. Judas, it seems, was the treasurer of the group, with the responsibility of managing their funds. When Jesus gives orders to cross to the other side of the lake, it is the disciples who make it happen.[8] On Jesus' entry into Jerusalem, he sends two of them out to find the donkey for him to ride in on. At the Feast of the Passover, he dispatches another two to find the upper room where they will share their final meal together. It is with his disciples as a (rather ineffective) protective group that Jesus spends the hours before his arrest, and it's at least one of his disciples who stirs into action in trying to defend Jesus against the arresting mob.

However, on a more important level, the disciples were sitting at the feet of their master and listening to his teachings and learning his ways. He chose them that "they might be with him and that he might send them out to preach and to have authority to drive out demons".[9] In other words, he was training them up to themselves become masters of the craft of preaching the message of Jesus. They frequently wrestled with his words and struggled to be like him. Jesus is rarely mentioned without his disciples being present. He is constantly commenting to them, answering their questions, challenging their ideas and even rebuking and correcting them for their misleading

8. Matthew 8:18.
9. Mark 3:14–15.

thoughts or words. The disciples were privy to Jesus' more private moments, explanations and conversations. Jesus revealed things to them about who he is and what he was doing, which is important, because these men would take over where Jesus left off. And so Jesus commissioned them and gave them authority and lengthy instructions about their mission: "Proclaim this message: 'The kingdom of heaven has come near.' Heal the sick, raise the dead, cleanse those who have leprosy, drive out demons."[10]

It is clear that during Jesus' three years of ministry, his disciples went out to various places and began to preach and heal as per their rabbi's instructions. But they did so even more powerfully after Jesus' death.[11] These men would in fact play an integral role at a key point in human history in terms of spreading the good news – the *gospel* – of Jesus. It was Jesus' disciples who would take the news of their master throughout the ancient world, throughout Palestine, Asia Minor, Europe, North Africa and eventually the rest of the world.

But it is sobering to reflect upon the fact that these disciples' ministry came at a cost. They all suffered hardships and imprisonments, hostile towns and angry mobs, and tradition dictates that only one of the disciples – John – died of old age. The others were martyred for their highly controversial message that a crucified man from Nazareth was the promised Messiah.[*] The eleven disciples (not including Judas) were said to have been tortured, beheaded, stoned, crucified, burned alive, crucified upside down, speared or clubbed to death.

But in terms of our narrative, that's a long way off for these men. At this point, they were young men who had just met the Messiah and were excited about the possibilities that lay ahead serving as disciples of the man they called their rabbi – Jesus of Nazareth.

---

10. Matthew 10:7–8; Mark 6:6–13; Luke 9:1–6.

11. Which you can read about in the book of Acts.

They were young men who had just met the Messiah and were excited about the possibilities that lay ahead serving as disciples of the man they called their rabbi – Jesus of Nazareth.

* Except for Nero, there is virtually no evidence whatsoever until the second century that Christians were martyred by pagans. Jewish persecution accounted for 90 percent of Christian martyrs in the first century.

When the news was announced that international supergroup U2 were flying to Australia in 1984, the response was immediate and enormous. Fans from all over the country stirred to action. *Have you heard? U2 are coming!* They made travel plans and bought concert tickets. They came by plane and car, by train and boat, by bus and on foot. They flooded the lounges and observation decks of airports. Fans followed the group around to their various public appearances. They besieged the stage door of concert venues and camped out at their hotels, generally accompanied by a cacophony of chanting, singing, squealing and screaming. It was a frenzy as people scrambled just to get a glimpse of their idols and be part of the action of the sensation that was U2.

Of course, with such crowds it was virtually impossible to get close to the band. Impossible, that is, unless you are a die-hard fan with a cunning plan to somehow meet them face to face. A die-hard fan like, say … Ben.*

One morning, Ben and a few of his mates dressed up in business suits and caught a taxi to the hotel where U2 were staying. Because they looked like corporate salesmen rather than adoring fans, they were allowed right through the screaming crowd and ushered straight into the hotel lobby, where they promptly headed for the bistro, where breakfast was being served. Their ingenuity and perseverance paid off. After a while, Bono and the lads turned up to have breakfast too, and to cut a long story short, the result was Ben and his mates got to chat with the band and had a few photos taken … before they got turfed out!

It is easy to think of Jesus as being something of a meek individual who wandered the landscape chatting with handfuls of people and gathering an underground following. It's easy to think of him quietly skirting around on the fringe of society without too many people noticing him before suddenly and inexplicably getting picked up by the Romans and executed for sedition.

But the accounts in the Bible convey a very different story. Here we read of a Jesus who built up a huge following and attracted enormous crowds wherever he went. He was a social phenomenon that was hard to miss, kind of like when U2 rolled into town. He turned the whole country on its head.

At the time of Jesus, there was a great sense of excitement and expectation about the arrival of a deliverer. Riding on the back of previous military occupations by the Babylonians and Greeks, the Roman occupation had suppressed the Jews into a disgruntled population, while Herod's extravagances,

> * Oh for goodness sake, do we have to hear this story again?     – Pete
>
> Beware, Pete, the green-eyed monster which doth mock the meat it feeds on.     – Ben

> Here we read of a Jesus who built up a huge following and attracted enormous crowds wherever he went.

taxes and violent purges had pushed them to breaking point. There were rebellions and flare ups, battles and clashes all over the region as groups agitated to try to wrestle back control of their own politics, religion and country. News of a potential new leader was met with great enthusiasm.

When word got out that a new prophet, John, had begun preaching in the desert, the population was electrified to action. Word spread through the temple courts, the markets and laneways. News passed between neighbours, family members and out on the roads between travellers along the trade routes to other towns and settlements. *Have you heard about the new prophet? Come and see!* "People went out to him from Jerusalem and all Judea and the whole region of the Jordan."[1] But John's message would have only fired up the crowds even more. John told people that he was *not* the one they were waiting for. He was just the messenger preparing the way for the true Messiah, who was just around the corner.

That true Messiah was Jesus of Nazareth. His first speaking engagement in his home synagogue was less than successful. Overnight he went from being local lad to social outcast. But he walked to the next town and began to speak. And then the next town. And the next. And it didn't take long for the word about this new rabbi with his authoritative teaching to spread from place to place. Over the coming months and years, he went "through all the towns and villages, teaching in their synagogues, proclaiming the good news of the kingdom and healing every disease and sickness."[2] His popularity soon built up a momentum that spread rapidly from region to region. Jesus was no fringe preacher drifting around the outskirts of society. He was a social phenomenon, and wherever he went, people came in droves to hear him.

Over the next few years, Jesus travelled around to the towns in Galilee – Korazin, Bethsaida, Capernaum, Gennesaret, Tiberius, Cana, Dalmanutha (also known as Magadan or Magdala) – and farther afield to the Mediterranean ports of Tyre and Sidon, the villages near the township of Caesarea Philippi, the towns of the region of Decapolis and down south to Sychar, Jericho, Bethphage, Bethany and eventually Jerusalem. He spent a great deal of time travelling with his team, or up mountainsides, or on or around the inland Sea of Galilee.

By now the rumours about this new sensation, this rabbi with amazing teachings and powerful healings and even the ability to perform miracles, had spread throughout all parts of society. Every time he performed a miracle, the word went out about him. After raising a girl from death, "news of this spread through all that region."[3] After two blind men were healed, "they went out

> Jesus was a social phenomenon, and wherever he went, people came in droves to hear him.

---

1. Matthew 3:5.
2. Matthew 9:35.
3. Matthew 9:26.

and spread the news about him all over that region."[4] On another occasion, after a spectacular healing, the crowd were "filled with awe; and they praised God, who had given such authority to human beings."[5]

Like a rock star who is suddenly unable to walk down the street without being mobbed, Jesus' popularity spread out of control. The crowds declared, "Nothing like this has ever been seen in Israel,"[6] and wherever Jesus went, masses of people turned up, running down the roads, sailing across the waters, crowding in, desperate to be near this rabbi, to see him, hear him, touch him. The scenes must have been frenzied. In one town, the people pressed against him so much that "the crowds almost crushed him."[7]

One day, when Jesus was staying in Capernaum (on the northwestern shore of the Sea of Galilee), the crowds had amassed so much "that there was no room left, not even outside the door".[8] Showing the same ingenuity that Ben showed in getting around the crowds and sneaking into that hotel to meet the guys from U2, some men were so desperate to meet Jesus that they got up on the flat roof of the house where Jesus was speaking and smashed a hole through the mud and thatch. Then they lowered their friend down on a rope into the room below.[9] On a different day, when Jesus entered Jericho, the crowds were so great that one resourceful fellow – a height-impaired tax collector named Zacchaeus – ran ahead and climbed a tree just so he could get a glimpse of this amazing man. On another occasion, when Jesus was on the shore of the lake, the crowd was so large that he even had to tell his disciples to get a boat ready to keep him from being crushed by the crowds.[10]

Even after he received news of the execution of his cousin John at the hands of Herod, and he sought out a private and solitary place to be alone, the crowds got whiff of his whereabouts and came pouring out of the towns to seek him out.[11] And we do mean *crowds.* We are not talking a small contingent of polite devotees, but a seething mass of humanity. Matthew numbers the crowds on this one occasion as being "about five thousand men, besides women and children".[12] Sometime later, Jesus is again on a mountainside when "great crowds came to him", Matthew numbering the people at "four thousand men, besides women and children".[13] No matter where he went, the word got out and people flocked to see him. The very next day, Jesus crossed

---

4. Matthew 9:31.
5. Matthew 9:8.
6. Matthew 9:33.
7. Luke 8:42.
8. Mark 2:2.
9. Mark 2:1–12.
10. Mark 3:9.
11. Matthew 14:13.
12. Matthew 14:21.
13. Matthew 15:38–39.

* Wow, Herod must have been really old by then!
– Pete

It was a different Herod, Pete.
– Ben

What is really amazing about this is the way Jesus' popularity and appeal spanned all strata of society.

the lake to Gennesaret but again found himself confronted by crowds. "When the men of that place recognized Jesus, they sent word to all the surrounding country. People brought all their sick to him."[14] Such events did not go unnoticed by the rulers of the land. Reports about Jesus even reached the ears of Herod the tetrarch,* the puppet king of Galilee and Perea.[15]

What is really amazing about this is the way his popularity and appeal spanned all strata of society. He was sought out and followed by people from all walks of life and backgrounds, from all income levels and cultures.

Jesus is, of course, well known for his dealings with the lowly and undesirable of society. In a society that was very hung up on social order and rules, Jesus openly went against the grain. He spoke with, touched, ate with and even stayed in the homes of the untouchables: the lepers and those with miscellaneous skin disorders, women of ill repute, the blind, the lame, the paralysed, the unclean, the demon possessed, the social outcasts, and even despised tax collectors.

It's convenient and easy to limit our understanding of Jesus' appeal to these lowlifes and outcasts. But Jesus also caught the eye of the powerful, wealthy and influential. On one occasion, a teacher of the law declared to Jesus that he would follow him.[16] To be a teacher of the law meant that this man was influential, learned and respected in his community. He was a teacher and a leader, a man who knew the scriptures and interpreted them for the people. Yet here is this man declaring his allegiance to *follow* Jesus, to be not a leader but a disciple. On another occasion, a ruler of the synagogue threw himself at Jesus' feet, pleading with Jesus to heal his daughter.[17] This man was a devout Jew, a senior executive member of society responsible for the administration of the synagogue. But again, here he is acknowledging and submitting to Jesus.

Perhaps the best example of Jesus' wide appeal is found in Nicodemus. He was a member of the Jewish ruling council, the Sanhedrin. This powerful conservative group met in Jerusalem and sat in judgment over matters of Jewish law and life. They were the most senior and powerful elders and priests in the land who were able to mete out punishments, including death, for violators of Jewish law. (It was the Sanhedrin who later on would grill Paul, Peter and John over their preaching about Jesus, and the Sanhedrin who executed Stephen.)[18] They did not take kindly to challenges to the established order. Nicodemus sought out and visited Jesus at night[19] – presumably because he

14. Matthew 14:34–35.
15. Matthew 14:1–2.
16. Matthew 8:18–22.
17. Mark 5:21–24.
18. Acts 6 and 7.
19. John 3:1–21.

did not want to be seen mixing with this troublemaker – and he made this telling comment: "Rabbi, we know that you are a teacher who has come from God. For no one could perform the signs you are doing if God were not with him." So the reports about Jesus had obviously grown such a profile that he was being investigated by this most influential and powerful ruling group within Jewish society.

Another truly telling indicator of the social impact Jesus had, and the reach of the news surrounding him, is found in the fact that Jesus was also sought out by people from *outside* Jewish culture. Just think about this for a moment. It wasn't just the Jews with their baggage of expectation for a Messiah who followed Jesus. It was also people of different nationalities who sometimes had opposite beliefs.

In Capernaum, a Roman centurion sought Jesus out and asked him to heal his servant.[20] On another occasion, in the coastal region of Tyre and Sidon, Jesus was approached by a Canaanite woman who called him Lord and asked him to heal her daughter.[21] This woman was a non-Jew, a despised pagan descended from another nation. Both of these people recognized in Jesus something powerful and amazing.

The magnitude of Jesus' popularity is nowhere better summed up, however, not in the words of his friends and followers but in the words of his enemies. When faced with the excited crowd flooding out of Jerusalem to meet Jesus, they exclaimed, "Everyone in the world is following Jesus!"[22]

However, behind the wild crowds and frenzied scenes, trouble was brewing. Not everyone was impressed with this charismatic and authoritative teacher and his huge following. He was a threat to the established order and was viewed as a troublemaker, a rebel and a blasphemer, a rogue rabbi who was rocking the boat in a politically fragile time. So while the crowds continued to grow, so too did the whispers and rumours and grumblings behind closed doors. Jesus soon found himself with powerful enemies who began to plot against him. The problem was that Jesus didn't fit the mould. So much did Jesus' teachings not fit into the established thinking of the day, we may well call Jesus a square peg in a society of round holes because of the radically inverted nature of his ideas.

Which we'll explore in the next chapter …

20. Matthew 8:5–13.
21. Matthew 15:21–28.
22. John 12:19.

> When faced with the excited crowd flooding out of Jerusalem to meet Jesus, they exclaimed, "Everyone in the world is following Jesus!"

# Chapter 11

# SQUARE PEG, ROUND HOLE
## Jesus' new way of looking at things

I have a dream that one day this nation will rise up ..."

"We will fight them on the beaches ..."

"To be or not to be, that is the question ..."

"Well may we say, 'God save the Queen ...'"

"Friends, Romans, Countrymen ..."

"Ask not what your country can do for you ..."

"Ladies and gentlemen, I give you *Kong*!"

The world has witnessed some pretty impressive orators and speeches over the centuries. Speeches and public oratory have the power to move, inspire, entertain, teach and change lives.

Yet of all the orators and speechmakers and politicians and preachers, the most impressive and certainly the most quoted figure in history would have to be Jesus. He was a masterful and powerful no-nonsense speaker who pulled no punches. His words have changed the face of the world more than any other's.

Many people imagine Jesus standing in a marketplace or on a hilltop or in a boat with his arms spread wide, delivering some pithy epigram, generally something nice and gentle like, "Turn the other cheek," or "Do to others what you would have them do to you," or something cryptic but grandiose like, "What does it profit a man if he gains the whole world but loses himself?" or, "Blessed are the meek." But Jesus' words are not some airy-fairy religious sugar-'n'-spice goobledygook. His sayings and sermons are beautifully crafted master-pieces that have continued to inspire and challenge millions worldwide.

Soon after he began travelling and speaking throughout Galilee, enor-mous crowds turned up to hear what this new rabbi had to say. It was on one such occasion that Jesus went up to a high point on a mountainside so he could address the large numbers of people. And it was here, in this address (which we now have given the rather grandiose but obvious title of "The Sermon on the Mount"), that Jesus delivered his magnum opus. This sermon – or rather, series of lectures – was probably given over a number of days and is remem-bered because it contains some of Jesus' most famous sayings. Even if you've never read the Bible, you may recognize some of these words:

"Blessed are the poor in spirit."

"Blessed are the meek, for they shall inherit the earth."

"Blessed are the peacemakers, for they shall be called sons of God."

"Love your enemies."

"This then is how you should pray: 'Our Father in heaven …'"

"Ask and it will be given to you, seek and you will find."

"Do not judge, or you too will be judged."

> The crowds were amazed at the authority of Jesus' teaching. They found it powerful and meaningful, not the empty rhetoric of other teachers of the law.

The crowds were amazed at the authority of his teaching. They found it powerful and meaningful, not the empty rhetoric of other teachers of the law.[1] In fact if you really want to get to the heart of who Jesus is and what he was all about, the best place to look is in his own words in his sermons, sayings, parables, debates and lessons.

It becomes very clear from early on that Jesus himself saw that his preaching and teaching were central to his ministry, and this is certainly reflected in the views of the people around him. He is constantly referred to as Rabbi and Teacher. In this respect, it would be wrong to think of Jesus as just a travelling miracle worker who spoke about a given subject every now and again. Rather, he was widely recognized and named as a preacher first of all, who then performed miracles.

As we have already mentioned (in the chapter "Rebel with a Cause"), a highly significant moment at the start of Jesus' ministry was when he read from a scroll in his hometown synagogue and then declared that he was the fulfilment of that prophecy. The scroll contained a copy of the book of Isaiah, and Jesus read a portion of it, which included these words: "The Spirit of the Lord is on me, because he has anointed me to *preach* good news to the poor. He has sent me to *proclaim* freedom for the prisoners and recovery of sight for the blind, to release the oppressed, to *proclaim* the year of the Lord's favor."[2]

This passage from Isaiah acts like Jesus' own mission statement. By saying this, Jesus was clearly indicating that this six-hundred-year-old prophecy was now being fulfilled and that he himself was this divinely ordained preacher and proclaimer. In fact, shortly after this pivotal moment, Jesus said to a crowd that was intent on preventing him from leaving their town, "I must preach the good news of the kingdom of God to the other towns also, because that is why I was sent."[3]

---

1. Matthew 7:28–29.
2. Luke 4:18–19 NIV, emphases added (see also Isaiah 61:1–2).
3. Luke 4:43 NIV.

So from this moment onwards, wherever he went, Jesus began to teach, preach, debate, lecture and tell stories on a whole range of issues. He tackled the big questions and was bold in declaring a new way of looking at things. Some of his messages were quite blunt and challenging. He didn't beat about the bush when he spoke about marriage, love, divorce, giving, making promises, judging others or revenge. He was critical of hypocrisy and religious pretension. He spoke out against evil thoughts, vulgar deeds, stealing, murder, greed, meanness, deceit, indecency, envy, insults, pride and foolishness.[4] He told people to reconcile broken friendships, to support the needy, to pray simply, to be faithful in marriage, to be people of their word, to love their enemies, to be humble. He told people not to worship money, not to be hung up on food and clothes, not to be proud and boastful and arrogant, not to backstab, not to be sexually immoral. He boldly spoke out against injustice and encouraged people to be compassionate. He spoke about God, sin, forgiveness, judgment, hope, temptation, desire, anxiety and the end of the world, just to name a few. He challenged established ways of thinking and provoked people to think about his words and inspired them to fresh thinking about God and the way they lived.

In the modern world, we have become a bit blasé about Jesus' words. To some, there is a nice middle-classness to them and they roll off the tongue pretty easily. We think that Jesus simply taught everyone he met to love one another and help little old ladies across the road. However, much of what he taught was challenging and demanding. His words were often confrontational, difficult, awkward, radical and controversial, often going against the grain of cultural and religious wisdom of the day. In an era when many people were hung up about rules and rituals * relating to food, he said that it is not what a person eats that makes them unclean but what is in their heart and what comes out of their mouth. In an era when strict religious types wouldn't even scratch themselves on their holy day because it was considered work, Jesus taught that it was okay to do good deeds and to eat on the holy day. In an era of violence and racial tension in an occupied nation, Jesus told his followers to love their enemies. He took laws of the Old Testament and common sayings of the day and infused them with new meanings that made them even harder, even impossible to keep. In the Sermon on the Mount, he taught that lust is adultery even if it never passes beyond the look of desire, and that hateful anger is murder even if blood is never spilled. He said if your eye causes you to sin, cast it out. If your hand causes you to stumble, cut it off.** He told a rich man to sell all of his possessions and give them to the poor.

---

4. As reported in Mark 7:21.

So from this moment onwards, wherever he went, Jesus began to teach, preach, debate, lecture and tell stories on a whole range of issues.

* Some of their motivation was driven by the fact that in their postexile world, the leaders of Israel did not want to make the same mistakes previous generations had made in being negligent about following the law. So in essence they began to err to the other extreme of "better safe than sorry".
** These, of course, were metaphors. Jesus was not promoting self-amputation or ocular removal!

But perhaps Jesus' toughest sayings were those concerning what it meant to be his follower and one of his disciples.

But perhaps his toughest sayings were those concerning what it meant to be his follower and one of his disciples. Remember that rabbis and their disciples were commonplace, and there were other rabbis who had their own groups of disciples who were following them. But Jesus' words about following him were somewhat less than appealing. After rebuking Peter in front of his disciples, Jesus said to them all, "Whoever wants to be my disciple must deny themselves and take up their cross and follow me."[5]

On another occasion, he said, "Anyone who loves their father or mother more than me is not worthy of me; anyone who loves a son or daughter more than me is not worthy of me. Whoever does not take up their cross and follow me is not worthy of me."[6]

In this day and age, we don't appreciate how radical these words were. The cross has become a central part of Christian iconography. There are crosses on top of churches, on the covers of Bibles, on the letterheads of organizations and around people's necks. It has become a comfortable, established symbol. In Jesus' day, however, crosses weren't used in art, architecture or jewellery. The cross back then was the instrument the Romans used for crucifixion, a form of execution reserved only for the worst criminals. It was a bloody, horrific and barbaric symbol to which the only response was shock, fear and revulsion.

So when Jesus initially called his followers to pick up a cross and follow him, it would have been an unpalatable shock, like hearing him say "pick up your noose" or "pick up your electric chair and follow me." It's easy for us to have an image of "picking up your cross" as being like "pick up that heavy backpack over there and lug it up this hill" as if it's some tough *Survivor*-style TV challenge. But it was a lot more confronting than that. It was a radical way of saying that following Jesus was no dabbling on the fringe of your life, no intellectual exercise. It was central to who you are. It meant surrendering your life.

Yep, Jesus didn't beat around the bush. His messages were often blunt and direct. But he didn't always speak with the subtlety of a sledgehammer. He is perhaps most well known for his powerful use of memorable stories and vivid metaphors to connect with his listeners. And it is to these *parables* that we will turn our attention next.

---

5. Mark 8:34.
6. Matthew 10:37–38.

# Chapter 12

# MUSTARD SEEDS AND LOST COINS
## Jesus uses parables

Back in the eighties, Ben was a long-haired rock-and-roll hero playing in a rock band. At the end of every gig, the band finished their set with an anthemic blues thumper called "Steamboat". The lyrics went a-something like this:

> Don't know the time, don't know the place,
>
> but I know there's a river moving through this place.
>
> You don't know, my friend, when it's comin' back again.
>
> Look down the river!...
>
> My ticket's paid, hope you're the same,
>
> 'cause there's a river sweeping out the days....
>
> There's a steamboat comin'.... Are you gonna be on it too?[1]

It was a big finish, although one might question why this very evangelistic Christian rock band would have as the high point of their performance a song about a person standing on a dock looking down a waterway, wondering about the ferry timetable and contemplating the fact that they have a ticket for the boat trip and wondering if their friend has a ticket and if they'll be on the boat too.*

As you have probably already gleaned, of course, the song is not *literal* but is what is commonly referred to in literary circles as *allegorical.* The literal story is actually a representation of something else; one thing is used to teach about another "hidden" thing. In this case, the song is about the return of Jesus, and the singer is expressing his desire for the listener to be prepared and ready.**

This is actually a very powerful tool of communication used by writers, poets, orators and singers throughout history. When Pete was at Uni doing his teaching degree, one of the first things he learned was that a good teacher uses things that are *familiar* to their pupils to help them understand the *unfamiliar.* Rather than trying to conceptualise a new idea out of nothingness, such a process gives the pupil a hook on which to hang a new concept. It uses the concrete and known to help us contemplate the abstract and unfamiliar. This is especially powerful if the connection

> \* Yes, I must admit I did often wonder what this boat song had to do with anything. Seemed a bit pointless, if you ask me.
> – Pete
>
> Mate, are you serious?
> – Ben

> \*\* Ohh, now I get it. Good one. – Pete

---

1. Lyrics by John Dickson, "Steamboat", 1987. Used with permission.

* Wow, I didn't know Jesus told the parable of the steamboat. That's so cool.        – Pete

No, Pete, he … I … oh, never mind.        – Ben

engages the imagination or is a highly vivid word picture or image (like a steamboat!).*

Without the benefit of a modern literature professor's advice, Jesus crafted his words and taught people – many of whom had little schooling – using not jargon or intellectual gibberish but clear and timeless stories and simple comparisons that conveyed complex universal truths.

Some people have a picture of Jesus as this kind of quirky smart-aleck guy who spoke in riddles and puzzles all the time, leaving his listeners bewildered and wondering what the heck he was talking about. Like every time he was asked a question, instead of just giving an answer, he looked off into the sunset and said cryptically, "Once there was a man who built a house …" or sagely declared, "The kingdom of God is like a mustard seed …" In part, this is true. But here's the important bit. **This kind of talk was not unusual.** It was a normal and accepted part of rabbinic teaching style and the language of politics of the time. Jesus' listeners would not have been caught off guard by this kind of talk. Having heard it before (from other rabbis, for example), they would have been familiar with it and accepted it as part of everyday public rhetoric. **Jesus spoke in the language of the everyday.**

Socrates, Plato and Aristotle were among many well-known Greek philosophers who hundreds of years before had used parables to explore ideas. There was also an extensive use of allegories (for the sake of simplicity, here used to cover all figurative speech) littered through the Old Testament scriptures, which, remember, were the bread and butter of Israelite society. For example:

- **The book of Daniel** uses the figure of a giant statue of gold, silver, bronze and iron to represent the empires of Babylonia, Medo-Persia, Greece and Rome.
- **In the book of Judges** (chap. 9), a furious Jotham addresses a crowd, telling them the story of a grove of trees that seeks to appoint a King of the Trees. This seemingly childish story is actually a criticism of Abimelech's climb to power by murdering his half brothers.
- **Psalm 78:1–3** acknowledges the long-established method of using parable in teaching:

> My people, hear my teaching;
> listen to the words of my mouth.
> I will open my mouth with a parable;
> I will teach you lessons from the past –
> things we have heard and known,
> things our ancestors have told us.

One of the most well-known stories about the most famous figure of Israelite history involved the telling of a parable.[2] One thousand years before Jesus, the prophet Nathan told the great Israelite king David the story of a rich man who, despite having large flocks and herds of his own, took the lone sheep of a poor man to kill and present to a guest. David was furious at the injustice of this, and it was then that Nathan revealed his trump card: the story was not about a rich man and sheep but really about David himself and the fact that he had taken another man's wife.

So when Jesus talked in parables and similes, he was not alienating his audiences with enigmatic fables, incomprehensible tales and mysterious yarns but rather using a teaching method that was relevant, comfortable and familiar to them.

## Why Parables?

Something like a third of Jesus' recorded words are parables,[*] which gives us an indication of how they featured in his public appearances. It also indicates how memorable and powerful they were to the writers of the Gospels, with Matthew recording on one busy occasion that "Jesus spoke all these things to the crowd in parables; he did not say anything to them without using a parable."[3]

Of course, the immediate question is ...

*Why?*

While there are certainly many instances when Jesus spoke openly and bluntly about all manner of issues, *why* did he spend so much time telling obtuse stories?

One reason is – as we have already suggested – it is simply an effective teaching tool. Speaking to a varied audience – made up of the wealthy, the learned, the powerful, the simple, the uneducated, the outcast – Jesus drew from the rural images and experiences of everyday life at the time.

Another reason is perhaps that Jesus was being cautious. Throughout history, many leaders of underground movements around the world have had to watch what they say publicly because of the spies of a harsh dictatorship lurking in their midst. In some countries, to speak anything controversial or of an insurrectionist nature against the ruling regime means that secret police visit your house and you are never seen again. Jesus was certainly in a situation in which his enemies were tracking him and trying to catch him out. He was a troublemaker and a threat, and they were waiting to hear him come out with blasphemous things so they could charge him and have him imprisoned or executed. So in some respects, using "innocent" parables allowed him to

* There is some small debate over what scholars actually define as parables. There are wider and more specific definitions of the word, as well as a bag of variations on a theme, including allegories, similes, exemplary stories, extended similes, metaphors, narrative parables, parabolic statements and – wait for it – metaphorical aphorisms. But, quite frankly, we will leave those arguments to people with more time on their hands, and we are happy to stick to the generic person-in-the-street understanding of a parable.

2. 2 Samuel 12.
3. Matthew 13:34.

Using "innocent" parables allowed Jesus to teach and to challenge his listeners while at the same time not giving his enemies any ammunition.

* An important event, recorded in three gospels: Matthew 13; Mark 4; Luke 8.
** Aussie talk meaning "argument" or "fight".

teach and to challenge his listeners while at the same time not giving his enemies any ammunition.

But the clearest reason for the use of parables comes from Jesus himself, in his own words. Imagine the scene: Jesus has gone out by the lake, and so many people have come to hear him speak that he has to get into a boat and float a bit offshore so he can address them all.* The disciples are there, possibly trying to organize things and do a bit of crowd management. This is a **big gig** for them, a huge opportunity for their rabbi to get down to business, to make his mark and declare himself as the Messiah. The crowd hushes, Jesus draws breath and ... tells a story about a farmer scattering seed around the place.

The disciples look at each other with raised eyebrows. Later on they ask him, "Why do you speak to the people in parables?"[4]

Jesus answers, "This is why I speak to them in parables: 'Though seeing, they do not see; though hearing, they do not hear or understand.' ... But blessed are your eyes because they see, and your ears because they hear. Truly I tell you, many prophets and righteous people longed to see what you see but did not see it, and to hear what you hear but did not hear it."

Jesus was speaking to people who wanted to hear and wanted to see. He was speaking to people who were interested in what he had to say. He was speaking to people who were searching, who were – to borrow Jesus' own words – "hungering and thirsting" after the truth.[5] He was speaking to people who would hang around and be bothered to contemplate his words and work through what they meant. He was speaking to people who had open hearts and minds. They were the ones who gleaned the truth out of his stories. They were the ones who would "get it".

Others, however, would disregard Jesus outright. They would hear but not understand, because they didn't want to. Such people had closed minds and hard and calloused hearts. Such people clung to their old ways and were not interested in allowing anything new to get through to them. They would consider Jesus' stories as fanciful nonsense because they wouldn't be bothered to think them through. If you've ever had a blue** with someone who stubbornly refuses to listen to reason but just blindly clings to the mantra of their unsubstantiated opinion, you know the kind of person Jesus is talking about. They are people who *hear* but don't *listen*.

### Parables: What Do They Teach Us?

Some people think that the parables are just quaint little ditties in the mould of fairy tales. They picture Jesus saying, "Let me tell you a parable. Once upon a time, there was a big castle, a foreboding forest, a wicked witch

---

4. Matthew 13:10–17.
5. Matthew 5:6.

and three bears … and the moral of the story is: chew your food properly before swallowing." On the surface, the parables do have something of a simple rustic quality about them. They are stories about seeds, pearls, wheat, bridesmaids, fishing nets, virgins, farmers, rich men, lost coins, lost sheep, lost sons.

But we must not confuse them for simple children's stories.

Rather, the parables were highly controversial, pointed and, at times, incredibly divisive. They often had cryptic but scathing undertones that acted as harsh rebukes to his listeners. They were messages with a sting. So much so that it was his parables that often left groups like the Pharisees wanting to kill him.

To get to the heart of the parables, we have to look beyond the surface meaning and consider the underlying teaching. Some people have referred to it as finding gold in the earth or the kernel in a nut, in that while the surface may not be promising, something of true value lies within.

So what is this marrow and gold that we find in the parables? In the parables, Jesus was illustrating and making clear his views about God's love, forgiveness and grace. He used parables to talk about heaven, judgment and the kingdom of God. But the one thing that they all seem to have in common is that they tell us something about Jesus – who he is and what he came to do.

Jesus often used parables in response to a particular situation, question or challenge from somebody who wanted to dispute or complain about something he had said or done. So the parables were often a clever reply that forced the person complaining to reconsider their opinion or that backed them into a corner, where the flaw in their thinking was exposed.

> To get to the heart of the parables, we have to look beyond the surface meaning and consider the underlying teaching.

## The Shepherd, the Woman and the Father

On one occasion, Jesus was socialising and having a meal with a number of outcasts and lowlifes (referred to as tax collectors and sinners) when some very morally upright and religious folk known as Pharisees and "teachers of the law" came by. They were shocked to see Jesus identifying with notorious outcasts and – horror of horrors – dining with them. In their minds, sinners and traitors like the tax collectors were to be despised and shunned for their immorality and unworthiness. So the Pharisees and the teachers of the law complained and muttered among themselves, "This man welcomes sinners and eats with them."

Jesus sensed their grumbling and told them three back-to-back stories that acted as a wonderful defence for what he was doing. He ended up telling them the story of a man who threw a dinner party for a terrible sinner. The parallel couldn't have been more obvious!

The three stories are actually part of the one parable[6] and function in the same way we might tell a modern joke. In a joke we might say, "There

---

6. Luke 15:3: "parable" is singular.

was a Canadian, an American and an Australian ..." The first two characters might do something in a similar way but the third character does something with a twist that delivers the punch line. In this case, there are three similar scenarios, but the twist (and lesson) comes most powerfully at the end.

Jesus began by including his audience in the first story (the parable of the lost sheep) and then posing the question: Imagine you are a shepherd with one hundred sheep, but you lose one. Wouldn't you go out and search for it? And after finding the sheep, wouldn't you be happy enough to celebrate because your lost sheep was found?

He then told a very similar story (the parable of the lost coin) about a woman (presumably without a husband) who owned ten silver coins but lost one of them and so searched carefully until she found it. Then in identical fashion, after finding her valuable coin, she celebrated by throwing a party.

Then Jesus delivered the simple point: In the same way, there is celebration when one of these sinners turns from ignoring God and gets back to living their life God's way. Jesus was saying that he was here not to ignore the lost but to **find and restore** them. He was on a search and rescue mission.

And then to make the point stick, he gave a third similar scenario, but this time there was a twist to rebuke his critics. He finished with the story of a father who had two sons. One rebelled by demanding his inheritance immediately, saying, in effect, that he wanted his father dead. This is an incredibly horrible demand in any culture, but it would have been particularly heinous in the eyes of Jesus' first-century Jewish audience, not the least the Pharisees.

Surprisingly, the father graciously complied despite this offensive request. Shortly after, this son took off to a distant land to spend the money as he pleased without the father's restraints. The son eventually went broke, spending all of his money unwisely on himself in what Jesus described as "wild living" and – like so many people who suddenly receive a large sum of money but have no skill in managing it – soon found himself beyond his means and in a worse situation. To survive, he ended up being the slave of a pig farmer. This was not only humiliating but culturally deplorable. Jews did not farm pigs, because they were considered unclean and therefore unholy. Even worse, the son's desperate and lost condition was emphasized by the fact that he was so hungry that he began to desire the pigs' slop he was dealing out. Yet in a rare moment of clarity, the son realised that even the workers at home ate better than him. He rehearsed his repentance speech and made his way back home, hoping his father would at least accept him as a servant on the family property.

Many people are familiar with the next heartwarming moment of the story. The father, looking to the horizon, saw his lost son coming home and immediately threw off all cultural norms and ran to his son to embrace him.

> Jesus was saying that he was here not to ignore the lost but to find and restore them.

The son began his repentance speech word for word but was cut off when his father, amazingly, called for new clothes to be brought out and a big party to begin. Like the shepherd who found his sheep and the woman who found her coin, the father celebrated that his lost son had come home.

But the story doesn't finish there.

The great twist was yet to come. Jesus' cryptic rebuke of the Pharisees and the teachers of the law came in the account of the older brother's reaction. He (like the Pharisees) was highly unimpressed about the meal with this sinner. He wanted the younger brother disciplined rather than welcomed. He protested by boycotting the party and sulking outside. In a subtle touch of irony, the father went looking for the older son, and when he found him, this older brother voiced his bitterness. The older son said that he had been good all his life and had never done anything so disrespectful, but never had his father thrown him a party like this. The magnitude of this son's anger is seen in how he described his younger brother. He said to his father that "this son of yours" (rather than "this brother of mine") is immoral and unworthy. But the father rebuked the older son by correcting his description of the younger son: " 'My son,' the father said, 'you are always with me, and everything I have is yours. But we had to celebrate and be glad, because **this brother of yours** was dead and is alive again; he was lost and is found.' "[7]

The whole parable acted as a brilliant, albeit not too subtle, defence of Jesus' ministry and his acceptance of and love for the outcast, the sinner and the lost. He was justifying his actions. Equally, it acted as a scathing rebuke to the Pharisees and teachers, who ought not to have looked down at these people Jesus was dining with as scum to be ignored but instead ought to have accepted them as brothers.

Many people who hear this parable immediately identify with the lost brother who returned to the father. But the barb in Jesus' parable was targeted at the other brother, aiming criticism at those who are self-righteous about their supposed exclusive claim to the kingdom of God.

## The Good Samaritan

Another example of the confrontational nature of the parables can be seen in Jesus' so-called parable of the good Samaritan. Many of us today miss the controversy of this story, but it would have been quite confronting and relevant to Jesus' contemporaries. Part of the problem is that in our Bibles, we are given the subheading "The Good Samaritan", and so we are effectively given the punch line before we begin. The great twist and surprise of the parable is that the **Samaritan**, of all people, was **good!** Jesus certainly didn't start the parable by saying, "Let me tell you a parable about a Samaritan who

---

7. Luke 15:31 – 32, emphasis added.

was good." That would be like a comedian beginning with the punch line ("Five: one to change the bulb and four to rebuke the spirit of darkness") before telling the joke ("How many Pentecostals does it take to change a lightbulb?"). Or a murder mystery movie that begins by showing us that the butler did it.

The parable this time is a response to a question posed to Jesus by a scholar of the law: "Who is my neighbour?" Everyone knew that the commandments said to "love thy neighbour"; the hotly debated question amongst Jews was, How you define *neighbour*? Who are the neighbours that we should love?

Jesus answered by telling them the story of a man who was robbed, beaten and left for dead by a gang of thugs on a country road. Some time later, a priest came along and found the injured man but crossed to the other side and continued on his way, giving no aid to the victim. A little later, a Levite also found the man, but he too offered no help and moved on. Jesus chose the characters of the priest and the Levite because they both were in highly regarded positions of authority and morality. They were involved in the running of the temple and were generally seen as fine examples of upstanding citizens and typical good Jews.

But then Jesus introduced a third man: a Samaritan.* In contrast to the first two Jewish men, this man stopped and was kind to the half-dead victim. He not only administered first aid but also provided accommodation for him.

It was this third man who was the surprise of the story. Not simply because he was good but because he was a Samaritan. Jesus touched a raw racial nerve here. Samaritans were seen as inferior half-caste** Jews because they were the descendants of both Jewish and Assyrian ancestors. They were seen as people who had been infected with pagan blood, so the hatred between Samaritans and Jews had a long history of conflict, which continued in Jesus' day. The idea of a Samaritan being good and providing a moral example would have been highly offensive to the lawyer who posed the question. The great irony was that the first two were the ones breaking the law by being bad neighbours, while the despised Samaritan was the one who truly kept the law. So the parable wasn't just a story about being kind to others. Rather it was a controversial stab at racism as Jesus radically redefined what a neighbour really is and what loving that neighbour really means. Jesus was challenging the established social order.*** He criticised the lofty and respected, and praised the despised. Many of Jesus' listeners would have been shocked at his offensive reinterpretation of the structure of Jewish life. In effect, he was saying that it doesn't matter who you are, but it does matter what you do.

## Thy Kingdom Come

Jesus also used parables to teach about the coming of God's kingdom, which we elaborate on in the next chapter. This was a hot topic in Jesus' day,

> \* If this were a play, this is where the crowd would boo and hiss.     – Ben
>
> To say nothing of the lobbing of rotten fruit. – Pete

** A term referring to a person born of mixed-race parents.
*** The lawyer could not even bring himself to utter the word *Samaritan* and instead called him "the one who showed mercy".

96

and people were very interested to hear what various rabbis had to say about the expected kingdom. Some of the parables include:

**The parable of the sower:**[8] Jesus tells of a farmer scattering seed – some of which lands among rocks, some where it is eaten by birds, some where it grows among thorns, and some which lands in the good soil. Jesus uses these images to explain to his disciples that people will have different responses to his message about God's kingdom. Some will not understand it in the first place. Some will respond enthusiastically, but their shallow faith won't stand the test of time. Some will respond, but after a while the troubles of life and work will distract them. And some will let the message change their life.

**The parables of the mustard seed and the yeast:**[9] Jesus incongruously compared the kingdom of God to these insignificant and small items. Both, however, are symbols of tremendous growth. Jesus was saying that God's kingdom would not arrive with a devastating thunderclap. Rather it would start small – indeed with a rabbi from a no-hoper town – and it would grow and become something huge, which we see today, when the followers of this Son of God represent the largest single global community of people on earth.

**The parable of the unmerciful servant:**[10] Jesus tells the story of a king who cancelled the equivalent of a ten-thousand-dollar debt of one of his servants. But then the servant went out and harangued a man who owed him only a few dollars. The king was furious when he discovered the servant's lack of gratitude and stinginess. According to Jesus, as servants under God's rule, people are to forgive as they have been forgiven. Much has been given to them, and the appropriate response is not to be measly, judgmental and hard-hearted but to be open, kind and giving.

**The parable of the tenants:**[11] Jesus' attack on the Pharisees continued in this parable, in which he controversially stated that the nation of Israel would lose its special place (and prophetically, that it would also kill the son of the landowner) and that instead God's blessing would fall to anyone who sought to follow him. Quite pointedly, he stated to the chief priests and Pharisees that "the kingdom of God will be taken away from you and given to a people who will produce its fruit."[12]

Jesus' words here are incredibly confrontational. He was basically saying to the face of the religious establishment that they had lost their rights to being part of the kingdom of God and that they had no role in God's

---

8. Matthew 13:1–23.
9. Matthew 13:31–33.
10. Matthew 18:21–35.
11. Matthew 21:33–46.
12. Matthew 21:43.

kingdom. Instead, it was open to anybody who sought after it – including the prostitutes and tax collectors. This teaching was unbelievable! *Shocking! Blasphemous!*

Jesus' teachings were offensive to the Pharisees, the chief priests and the teachers of the law. Their response was suitably aggressive: "When the chief priests and the Pharisees heard Jesus' parables, they knew he was talking about them. They looked for a way to arrest him."[13] His words made him a marked man in the eyes of the establishment, and he became the subject of their anger. Conversations took place and plots were hatched to get rid of this rabbi from Nazareth.

It soon became obvious that Jesus thought the kingdom of God was a significant and important topic. He spent a great deal of time talking about it. But what exactly is this kingdom of God? Where is it? What is it? And what's it got to do with me anyway? These well-timed rhetorical questions are just the thing to segue us into the next chapter.

---

13. Matthew 21:45–46.

## Part 4

# NOT OF THIS WORLD

Ladies and gentlemen … *the kingdom of God!*

It inspires visions of heavenly rolling landscapes of majestic rivers and awesome mountains with Neuschwansteinesque castles* in the clouds and numberless armies of creatures surrounding God (complete with sceptre and crown) sitting on a throne grandly surveying his kingdom below – earth. *Behold! The kingdom of God!* **Into battle, ho!**

It is an expression Jesus used again and again, often at pivotal moments. Sometimes he said, "The kingdom of God is at hand," or, "The kingdom of God has come upon you." Other times, he began a story or parable by saying, "The kingdom of God is like …" or, "The kingdom of God can be compared to …" Sometimes one of the gospel writers states in summary fashion that Jesus simply "spoke about the kingdom of God" or that he "went about preaching the good news of the kingdom".

With the gospel writers quoting its use about eighty times, it soon becomes clear that this phrase – "the kingdom of God" (or sometimes, "the kingdom of heaven") – wasn't some religious throwaway tagline for Jesus but rather a concept that was central to his message and purpose. Luke records that at the start of his public preaching, Jesus announced to a crowd, "I must preach the good news of the kingdom of God to the other towns also, because that is why I was sent."[1]

The word **kingdom** is actually a combination of two words: *king* and *domain*. For example, if Pete were the king of a certain country and Ben were a citizen of that country, you could say that Ben was in Pete's domain, his king-dom. He would be subject to the laws of Pete's kingdom and under Pete's influence and rule, and he would have to do whatever Pete said no matter how ridiculous it seemed.** But he would also experience the benefits of that kingdom. So another way of describing the kingdom of God is "the time and place in which God's ways are supreme". It is the domain or realm where God's authority is sovereign and where people are living with God as their Lord.

It's sometimes difficult for us in the twenty-first-century West to understand this ancient concept of kingship. After all, in our democratic countries, it is we the people who vote our leaders into and out of power. Even many modern kings are figureheads behind their countries' political systems. They

* Neuschwanstein is the castle in southwest Bavaria on which Disney modelled their Sleeping Beauty Castle.    – Pete

And which also appeared in *Chitty Chitty Bang Bang*!    – Ben

Well, someone knows their architectural trivia!    – Pete

** Oh yeah? Well, I wouldn't.    – Ben

Off with his head!    – Pete

---

1. Luke 4:43 NIV.

come and go, and while they contribute much to the international community, to civic life and to various charities, many people perceive modern kingship as anathema. But in traditional societies, the king was the centrepiece of social order. The birth or coronation of a king was met with much celebration and hope. The death or even the serious sickness of a king brought great calamity and uncertainty that trickled to all levels of society, throwing the populous into doubt and despair. Kingship in these societies wasn't just some nicety celebrated in trashy supermarket magazines. Kingship was everything. The king was responsible for his nation's order, justice, direction, health and prosperity.

As we have already mentioned, the Jews of Jesus' day weren't a singular organized group. However, based on numerous prophesies and other Jewish writings, just about every practicing Jew believed and hoped in one thing: that one day the kingdom or rule of God would dramatically and physically come and overthrow God's enemies. The one to bring in this new era would be a divinely appointed leader (or Messiah) – a physical and military-style conqueror – who would rule on God's behalf and establish his kingdom like it was in the good old days under Kings Saul, David and Solomon, one thousand years before.

We are familiar with this idea, appropriated in the fiction of J. R. R. Tolkien. In *The Lord of the Rings*, the period of the great kings comes to an end and the land of Middle Earth falls into a time of despair. A lot of time is spent waiting for the return of the king while dark forces rule the earth, until finally the young warrior-king Aragorn emerges, seizes power, looks rugged, rallies the troops and smashes the enemy in a series of monster battles. He is crowned king and gets the girl. The ring of power is destroyed and the balance of the universe is re-established and everyone is happy. Roll credits.

This is not unlike the hope that the nation of Israel had. And then, a young man from Nazareth, a rabbi with a growing following, began travelling around the region of Galilee making the following incredible pronouncement: "The time has come … The kingdom of God has come near! Repent and believe the Good News!"[2] In doing so, Jesus heralded the dawning of a new age, an age of God's authority on earth **now.**

But here's the clincher. Jesus radically challenged the traditional view of the coming of the kingdom of God. He said that the arrival of the kingdom of God was not so much a **physical** event as a **spiritual** one. He said that the real enemy of God's people wasn't the pagan Roman Empire but the broken relationship that people had with God. The problem was not in the streets or the palaces but in people's hearts and minds and with their attitude toward God in the first place. The kingdom of God wasn't about massive physical battles, political power and self-affirmation but about love, humility, service

2. Mark 1:15.

and self-sacrifice. It was about people living under the authority of God as ruler.

These thoughts were radical, extreme, unheard of. Rather than affirming yourself, picking up your sword and conquering your enemies, Jesus taught that the way of the kingdom of God is all about denying yourself, picking up your cross and loving your enemies.

To us in the twenty-first century who live safe and comfortable lives and who are riding on the back of two thousand years of "Jesus is Lord and Saviour" ideology, this is pretty easy to swallow. However, it was completely different from what most contemporary Jews believed and taught. This whole idea was new, uncomfortable, difficult. Jesus said that as the Messiah, he had come not to rule and kill his enemies but to love and lay down his life for them. He taught that he had come to be not the mightiest but the lowliest. He came not to sit on a throne but to hang on a cross. Speaking of himself, Jesus said:

> "For even the Son of Man did not come to be served, but to serve, and to give his life as a ransom for many."[3]

> "I am the good shepherd. The good shepherd lays down his life for the sheep."[4]

Can we imagine how incomprehensible this must have been to some of Jesus' listeners? Even those closest to him found the idea of a suffering Messiah and his teaching about self-denial and servanthood hard to understand. Their problem was that they did not see the awaited Messiah and Isaiah's Suffering Servant as one and the same person.

Nowhere is this more clearly seen than at a pivotal moment when Jesus turns to his disciples and asks them, "Who do you say I am?"[5] Peter, on behalf of the others, steps forward and confidently says, "You are the Messiah." It was at this point that Jesus told them about his mission: to suffer, die and rise again. But this puzzled the disciples. Their puzzlement was not a mild intellectual curiosity as much as a total dumbfoundedness, a mouth-open "say what?" lack of connection as if Jesus were speaking on the other side of a great chasm with a bucket over his head.

Upon hearing these words, Jesus' friend and companion Peter responded by taking Jesus aside to correct him. We are not told exactly what Peter said, but it would have been something like, "Look Jesus ... um ... we know you're the Messiah, the Christ of God come to rule the world and bring about God's kingdom, but Messiahs don't suffer and die. They conquer and reign in glory. Now stop talking all this nonsense about dying and let's get on with conquering the world."

---

3. Mark 10:45.

4. John 10:11.

5. Mark 8:27–33.

Jesus responded to Peter's objections in spectacular fashion: "Get behind me, Satan!... You do not have in mind the things of God, but the things of men."[6]

From this moment on, the disciples understand glimpses of what Jesus had come to do. It wouldn't be till much later, however, after they had come to terms with their friend and rabbi actually returning after his execution that all of the pieces of the puzzle would come together for them. His suffering and death made sense only once they saw the big picture.

Jesus also challenged the popular opinion and established social order that the true people of God were the morally upright, the wealthy, the spiritually clean and the good. Jesus said virtually the opposite. The ones who recognized their own shame, sin and spiritual poverty – the ones who acknowledged and submitted to God's authority and power – were the ones who were part of the kingdom of God. The proud and self-righteous who wanted to stand on their own two feet were actually the ones who were excluded from God's domain.

Jesus said:

> "I tell you the truth, anyone who will not receive the kingdom of God like a little child will never enter it."[7]

> "If anyone wants to be first, he must be the very last, and the servant of all."[8]

> "Whoever finds their life will lose it, and whoever loses their life for my sake will find it."[9]

> "I tell you the truth, unless you change and become like little children, you will never enter the kingdom of heaven. Therefore, whoever humbles himself like this child is the greatest in the kingdom of heaven."[10]

Some of his harshest comments were directed at those people who were trying to perfect themselves and earn God's favour by doing the right thing and following complicated lists of ridiculously rigid doctrines and rules. Jesus was particularly critical of the unloving and harsh hypocrisy of some of the religious leaders. (More of that later.) He said that the religious establishment was rife with people who were more interested in showing off in front of others than in genuine piety. He was critical of their self-interest and the way they showed off when they prayed or donated money, while on the inside they were hard-hearted. In that era, such criticism of leaders was scandalous and shocking.

Jesus was particularly critical of the unloving and harsh hypocrisy of some of the religious leaders.

6. Mark 8:33 NIV.
7. Mark 10:15 NIV.
8. Mark 9:35 NIV.
9. Matthew 10:39.
10. Matthew 18:3–4 NIV.

As we've been saying, Jesus was a rabbi who travelled far and taught a lot. He moved from town to town, using synagogues and marketplaces and hillsides as his platform. His words were powerful and had a great impact. But there was something distinct about Jesus that separated him from the other rabbis, something that excited the population and caused crowds to flood to him in droves. Jesus began to *do things* – things that ordinary people could not do. He began to show that he was unique and had amazing abilities and incomprehensible powers by which he could manipulate the actual fabric of our world. Jesus began to do things that showed that he was not of this world. They can only be summarised in one word: **miracles.** It was the dawning of a new era. The kingdom of God had arrived.

# Chapter 14

# WINE, STORMS AND A HANDFUL O' FISH
## Jesus did amazing things

Scenario 1: Peter comes home from a day at work. He walks in the door to find that his daughters have unpacked their school bags and put their dirty sports gear in the laundry basket. They have completed their afternoon chores as well as their music practice. The dinner table is already set, and they are sitting contently doing their homework. Peter falls to his knees, raises his hands in the air and cries, "It's a miracle!"

Scenario 2: Ben comes home from a day at work. His wife, Karen, meets him at the door and says, "Let's watch a game of rugby tonight, followed by an Arnold Schwarzenegger movie, and eat fattening food together! I've put some Guinness in the fridge for you." Ben falls to his knees, raises his hands in the air and cries, "It's a miracle!"

The word *miracle* gets bandied about a lot these days. People use it all the time in reference to an event that is slightly surprising. It's a miracle when your favourite team end a losing streak by beating the number one team. It's a miracle that someone could survive that car crash. It's a miracle that the sun came out on a rainy wedding day. It's a miracle he completed school and got into Uni.* It's a miracle she got the promotion. It's gonna take a miracle for us to get to the airport in this traffic.** We talk about the miracle of birth whenever a baby is born. The word even permeates our entertainment culture, with TV specials and series showcasing miracles and amazing stories ("Miracle Dog Survives Fire!" "Miracle Baby Born without Body!") and numerous songs about miracles, performed by the likes of Whitney Houston, Queen, the Foo Fighters, Bon Jovi, Celine Dion and Bruce Springsteen, to name just a few.

The immediate effect of this is that we have become blasé to the real power of the word. It has lost a lot of its punch. However, when the men who wrote the records of Jesus' life tell us that he performed miracles, they aren't using the term loosely or in a metaphorical sense like we might today. They report that Jesus performed some real, astonishing, jaw-dropping, eye-popping, remarkable feats and displays of otherworldly power. He did things that were, in the true sense of the word, miraculous, things to which the only response could be awe, wonder and sometimes even fear. Even Josephus (the Jewish historian who lived and wrote shortly after Jesus) said that he was a man "who performed startling feats".[1]

It's these miracles that make Jesus truly unique on the world stage and set him apart from just about every other religious leader or guru. He wasn't just

> \* Hey Pete, that's what your folks said about you!
> – Ben

> \*\* It's a miracle we finished this book. – Pete

1. Josephus, *Antiquities of the Jews* 18.3.3, written about AD 93–94.

* Writers such as David Hume, David Strauss, Friedrich Nietzsche, and, more recently, scholars such as John Dominic Crossan and novelists such as Dan Brown have all called the gospel accounts and the miracles of Jesus into question, and this has had its effects.

He did things that broke the barriers between the natural world and the world beyond – *the supernatural* – and that bent the laws of the universe.

an amazing teacher and speaker – 'cause let's face it, there have been many of those – but he also did things that were incredible, unique and almost incomprehensible. He did things that broke the barriers between the natural world and the world beyond – **the supernatural** – and that bent the laws of the universe. In doing so, he showed that he was **not of this world.**

But let's be honest. For many of us, the miraculous side to Jesus can be a little hard to swallow. After all, in today's world, real miracles are hard to come by. Even if we may have seen an amazing event or know someone who has made a surprising recovery from an illness or accident, miracles of New Testament proportions are rare. When was the last time you were at the beach and you saw someone walking on water? Or who's ever been in a plane during a storm and seen a flight attendant get up and command the lightning to stop? Or been at a party where one of the guests starts pouring a nice cabernet sauvignon out of the water jug? No one has ever come up to us and said, "Hey Ben and Pete, come to my party this weekend. I want you to meet Fred. He died in a car crash the other week and we had a funeral for him, but he climbed out of the grave four days later and now he's back at work."

Over the last three hundred years or so, and especially since the rise of modern science and the dawning of the Enlightenment, Jesus' miracles have come under the microscope by a number of cynics and critics. In the nineteenth century, Darwinism and the theory of evolution began to question the credibility of the opening book of the Bible – Genesis. The theory of evolution was regarded by many as the fatal blow for belief in the existence of God. Then along came German philosopher Friedrich Nietzsche, who tried to play mortician, supposedly climbing up onto the corpse of God and declaring him dead. It wasn't long after God's funeral, so to speak, that the knives came out for his Son and dark clouds of scepticism began to form over the Gospels and their claims that Jesus performed miracles. Now hundreds of books have been written that question the reliability of the Gospels and their claims that Jesus performed miracles.*

Some people believe that Jesus' miracles are the point where the Jesus of history becomes the Jesus of fairyland. They are willing to accept that there was a good man and great teacher named Jesus who lived two thousand years ago and spoke about God, love and forgiveness, but they squirm when it comes to the Jesus of the Bible who performed miracles. And so, more often than not Jesus' miracles are simply argued away by saying that the ancient world was just full of simpleminded, gullible people. When Jesus was walking on water, he was really just walking on a sandbar. Or when he raised someone from the dead, they weren't really dead but were just narcoleptic.

Others suggest that the disciples were so enamoured with Jesus that they exaggerated the stories. So for example, when Jesus fed the five thousand with a couple of fish and some bread, he really did it with a small bakery and two whales; and there were only fifty people, but somewhere along the way, more zeros got added to the number.

Then there are others who want to point the finger directly at Jesus and say that he used ancient forms of trickery and magic to deceive the crowds. They say that Jesus wasn't a performer of genuine miracles but was a skilled charlatan, an ancient travelling snake-oil salesman deceiving the crowds with magic and clever deception. After all, it appears there were many others of the time who performed various tricks and stunts. The Old Testament is littered with references to sorcerers and magicians, even working within the courts of kings and pharaohs.

Finally, there are even a few who argue that the stories of Jesus' miracles were never meant to be taken literally but that they were actually coded stories describing normal events in symbolic ways. So, for example, some have argued that when Jesus restored sight to the blind, he wasn't really healing a medically blind person; this was just a metaphorical way of describing how Jesus' teaching gave someone a whole new perspective.

**So where does that leave us?** We can't prove that Jesus performed miracles, but there's enough evidence to believe that the gospel writers were telling the truth. Their claim is that they are writing true and accurate historical accounts of eyewitnesses. So here are some things worth considering:

**First** of all, it's worth knowing that the accounts of Jesus' miracles are placed within the context of many precise historical references. They don't come to us in a nebulous void. The birth, life, sermons, miracles, trial, death and resurrection of Jesus are all carefully recorded alongside specific dates, geographical references and the names of contemporary leaders, such as emperors, governors and Jewish officials. This means that for many of Jesus' miracles, the writers provided details of where they occurred, when they occurred, and who witnessed them. So the gospel accounts of Jesus' miracles are located firmly in the context of a tangible history.

**Secondly,** it's not only the Gospels that tell us that Jesus performed miracles. A couple of contemporary non-Christian sources outside of the New Testament tell us that Jesus was widely known as a miracle worker of some sort. As mentioned before, Josephus tells us in a fairly matter-of-fact way that Jesus was "a man who performed startling feats". And the Jewish Talmud* confirms that Jesus was known for performing some sort of supernatural deeds: "On the eve of the Passover they 'hanged' [on a tree; ie, crucified] Jesus the Nazarene because he practiced sorcery and enticed and led Israel astray."[2] What is interesting here is that even though this account of Jesus' miracles might seem negative, even his opponents didn't try to deny Jesus' miraculous side. They just wrote it off as sorcery.

---

2. *Baraitha Sanhedrin* 43a.

*The Talmud is the Jewish book that records rabbinic discussions and interpretations of law, stories, customs and ethics.

## Jesus performed many different types of miracles.

**Thirdly,** Jesus performed many different types of miracles. It's not as though he had one favourite trick like a travelling magician ("Hey you guys, watch me pull a rabbit out of this hat!") and then just repeated it wherever he went. There were miracles of all kinds in response to various situations. He healed lepers, the blind, the lame and those with fevers (more about this in the next chapter). He performed numerous exorcisms under different circumstances; he calmed a storm, turned water into wine, walked on water, raised at least three different people from the dead and even came back to life himself. These miracles show us that in a way almost too difficult and mysterious for us to comprehend, Jesus could manipulate and control the reality of our physical plane.

**Fourthly,** there were many eyewitnesses to his miracles. We might have every right to be sceptical if Jesus did his miracles only to a select few behind closed doors, but in many cases, he did things in front of large crowds. At least five thousand people witnessed his transformation of the loaves and fishes into lunch for everyone.* Large crowds witnessed him heal a leper, raise Lazarus from the dead and cure a paralytic. The stories about this man and his miracles spread from town to town, and it didn't take long before frenzied crowds were turning up wherever he went. The writers of the Gospels use phrases that convey the excitement that surrounded Jesus because of his miraculous works: the crowds were "filled with awe"; "The crowd was amazed and said, 'Nothing like this has ever been seen in Israel'"; "The people were amazed when they saw the mute speaking, the crippled made well, the lame walking and the blind seeing." There are many times when Jesus found himself almost crushed amongst the mob that wanted to witness for themselves the amazing powers of this man. Furthermore, the apostle Paul tells us that after Jesus rose from the grave, he appeared to over five hundred people.[3] And not only did Jesus perform most of his miracles publicly, but on many occasions he did them in front of sceptical critics. Pharisees, Sadducees and other enemies of Jesus were all present and witnessed some of his most impressive miracles, and yet they didn't deny them.

**Fifthly,** it is worth bearing in mind the reaction of those who witnessed these amazing events. In no way did they seem to think that Jesus' miracles were just metaphorical. It's actually quite refreshing to see that Jesus' followers were just as sceptical as we would be. They weren't gullible zombies ready to believe anything they saw. When the initial reports of Jesus' resurrection reached his followers, just about all of them (not just Thomas) doubted the news, and some of them even began to travel back to their hometowns. Even his closest companions – the twelve disciples who had front row seats to just

---

3. 1 Corinthians 15:6.

about all of his miracles – were at times amazed, confused and frightened and doubted what they were witnessing.

**Lastly,** and perhaps most impressively, many of Jesus' followers were executed for their uncompromising belief that Jesus performed miracles and rose from the grave himself. Admittedly, the sources are a little hazy, but it seems that most of the apostles were martyred for what they believed and preached. Only the apostle John seems to have avoided execution for his faith and died from old age.

So with that off our chests, we can now look at what the miracles were all about.

### The Purposes of the Miracles

Have you ever wondered why Jesus didn't fly from town to town or breathe fire or make himself really muscly?* That's because the miracles weren't just random tricks that Jesus did to show off and impress people. They weren't an amusement so that he could simply get some attention and draw a crowd. Jesus didn't feed the five thousand because he had nothing better to do. He didn't turn water into wine because the party was getting boring. And he didn't walk on water just because he wanted to take a shortcut across the lake.

Many of Jesus' miracles, especially his acts of compassion in healing people, were spontaneous reactions to specific situations and encounters. The miracles were his response to people and their needs. At the same time, however, Jesus' miracles were often calculated to reveal who he was and what his mission was. From who was present, to who was involved, to where, when, how – all of it revealed that Jesus was indeed the Son of God. The gospel writers even narrated the miracles in such a way as not to just tell us what happened but to teach us something about Jesus. In some ways, the miracles acted like his business card.

Perhaps this can best be seen from John's perspective. John even calls the miracles "signs" because he clearly wants us to know that they are far more significant than just neat party tricks. Furthermore, when Jesus performed a miracle or a "sign", more often than not he followed it up with a lesson or sermon. In this way, his miracles acted as illustrations to his talks. So John tells us that shortly after Jesus miraculously fed the five thousand, he declared to the crowds, "I am the bread of life ... come down from heaven",[4] indicating that he wasn't just the divine provider but the provision itself. And after he raised Lazarus from the grave, Jesus proclaimed that he was "the resurrection and the life".[5] The miracles reveal who Jesus is and what he came to do.

---

4. John 6:35–58.
5. John 11:25.

> It's actually quite refreshing to see that Jesus' followers were just as sceptical as we would be.

> * That's what I'd do!
> – Ben
>
> Yeah, you need to! – Pete

\* This is also the role God plays in the Old Testament, often described there as the Great Shepherd. Psalm 23 is a classic example: "The Lord is my shepherd …".

### Changing Water into Wine

John records that at the start of Jesus' ministry, he performed a significant miracle.[6] Along with his mother and followers, Jesus was invited to attend a wedding in Cana, and it was at this celebration that Jesus famously changed water into good wine. But as we've been saying, this wasn't just a trick Jesus pulled to save the hosts from embarrassment or simply to provide entertainment at the wedding reception.

The key to comprehending the significance of the miracle is to understand something about the water Jesus chose to change. We are told that the water wasn't just drinking water but water used for ceremonial cleansing for guests at the wedding. It was a custom to have huge jars of water at such an event, particularly when food was being served, so that people could cleanse themselves and make themselves "pure". Jesus claimed that he was ushering in a whole new system under which people could be made clean.

Secondly, there was plenty of it. John tells us that each of the pots of water contained twenty to thirty gallons. This means that the combined capacity of the waterpots was about 150 gallons. Reckoning a half-pint to a glass, these vessels would contain about 2,400 servings of wine! The sheer quantity of water turned into wine then becomes symbolic of the overwhelming abundance of provision in this new era.[7]

So the whole miracle is telling us something about Jesus' mission: that a new and plentiful age of cleansing has begun, replacing the old system with a new one. It is also interesting to note the immediate effect upon his band of disciples, who were in these early days still perhaps trying to get a feel for what their new rabbi was all about. This miracle would have left them in no doubt that they were in the presence of someone extraordinary. John records that "he revealed his glory; and his disciples put their faith in him."[8]

> The whole miracle is telling us something about Jesus' mission: that a new and plentiful age of cleansing has begun, replacing the old system with a new one.

### The Feeding of the Five Thousand

Apart from his resurrection, the feeding of the five thousand is the only miracle that is recorded by all four gospel writers.[9] We are told that a great crowd had poured out of the townships and followed Jesus out to the inland sea. They came in their thousands, and we are told that Jesus felt compassion for them because they were like "sheep without a shepherd". This sets up the miracle beautifully as Jesus takes the role of a compassionate shepherd and "feeds his sheep", so to speak.\*

The miracle narrative proper begins with the disciples coming to Jesus with their concerns about a lack of food amongst the crowd while they are

---

6. John 2:1–12.

7. D. A. Carson, *The Gospel according to John* (Downers Grove, IL: IVP, 1991), 174.

8. John 2:11.

9. Matthew 14:13–21; Mark 6:30–44; Luke 9:11–17; John 6:1–14.

in the wilderness far from their towns and villages. They suggest that Jesus should send them all away to get what they need. However, Jesus wants to show both the disciples and the crowd that he is the Great Shepherd and provider and there's no need for them to leave. He asks the disciples how much food is available. The scene is almost comical in the context of the thousands of people milling around when the best they can produce is five loaves of bread and two fish.

Then Jesus does the impossible. He turns the small amount of provisions into enough food to feed over five thousand people. Just like the miracle of turning water into wine, there is an abundant supply. The food just keeps on coming. This is emphasized by the fact that not only did "all eat and were satisfied" but that there were twelve baskets full of food still left over. There was more than enough for everybody.

What an amazing event. What an incredible scene. Thousands of people – people as far as the eye can see, sitting, standing, moving, pushing forward, talking – all curious about this new rabbi. And then this. *Out in the desert! Food!* The crowd would have quickly realised they were in the presence of someone very special. They were in the presence of God in human form – the Great Shepherd and provider of his people.

### Jesus Calms a Storm

Jesus and his closest followers enter a number of boats to cross the Sea of Galilee.[10] But after they have set out from the shore, a fierce squall comes up, causing waves on the lake to break over the side of the boats. This was no ordinary storm. We know that several of Jesus' disciples were professional fisherman of this lake and were highly accustomed to its weather patterns. They would have experienced a lot of rough weather in their time and they wouldn't normally have been so concerned, but it seems the wind and the waves were so fierce, they were frightened they were going to drown.

In complete contrast – and in something of a comical scene – Jesus is asleep in the stern of the boat. Astonished at Jesus' complacency and in complete desperation, the men wake him and demand, "Don't you care if we drown? Save us!"[11] With this, Jesus does one of the most extraordinary things in recorded history. He simply says, "Quiet! Be still!" and the storm stops. There was no magic formula such as "abracadabra " or some lengthy spell; there was no hocus-pocus or the quick performing of a ritual. Jesus doesn't even pray. His simple direct words alone are enough to calm the storm.

Again, imagine for a moment actually seeing that happen. You'd be pinching yourself or rubbing your eyes to make sure you were seeing things properly. This was an extraordinary miracle, impossible to fake. You would

> The crowd would have quickly realised they were in the presence of someone very special. They were in the presence of God in human form – the Great Shepherd and provider of his people.

---

10. Mark 4:35–41; Matthew 8:23–27.
11. Mark 4:38; Matthew 8:25.

very quickly realise that you were in the presence of a man who was different from other men and that somehow, mysteriously, this man had a power over creation that no one else did. This person could control water, air, waves, rain, clouds, thunder, tides, wind. He obviously had some sort of *super*natural connection.

The magnitude of the miracle is seen in the disciples' reaction. Keep in mind that they have already witnessed Jesus performing some pretty impressive healings and exorcisms, but none of the disciples reacted to those events like they do with this one. They turn to each other in awe and fear and say, "Who is this? Even the wind and waves obey him!"[12]

Jesus was taking things to another level. And the reason for their reaction was this: In several passages in the Old Testament, we are told that God alone is the master of the elements and that he controls the wind and the waves.[13] And add to that, perhaps the most famous miracle in Israel's history was the parting of the waters of the Red Sea during the exodus. Jesus' closest companions would have looked at him with new eyes after that day.

> The disciples turn to each other in awe and fear and say, "Who is this? Even the wind and waves obey him!"

These big miracles – changing water into wine, calming a storm, feeding thousands of people – were spectacular and truly miraculous. However, perhaps the biggest impact Jesus had upon the people of the region was not in the epic miracles. Where we see people getting really excited about Jesus is in the multitude of smaller, more personal miracles, when he deals with people one on one. It was an excitement that caused people to seek Jesus wherever he went, dragging their sick friends and family members with them – across lakes, down roads, into houses.

And it's these miracles that we will look at next.

---

12. Mark 4:41.
13. Job 9:8 – 10; Psalm 107:25 – 29.

Some years ago, Pete hurt his back. In a perfect storm of stupidity mixed with naivety and a misguided sense of indestructibility, he lifted a bag of concrete while bent over and twisting sideways. The result was that a muscle snapped its way in between two of the vertebrae in his spine. He described it later as like being hit by a truck and a bolt of lightning at the same time. He crumpled to the ground, where with boggle eyes, mouth agape and face pressed into the dirt, he was able to reflect upon his new understanding of phrases like "crippling agony", "suffering without end", "white hot pain" and "stupid idiot".

He was barely able to move, and every breath brought on a sensation akin to having one's back cleft in two by a woodsman wielding an enormous axe. So unforgiving and all-encompassing was the pain that Pete would have *paid anything* and *done anything* to make it stop. ***Anything.*** He was desperate. He ended up later that day on the workbench of a special physiotherapist who performed a series of stretches, poundings, twistings, massages and crackings on Pete's back.* While there was inflammation and damage and still a lot of pain, the partial relief was immediate and wonderful, so much so that Pete was moved to tears. Here was a person who could fix him up, a person who had the skills and the power and the knowledge to provide relief, to make the pain and the problem go away. Over the coming weeks, Pete enthusiastically looked forward to his return visits, each time getting a bit better. He felt an incredible sense of gratitude and awe towards this physio who could provide such relief and comfort and healing.

> \* I would have done that to you for half the price.
> – Ben
>
> Yeah, but with twice the pain! – Pete

What an amazing age we live in. When we get sick or injured, relief and healing are generally little more than a phone call away. A doctor or chemist** can give us a tablet or gel or cream or spray or lotion or powder, and before we can say "health insurance", we are back on deck and whistling Dixie. Even if you are seriously ill or badly hurt, there are scores of learned doctors and dentists and podiatrists and physiotherapists and specialists and orthodontists and surgeons and nurses and obstetricians and neurosurgeons and plenty of others with impressive certificates on their wall and lots of letters after their name who can do the Humpty Dumpty on you. In fact, there isn't much on the scale between ingrown toenail and brain tumour – with a few obvious exceptions – that can't be sorted out with antibiotics, paracetamols, anaesthetics, vaccines, antidotes, penicillin, antiseptics or a session under the scalpel in a hospital full of machines that go *beep* and *ping*. So intrinsically

\** Aussie talk for "pharmacist".

intertwined have sickness and healing become that we have come to assume they are a package deal. They are inseparable. You get sick. You get better. *Fait accompli.*

But imagine it weren't like this. What would your life be like if you lived in an era when rather than pills and doctors and surgery to ease your pains and soothe your woes, there was ... nothing. Imagine if the only response to sickness or injury was to grin and bear it and cross your fingers. Even the most insignificant things, like a headache or an impacted molar, could become ongoing and catastrophically painful, while asthma or diarrhoea could leave you dead. If they didn't kill you, then diseases, infections and fevers could leave you permanently disabled or scarred ... to say nothing of the certain death that would come with such things as diabetes, appendicitis or complications in childbirth ... never mind even getting into the league of tumours, cancers or heart attacks.

This is life two thousand years ago, at the time of Jesus. It is an era when sickness and injury and disease take on a lot more sinister aspect than being just minor inconveniences. It is an era when if you lived to thirty, you were doing pretty well.*

The ancient world was not totally in the dark about medicine. Early civilisations such as those in Mesopotamia, Rome, Greece and Egypt had a preliminary understanding of human anatomy and organs. There were physicians and midwives and basic surgical tools such as scalpels, probes, forceps and hooks. They were able to treat broken bones, amputate limbs, stitch wounds and treat minor ailments with herbal remedies. But there were also a lot of misconceptions and folk remedies that would not have done much good at all. For example, at various times, there were beliefs about the heart being the source of intelligence, and the arteries carrying air around the body. Women in labour today have a number of options when it comes to relieving the pain of childbirth and encouraging the process of labour. At one stage in the ancient world, however, the best at your disposal were options like inhaling the fumes of burning animal fat, drinking urine or powdered dung, or having various animal body parts draped over you. The mortality rate of newborns was very high in this era.

Many implications came with being sick or injured. If you didn't die, it was likely that a sickness or injury would be with you for a long time, if not for life. Once you caught a disease, for example, that was it. You had it. So people would do anything to stay away from other sick people for fear of contagion. In addition, sickness was sometimes associated with demon possession. Sick people were shunned, especially if the disease or infection was highly visible, such as a skin disorder. Such people were ceremonially unclean according to Jewish law, and as such, they were unable to participate in religious rites and practices. But in addition to that, they were seen as a

* I wouldn't have lived past six when I was hospitalised with infected tonsils.          – Pete

And I would have checked out when I was sixteen and fractured my back.
                                    – Ben

It is an era when sickness and injury and disease take on a lot more sinister aspect than being just minor inconveniences.

highly visible threat and danger to the population. If you contracted leprosy (which is highly contagious and debilitating), you would become an outcast, literally "cast out" of your town and shunned from normal social life and human contact. Jewish law[1] dictated that a person with an infectious skin disease should live alone "outside the camp" and cry "Unclean! Unclean!" as they walked along. There would have been considerable apprehension from onlookers, and parents would have held their children tightly, such was the fear and danger associated with this sickness.

It is important to remember too that there were no hospitals or retreats or community services departments as we know them today. (And indeed, no Christian charity organizations!) If you were born with a disability or became permanently injured in an accident, or if a fever led to brain damage or loss of sight, then you were at the mercy of other people to look after you. If you were lucky, this might be in the form of your family. But more often than not, the gospel writers describe many people whose only sorry option in life was to park themselves in a public place and beg for people to give them some food, assistance or money.

Now, so far this chapter has panned out like a quirky history lesson. But it has all been setting the context and building up to this all-important point. Imagine being a sick person living at the time of Jesus. Imagine being lame or blind or having a crippling disease. Imagine if pain and discomfort and social rejection and the ever-present threat of death were just everyday realities for you and that is the way it would be for the rest of your life.

Then, imagine you hear a rumour.

The word comes through your town. All the people are talking about it. There's a rabbi who is travelling around who has done some amazing things. He seems to have powers that others do not have. Here it is in a nutshell: he can **heal.** He can make sick people well. Apparently, he has made skin diseases disappear. Someone says they heard that a paralysed man is now walking. Another person says they met a man who was blind who can now see. It turns out this guy claims to be the Messiah and is forgiving sins!* This is the biggest news you have ever heard in your life. This news is wondrous, awesome, amazing, unbelievable … indeed, miraculous.

Little wonder, then, that the writers of the Gospels describe that people who witnessed these incredible healings were amazed, shocked, speechless, awestruck, overcome with joy and even frightened. These were staggering events that moved many to praise God and left even Jesus' strongest critics astonished. It was Jesus' healing miracles that seemed to have made the biggest impact on the crowds, and why not? Like Pete with his injured back, you would be so excited and grateful and hopeful at the thought that someone could fix you up. If you met someone who could heal a friend who was blind

---

1. Leviticus 13:45–46.

Sick people were shunned, especially if the disease or infection was highly visible, such as a skin disorder.

* In the ancient world, sickness and sin were often associated. When confronted by a sick person, Jesus often first said, "Your sins are forgiven!" Such a claim was blasphemy to the Jews, so the natural reaction of the sick person may have been, "Yeah, right, that's what I need right now!" Jesus then supported his claim by actually healing the person.

As soon as Jesus began to heal people, whole towns would come to see him and bring out those who were ill or injured.

or sick with a terminal illness, wouldn't you want to drag that person out to see if he could heal them? Wouldn't you do anything to try to see him? That was exactly the case in Jesus' day. The gospel writers tell us that as soon as Jesus began to heal people, whole towns would come to see him and bring out those who were ill or injured. The scenes were frantic, desperate and wild.

Mark describes one event when a large crowd followed Jesus and was pressed up against him.[2] He writes, "And a woman was there who had been subject to bleeding for twelve years. She had suffered a great deal under the care of many doctors and had spent all she had, yet instead of getting better she grew worse. When she heard about Jesus, she came up behind him in the crowd and touched his cloak, because she thought, 'If I just touch his clothes, I will be healed.' Immediately her bleeding stopped and she felt in her body that she was freed from her suffering." This was the kind of excitement and expectation that had formed around Jesus.

On another occasion (which we mentioned in passing earlier), Jesus was teaching in a house in Capernaum.[3] People had poured out of villages from all over Galilee and Judea and from Jerusalem to be there, and it was standing room only. In fact, there were even crowds outside who couldn't get in. Luke writes that "some men came carrying a paralyzed man on a mat and tried to take him into the house to lay him before Jesus. When they could not find a way to do this because of the crowd, they went up on the roof and lowered him on his mat through the tiles into the middle of the crowd, right in front of Jesus."

Can you picture this? These guys are so keen on getting their mate healed, so much do they believe that Jesus can actually fix him, that they will not let anything deter them. They are men of action who will find a way in, no matter what. You can almost imagine the people inside getting covered in flecks and falling debris as a gap appears above their heads, a beam of sunlight suddenly pouring through. You can imagine the commotion as people jostle to make room for the body that drops down from above their heads into the already packed room.* And then this: Jesus heals the guy. Right there in front of everyone, no doubt accompanied by a host of wide eyes and drawn breath, the paralysed man *stands up*. Luke says that the man "went home praising God. Everyone was amazed and gave praise to God. They were filled with awe and said, 'We have seen remarkable things today.'"[4]

This is just one of many stories about Jesus healing people. And it certainly gives us insight into why huge crowds began seeking Jesus out wherever he went. The Gospels tell us that Jesus miraculously healed people from a whole range of diseases and injuries. And they weren't just run-of-the-mill

* You can also imagine the house owner looking at the new skylight in his roof and thinking that maybe things were getting out of hand!   – Pete

If it was a rental, I think he'd lose his bond.   – Ben

---

2. Mark 5:21–34.

3. Luke 5:17–26.

4. Luke 5:25–26.

illnesses or infirmities either. He didn't heal only people with headaches or a runny nose or ambiguous lower back problems. He healed people of blindness, deafness, dumbness, epilepsy and all sorts of skin diseases.[*] He healed a woman with a severe curvature of the spine, a man with a shrivelled hand and others who were paralysed. His healing even went to the extreme of dealing with the ultimate sickness: death itself. On three occasions, Jesus showed his power by actually restoring a dead person to life. Yes, Jesus performed some spectacular, jaw-dropping miracles on the sick and injured. So it shouldn't surprise us that some of the most emotional and moving scenes in the Gospels are found in the context of healings.

**Jesus healed people for a number of reasons.** Clearly Jesus healed people because he loved them and was concerned about their well-being. One of the most famous verses (and, as an interesting aside, the shortest verse) in the Bible is this simple statement: "Jesus wept."[5] It was his immediate response to the death of a friend (Lazarus) and the tears of his family. Amongst other reasons, it was out of his sorrow and compassion that he brought him back to life again. Similarly, Matthew tells us that when Jesus got out of a boat on the shore of the Sea of Galilee and saw a crowd waiting for him, he simply "had compassion on them and healed their sick".[6]

Another purpose of the healing miracles was, in a very tangible way for those present, to demonstrate the arrival of the kingdom of God. As we have said, Jesus taught that his arrival on earth ushered in a new era and the arrival in part of the kingdom or rule of God. In this sense, it was a taste of things to come. The Bible tells us that for the believer, life beyond the grave will be free from suffering, pain and disease. Jesus was marvelously demonstrating to all what that life would be like.

The miracles also certainly displayed his power and authority. Here was a man *like no other.* Here was a man who had power over disease, pain, suffering and even death. Here was a man with an almost incomprehensible connection with the fabric of our physical world. With just the touch of his hand or by a single command, Jesus could heal people or restore life where there was death. He didn't need medicine or chants or several days to heal people. He was so powerful that just by a single command or by a gentle touch, people were instantly healed.

Healings were Jesus' business card, showing us who he is and what he came to do. The healing miracles demonstrated with no doubt that Jesus is God's great healer and restorer. Jesus came to heal the brokenhearted, to cleanse us from the disease of sin and to free us from the malady of a broken relationship with God. He came to give us life and open our eyes to the truth.

> Another purpose of the healing miracles was, in a very tangible way for those present, to demonstrate the arrival of the kingdom of God.

[*] The word translated as "leprosy" in the New Testament was used more broadly than today to describe a whole range of skin diseases.

5. John 11:35.
6. Matthew 14:14.

### The Healing of the Leper

One of Ben's favourite miracles was also a favourite amongst Jesus' first followers. Three of the four gospel writers chose to record this event.[7] When Jesus was being followed by a large crowd, a man with leprosy came up to him and knelt before him for all to see and said, "If you are willing, you can make me clean."

This was a gutsy move. Remember that lepers were shunned by society and forced to live as outcasts on account of their contagious illness. Most were unemployable and so etched out an existence by begging and scavenging for food. Also, because of their contagious disease, people kept their distance so they would not be contaminated. Imagine the humility and loneliness that came with that kind of a lifestyle. Yet despite these hurdles, this man had enough faith in Jesus to kneel before him and ask him to heal him in front of a crowd that no doubt kept their distance.

Furthermore, his public kneeling may seem like an incidental aspect to the story, but it speaks volumes on how this man viewed Jesus. He didn't stand upright before Jesus so he could address him on equal terms, nor did he seek him out on a less public occasion. He saw Jesus as far superior and was willing to publicly acknowledge his faith in Jesus' ability to heal him.

Jesus was moved with pity and stretched out his hand and touched him.

This is an incredible scene. Here was this lonely man, who in all probability hadn't been touched by anyone in years, now feeling the warmth of another human being's hand. And there was Jesus with this poor bloke before him and the two of them encircled by a huge crowd who stood there stunned at seeing something you just didn't see. Someone was ... touching ... a leper!

With his hand upon the man, Jesus said, "I am willing.... Be clean!" And there, in front of the crowd, for all to see, the man was healed. Rather than the leper infecting Jesus, the very opposite happened – Jesus infected the man.

The miracle wonderfully illustrates Jesus' greater purpose and the right response to him. Each and every one of us has a form of leprosy, a disease that makes us unclean and tarnished before God. In a sense, we are all unclean. Yet Jesus is both willing and able to make us clean. So when we come to him humbly and ask him, just like the leper did, to heal us and make us clean, he in effect says, "I am willing," and does so. This is both the simplicity and the beauty of what it means to follow Jesus.

> Rather than the leper infecting Jesus, the very opposite happened – Jesus infected the man.

### The Raising of Lazarus

The raising of Lazarus from the dead is one of the most memorable and stirring miracles.[8] It wonderfully displays Jesus' power over death.

---

7. Matthew 8:1–4; Mark 1:40–45; Luke 5:12–16.
8. John 11.

Lazarus, the brother of Mary and Martha, was a good friend of Jesus. John tells us that Lazarus – like so many of his day – fell ill to a serious disease. Whatever the disease, it was serious enough for the sisters to summon Jesus (most likely via a messenger) to come and heal their brother at once. The great surprise in the story, however, is that Jesus didn't respond immediately to the call, instead deciding to stay where he was for a few more days.

To any onlooker at the time, this must have seemed like an odd thing to do. Jesus clearly had the power to heal the sick, but even though his good mate was dying, he didn't rush to get there. After a couple of days, Jesus and his disciples finally made their way to Lazarus's house in Bethany. And on the way, Jesus told his friends some disturbing news: "Lazarus is dead." In fact, when they arrived, he had already been buried in a tomb and his family and friends had gathered at the house to mourn his death.[*]

When Jesus saw Martha, he had words of comfort for her. He told her that Lazarus would rise again. She acknowledged this and said she knew he would live again in the afterlife. But it appears Jesus meant something different entirely. So Jesus said to her, "I am the resurrection and the life. Anyone who believes in me will live, even though they die." The miracle was going to prove his point. Yet she didn't understand what he meant.

The death of a loved one is no easy matter. Both of us (Ben and Pete) have lost a parent, and a number of our close friends have died at an early age. Anyone who has experienced a loss like that knows just what the family of Lazarus was going through. It is not hard to imagine the sad faces, the tears, the pain, the gravity of loss and all the disorienting emotional lows the family was feeling at this time.

Sadly, Jesus has often been portrayed as being a cold, stone-faced, unemotional figure, a man who never laughed or smiled or cried or had emotions. More often than not in art and sculpture he looks glum and morbid. John wants us to know that this couldn't be farther from the truth. When the rest of the family came out to see Jesus, he didn't just stand there and coldly tell them to have more faith. He didn't look at them all without any emotion or stand there with a smirk on his face knowing that all would be different in a little while. John tells us that when Jesus saw the family weeping and in pain, he was deeply moved and troubled by the whole scene.

But there is more to John's description than meets the eye. The words John uses in the Greek to describe Jesus' emotions here are not just words of sadness but also words that contain an element of anger. But if that is the case, why is he angry as well? It is hard to say. It could be that Jesus is upset by their lack of faith. Or it could be his anger with sin and its consequences of suffering and death. Perhaps it is some combination of both. Certainly Jesus doesn't like death, and that shouldn't surprise us. Again and again the gospel writers tell us in various ways that Jesus loves people and cares for all mankind. And so if death is our greatest enemy, it is little wonder that Jesus was not only saddened but even angered by it.

After this emotional scene, Jesus asked to be taken to the tomb where Lazarus had been buried. Perhaps everyone thought that Jesus was simply going there to pay his last respects. No one would have expected what happened next.

When everyone arrived, Jesus said something shocking and offensive: he told them to remove the stone in front of the tomb. The tomb was a burial cave with a large stone used as a door to cover the entrance, not dissimilar to the one Jesus would be buried in. This command was most unusual. Lazarus had been buried there for four days and – especially in that hot climate – his body would have begun to decay. This would not be a pleasant scene. Martha objected, saying that the corpse would smell.

But when the stone was rolled away, Jesus prayed. And then he commanded Lazarus to come out of the tomb.

Can you imagine the family and friends of Lazarus at that moment? Each of them standing there transfixed on the opening of that tomb, waiting for any sign of movement, and then watching in stunned disbelief as Lazarus made his way out of the entrance of the tomb into the arms of those closest to him. The sense of joy and astonishment must have been overwhelming. John tells us that as a result, many of the Jews who were visiting Mary put their faith in Jesus.

The miracle not only acted as a brilliant illustration of Jesus' mission to give new life. It proved it! He was and is the life-giving Lord who rules over sickness and death.

There are so many other miracles in the Gospels that we'd love to tell you about, but hey, why don't you just read them for yourself? Remember as you read that when Jesus healed people, he clearly displayed who he was and bluntly revealed to people in a most visible way what his mission was all about. These miracles of healing show his compassion; they show us what life in the kingdom of God is like; they demonstrate his power and authority over sickness and death. In context, Jesus' miracles also make it easier for us to understand just how much he had an impact on the people around him. We can understand why people poured out of their homes and villages, traipsed across the landscape and followed him in droves wherever he went in a desperate attempt just to be near him, touch him and follow him.

But it wasn't just physical sickness that Jesus wanted to heal. There were also people who were spiritually sick. There were people who had fallen prey to spiritual forces beyond our comprehension. Which is a perfect segue into our next chapter.

> The miracle not only acted as a brilliant illustration of Jesus' mission to give new life. It proved it!

# Chapter 16

# GETTING TOUGH WITH EVIL
## Jesus' power over the dark side

You've got your ticket in your pocket, a drink in one hand and enough popcorn to feed a small country in the other. You sit down in a comfy seat in the theatre as the curtains draw back and the movie begins: *The Creatures from the Black Lagoon 3*. It's full of slimy monsters with two heads, green eyes and six arms. They all have ugly faces, with long teeth, pointy ears, yellow skin and visibly bad breath. They're hideous to look at, and they speak with bone-chilling voices. On cue, the audience shrieks, screams, yells and squirms, the whole time thoroughly enjoying it. The movie finishes, the lights come up. Some sit there still stunned, while others hold their hands over their quickly beating hearts, and others walk out smiling about the schlock.

But here's the thing: you don't leave thinking that what you've just seen is real. Even if you are a bit freaked out when, later on that night, you turn the light off in the bathroom and make a mad dash to your bed hoping that the Black Lagoon creatures haven't somehow inexplicably and randomly appeared in your hallway, deep down you know that it is not real. You've seen the DVD special features of the makeup and special effects. You know it's just fantasy and Hollywood at its finest (or worst).

Hollywood hasn't done us any favours when it comes to our understanding of demons and evil spirits and the people who have to face up to them. Aside from the classics *The Exorcist* and *The Omen*, there is a panoply of films out there with alluring titles – *Demon Island*, *Night of the Demon*, *Demon Knight*, *Demon Headmaster*, *Demon Doctor*, *Demon Classroom*, *Demon Planet*, *Demon Cathedral*, *Demon Slayer*, *Demon Fighter*, *Demon Killer*, *Demon Cop*, *Demon Lover*, *Demon Barber*, *Demon Dolls*, and our personal favourite title, the 1915 silent film *Dicky's Demon Dachsund* – that exploit the horror genre and play with the idea of dark forces in the world.

On top of that, there are thousands of films with the words *evil* or *devil* in their title (including the curiously named *Night of the Day of the Dawn of the Son of the Bride of the Return of the Revenge of the Terror of the Attack of the Evil, Mutant, Alien, Flesh-Eating, Hellbound, Zombified Living Dead Part 2: In Shocking 2-D*), and of course where would we be without the zombie films, like *I Was a Teenage Zombie*, *Psycho Zombie Love Butcher*, *Zombie Honeymoon*, *Zombie Beach Party*, *Zombie Farm*, *Zombie Vegetarians*, and *Punk Rock Kung Fu Zombie Catfight*. Our technological age has even heralded in a swathe of zombie/demon/evil-dead console games, including one in which you get to possess bodies, eat people, use your head as a grenade and play with the function called "eat brain". Together, these films and games have degraded our concepts of evil and spiritual forces into the comical realm of B-grade monster flicks, having packaged them up as pithy entertainment.

Part of the problem is that in the Western world, we have become blasé, immune and desensitised to things beyond the realm of what we can see, touch and hear. In some respects, our hectic lifestyle and absorption in science and technology act like blinkers on a horse, preventing us from seeing or contemplating a world or spiritual plane beyond our immediate lives. It doesn't help either that many people have never moved on from the childish picture in their head of ultimate evil in the world – the devil – as a cute character with a forked tail and pitchfork who sits on your shoulder and encourages you to be naughty, kind of like a mischievous cousin. Evil has been reduced to a kind of appealing naughtiness, with ice creams and chocolates marketed as "deliciously evil" and film characters, such as the much mimicked Dr Evil, portrayed as lovable rogues. So the idea of evil and its various manifestations are treated with disregard, humour and nonchalance in our culture. Nowhere do you see this more than in the fact that the biggest toy manufacturer in the world – the same company who make Scrabble and Monopoly – makes a "ouija board" (now with "glow in the dark gameboard") so the whole family can enjoy some paranormal fun together.

People in the Bible take evil and demons a lot more seriously.

The New Testament affirms that there is an active spiritual world that includes a devil, demons, evil spirits and angels, and that they are actively involved with the physical world we live in. Jesus taught not only that both angels and demons exist but that they are active in numerous ways in human affairs.

When we come to reading about demons in the New Testament, we encounter stories of evil spirits overwhelming people, speaking out from within them and causing them to perform uncontrollable acts.* And we also read about Jesus healing people by forcing demons to come out. The technical term for this is *exorcism*, a word that has its roots in binding demons with an oath. But as soon as we use the word *exorcist*, it's easy to fall into the trap of thinking about zombie-style horror scenarios with Jesus wielding a crucifix hopefully in front of him while objects fly around the room and people's heads spin around spewing bile. It's easy to package the whole lot up as fantastic fiction.

However, the four men who wrote the accounts about Jesus were under no such delusion. Like Jesus' other miracles, his exorcisms are recorded as history, accompanied by geographical references and names of individuals as the writers try to convey that this isn't fiction but fact. And as we have said elsewhere, it wasn't just his followers who claimed that Jesus performed

* Incidentally, the New Testament draws the distinction on numerous occasions between those who were ill (including those who had seizures) and those who had demons. See Matthew 4:24; Mark 1:34.

Jesus taught not only that both angels and demons exist but that they are active in numerous ways in human affairs.

miracles and exorcisms, but it was also his sceptical enemies. The question on the lips of his opponents was not, "Does he really perform exorcisms?" but, "By what power does he do them?"

## Jesus Did Not Tolerate Evil

On many occasions, we are told that Jesus directly dealt with evil spirits in people. However, only six encounters are recorded in detail. While each case is unique, all of them clearly indicate that Jesus was in control of the demon and the person possessed. There is a consistent sense that he rules over the spirit world and that demons as such are all subject to him. Similar to his power over nature, Jesus' power over the world of spirits again testifies that Jesus was no ordinary person but that he stood in the breach between our everyday world of the senses and the somewhat elusive and mysterious world of the spirit. He dealt with spirits and commanded them gone, just like he did with various sicknesses. These exorcisms were marvelous displays of his authority in and over the spirit world, and this can be seen in a number of ways:

**First** of all, he did not tolerate evil. When confronted by a person who was – to use our modern term – possessed, he didn't turn the other way. He didn't suddenly find other things to do or try to divert attention somewhere else. He didn't shuffle his feet or look confused or feel embarrassed or anything like that. Instead, he went for them, straight up. He recognized evil spirits as an aberration in the order of things, and he dealt with them. He faced up to evil spirits and commanded them in a no-nonsense authoritative way.

**Secondly,** his exorcisms didn't take long. It's not as though there was a great struggle between Jesus and the spirits that went on for days. He didn't have to pray for hours or wrestle with the subject in a great physical battle for long periods of time. Rather, there was usually just a single command from Jesus, and then the demons went. It has been said that if Jesus starred in *The Exorcist*, the movie would be short because he would turn up and say, "Come out," and it would all be over. Roll credits.

**Thirdly,** he didn't need to use any formulas or spells to cast out demons. Nowhere do we find Jesus saying "abracadabra" or chanting long spells or using holy water, amulets or incense, or wielding a crucifix like a light sabre, or invoking magic formulas, or slaying animals and painting their blood into geometric shapes. He didn't need to do any of that. He simply ordered the demons as he pleased with his own words.

**Finally,** the demons were all subject to his commands and were frightened of him. They cowered, cried out and begged Jesus not to harm them. In every case, Jesus was in full control of the situation, and the demons were subject to his every word. So commanding was Jesus over the demons that the

> Jesus' power over the world of spirits again testifies that Jesus was no ordinary person but that he stood in the breach between our everyday world of the senses and the somewhat elusive and mysterious world of the spirit.

Pharisees thought he must be working in conjunction with them. When Jesus healed one particular man with a demon, the Pharisees said that it was "only by Beelzebul, the prince of demons, that this fellow drives out demons".[1]

## Jesus versus the Devil

A key to understanding the impact of the exorcisms of Jesus and his battle with the devil is to see how they symbolically relate in Israel's history to King David.

David, who lived about a thousand years before Jesus, was perhaps Israel's most famous and popular king. Despite some of his moral mistakes, he was regarded as a great leader and hero to the Israelites. Shortly after David received his divine appointment as the new "anointed one of God" (Messiah), he performed two great signs that displayed God's special favour on him as king over all of Israel.

The first thing David did as the anointed one was to exorcise a tormenting spirit that had begun to harass King Saul. At the time, David was a musician (a kind of ancient guitar player) who was summoned by Saul to play his instrument to soothe away the evil spirit.[*] David's power as the anointed one was shown in that whenever he played, the spirit left.

> * As a guitar player, I can relate to that.     – Ben
>
> Yeah, but *his* playing was soothing!     – Pete

Secondly, immediately following this, David performed his most famous "miracle". He fought the great Philistine soldier Goliath. This famous event reads like a scene out of the movie *Braveheart*.[2] The armies of the Israelites and the Philistines face one another in a big valley ready for battle. Goliath – famous for his strength and size – breaks forth from the battle line and challenges the Israelites to come down and fight him. We are told that this went on for forty days and nights.

Young David arrives on the scene having had no battle experience, yet he decides to take up the challenge. He doesn't place his confidence in his strength or his ability as a fighter. Instead, David simply trusts in God's protection. So David fights Goliath and famously kills him with his shepherd's sling. He then becomes a national hero and his journey to the throne begins.

Like David, Jesus was anointed by God. His anointing was in his baptism, and the first few things he did as the newly commissioned king (although in reverse order) were to fight the great enemy of God's people – the devil – and then cast out demons.

Like Goliath, the devil taunted Jesus for forty days and forty nights, and like David, Jesus fought him and won, not with a stone and sling but with the word of God. And according to Mark, one of the first miracles Jesus performed after his duel with the devil was the exorcism of an evil spirit from a

---

1. Matthew 12:24.
2. 1 Samuel 17.

man in Capernaum. The parallel is striking. Jesus' battles with the devil and demons displayed that he was the new king, the great divinely Anointed One (Messiah or Christ) of God.

## The Exorcism at Gerasenes

The exorcism on the man in the region of the Gerasenes is perhaps the most famous and controversial of Jesus' exorcisms. It is recorded in a fair amount of detail in three of the Gospels.[3]

Shortly after Jesus calmed a storm on the Sea of Galilee, he and his disciples came into the region of Gerasa* on the southwest side of the lake. When they came ashore and Jesus got out of the boat, he was confronted by a man who was possessed by a demon.

According to Mark, this demon, or "unclean spirit", had such an effect over the man that he was supernaturally strong and was a danger to both himself and others. In fact, Mark tells us that no one, even with the aid of chains and shackles, could control him. As a result, he lived as an outcast in a graveyard amongst abandoned tombs.

Mark gives us all of this information not because he wants to make the story frightening but rather because he wants to highlight Jesus' power and authority. After telling us in the example of Jesus' calming the storm that Jesus was a man who could control the physical world with tremendous ease, Mark continues to tell us that he also controlled the spiritual world. And so the uncontrollable man confronts the man who is fully in control.

As with the other exorcisms, this is all wonderfully displayed in the ease with which Jesus controls the man and the demon. From a distance, Jesus addresses the demon and simply says, "Come out of the man, you unclean spirit!"** And with that, the man runs over to him, worships him and cries out in fear and submission, "What do you want with me, Jesus, Son of the Most High God? Swear to God that you won't torture me!" With a single sentence, the uncontrollable man is now impressively under Jesus' control.

We are then given a bit of insight into why the man was so uncontrollable and destructive. Mark tells us that Jesus asks the demon, "What is your name?" and he replies, "My name is Legion, . . . for we are many." A legion in the Roman army was about six thousand men.*** It is highly unlikely that the man was possessed by six thousand demons, but the point is that this man has many demons in him.

At this point, the demon makes a curious request. It asks Jesus that it be cast out into a herd of nearby pigs.

To understand what happens next, we need to know a few things. The New Testament writers often describe demons as unclean spirits that cause

_____

3. Matthew 8:28–34; Mark 5:1–20; Luke 8:26–39. Quotations are from the NIV.

> Jesus' battles with the devil and demons displayed that he was the new king, the great divinely Anointed One (Messiah or Christ) of God.

* Modern-day Jerash.
** "Unclean" from the Greek.
*** The number varied between four and six thousand, but in Jesus' day, a legion in the Roman army was normally six thousand men.

impurity. That was certainly the case for this man. He lived in unclean tombs in a cemetery and he also cut himself with stones so that his skin was unclean. He was unclean to himself, to others and to God. The pig was also a forbidden animal that was symbolic of uncleanliness amongst the Jews.[4] Israelites were forbidden to eat pork, and many still abstain from it today.*

* Well, what do they eat for breakfast then? – Pete

Ever heard of cereal? – Ben

This extraordinary request is granted by Jesus. Immediately after the demons enter the pigs, all of them run down the hill and into the lake, where they drown.

The whole event was so bizarre that some who were present ran to tell their friends about the amazing event they had witnessed. People came from their homes to see for themselves what had happened. Imagine the scene that confronted them: a previously frightening social outcast now behaving normally, a rabbi, and a foreshore deep with the carcasses of pigs. Rather than being happy for the man and pleased that the demons had gone and curious about the whole rubric surrounding exorcism, their thoughts were more mundane. Here was the rabbi whom everyone had been talking about who had done something that showed he was different. He was working on a whole new plane, one that they could not comprehend. So their reaction was fear. They all became extremely frightened of Jesus and asked him to leave.

The exorcism is the story of Jesus' not only cleansing a man from unclean spirits but cleansing the land from all things unclean. The story then leaves us with Jesus not only having authority over evil spirits but also being one who is able to make *all things* clean. According to Mark, immediately after this, Jesus goes on to heal two more unclean people as he heals a woman who had been bleeding for twelve years and raises a dead girl to life. In both cases, Jesus touches them, but he isn't made impure. Rather, his touch makes them clean.

Events like this don't come by every day. The word continued to spread about this rabbi who could not only teach and interpret the law but could do things that showed he was beyond this world, things that no one else could do. People headed out of their homes and villages and farms. They dragged their friends and relatives with them. They poured down the roads and across the hills to seek out this man who could heal skin diseases, raise people from the dead, control evil spirits, and even manipulate the weather. He was a social phenomenon. He was Jesus.

> The word continued to spread about this rabbi who could not only teach and interpret the law but could do things that showed he was beyond this world, things that no one else could do.

---

4. Leviticus 11:7–8.

## Part 5

# FOR MY FINAL ACT

# Chapter 17

# PUBLIC ENEMY NUMBER ONE
## Jesus' enemies gather

In children's picture books, Jesus is often portrayed as a male version of Snow White. So there's Jesus, meek and mild, sitting on a rock in the middle of a flowery meadow, surrounded by children and cute forest animals and maybe even with some butterflies overhead. Jesus is saying something like, "Be good, 'cause it's good to be good. Eat your vegetables, and when you grow up, don't cheat on your taxes." The scene has a certain majestic serenity and satisfying wholesomeness to it. It's a scene that says Jesus is a nice guy and everything about him is comfortable and cheery and rosy.

So it is surprising to some people to discover that Jesus had enemies who fiercely opposed what he taught and claimed. As he travelled and his popularity grew, there were lots of people and groups who got their noses out of joint. To his opponents, Jesus was a troublemaker who posed a threat to the religious order. He challenged much of what mainstream Judaism taught, and he undermined the authority of the religious elite. That made a lot of powerful people very nervous. Not only that but they thought Jesus' teachings – many of which openly struck at the bedrock of Jewish life and faith – were blasphemous, wrong and misleading. Some even thought his teachings were *criminal*. So it didn't take long before this travelling preacher became public enemy number one and his enemies began plotting to have him executed.

So let us begin by dispelling a myth. Yes, Jesus did on occasion attract children. And he did draw large crowds. He was *popular*. Some of his teachings are the most comforting, inspiring and peaceful sayings in history and literature. However, much of what Jesus did and said was controversial and confrontational. Rather than always being a great comfort, he was a "difficult" person who caused division, disagreement and debate in the community.

One of the problems we face in the twenty-first century looking back at Jesus through the goggles of history is that our vision has become somewhat blurred by two thousand years of religion. In our Western culture, the church has become "the establishment". It is considered by some as an old-fashioned conservative watchdog with Jesus as its pious big-brother figure safeguarding morals and maintaining social order.

The irony is that in the conservative society of Jesus' time, Jesus' teachings were radical and challenging. Jesus went *against* the grain of the established order and caused a stir with his "new way" of looking at things – a new way, we might add, that has been perhaps the single most influential factor in

> To his opponents, Jesus was a troublemaker who posed a threat to the religious order.

shaping the society and culture in which we live today. Rather than being a comfortable conservative, Jesus was an outsider, a stirrer, a highly vocal thorn in the side of the establishment.

The important thing to note is that Jesus' enemies weren't a unified body, although eventually some groups did work together to have Jesus arrested, tried and executed. This group was actually made up of a number of smaller groups that differed from each other in the way they interpreted the Old Testament.

### The Pharisees

The most prominent and perhaps the most famous group of Jesus' enemies was the Pharisees. They were a prominent and influential religious and political sect of Jews, and in Jesus' day they numbered around six thousand. Strictly speaking, there were two schools of Pharisees, but all of them were notoriously concerned with a precise keeping of the purity laws of the Old Testament, especially those concerning the preparation and eating of food and the keeping of the Sabbath. They were heavily bound up with numerous rules about purity and restrictions about what people could and could not do. So concerned were they about keeping these laws, they even added some rules of their own just to be sure.* They fastidiously sought to be separate in order to stay detached from the unclean and "sinful" of society.

In some ways, the Pharisees considered themselves the spiritual elite of their people. They believed that they alone were the teachers of Israel because only they had a correct understanding of the Old Testament laws. In turn, many of them seemed to pride themselves on their own status and supposed holiness. The very word *Pharisee* can be traced to a Hebrew word meaning "separatist". So they certainly wouldn't have shared a meal with sinners or non-Jews.

This was the opposite of Jesus, who seemed to go out of his way to mix with the untouchables and the lowly. Accordingly, it was the Pharisees who took most offence at Jesus' sitting and eating with so-called unclean people such as prostitutes. To them, he was a blasphemer who was in league with the "prince of demons" and who was "possessed by Beelzebul".[1]

Jesus openly criticised these Jewish elite and radically challenged traditions about how to interpret some of the Old Testament laws. This was like a red rag to a bull for the Pharisees, who were incensed by Jesus' blasphemous actions and radical teachings. For example, the Pharisees had taken the fourth of God's commandments** to a ridiculous extreme by not permitting virtually *anything* to be done on that day. So they criticised Jesus for letting his disciples pick grain on the Sabbath when they were hungry.[2] They criticised

---

1. Matthew 9:1–8, 34; Mark 3:22.
2. Matthew 12:1–8.

> Jesus' enemies weren't a unified body, although eventually some groups did work together to have Jesus arrested, tried and executed.

* As we said before, they were paranoid about the possibility of "losing their religion" as their ancestors had once done before, which led to the disastrous exile era.
** "Remember the Sabbath day by keeping it holy. Six days you shall labor and do all your work, but the seventh day is a sabbath to the Lᴏʀᴅ your God. On it you shall not do any work" (Exodus 20:8–10).

him for healing a man's hand[3] and for healing an invalid on the Sabbath.[4] In flagrant opposition to their teaching, Jesus stated it was lawful to do good on the Sabbath and that he was actually Lord of the Sabbath.[5]

## The Sadducees

The other major group of Jesus' enemies were the Sadducees. Like the Pharisees, the Sadducees were a Jewish religious movement and political party active in Judea. They were not as numerous or as popular as the Pharisees but were more powerful because they dominated the Sanhedrin (the main judicial council of the Jews). And like the Pharisees, they were highly nationalistic and considered themselves the elite religious teachers of the day.

The Sadducees didn't see eye to eye with the other groups, like the Pharisees. For example, they considered only the first five books of the Old Testament as scripture, and they rejected the concept of angels and demons. Most notably, the writers of the New Testament tell us that they did not believe in the resurrection of the dead.

## Other Groups

There were other groups within Jewish hierarchy and administration that also began to oppose what Jesus was doing: individuals among the chief priests or the Jewish elders and the scribes. Sometimes in the Gospels they are simply collectively called "the teachers of the law". Like the Pharisees and the Sadducees, these were various Jewish groups who taught and led their people in both religious and political matters. At times they seemed to have acted independently of each other, but certainly toward the end of Jesus' life it becomes clear that some of them joined forces to plot to have Jesus arrested and executed.

Again and again, as Jesus travelled through ancient Palestine and taught the masses, his opponents would turn up to try to trap him with trick questions or to enter into debate with him. They continually tested him and "laid plans to trap him in his words".[6] They challenged him about his authority and right to speak[7] and harangued him about his views on matters of law, such as divorce,[8] the ceremonial washing of hands,[9] the payment of taxes to Caesar,[10] his interpretations of ancient scriptures[11] or about fasting and eating.[12] They criticised

> Jesus openly criticised these Jewish elite and radically challenged traditions about how to interpret some of the Old Testament laws.

---

3. Mattew 12:9–13.
4. John 5:1–10.
5. Matthew 12:8, 12.
6. Matthew 22:15–22.
7. Mark 11:27–33.
8. Mark 10:1–12.
9. Mark 7:1–8.
10. Matthew 22:15–22.
11. Matthew 22:34–46.
12. Luke 5:33–39.

him for keeping company with the outcasts of society – for dining with tax collectors and other sinners[13] – and tried to get him to prove himself by performing signs.[14] Yet so often Jesus dispelled their arguments and traps with just one sentence, leaving his enemies to walk away with their tails between their legs. Other times, Jesus would respond with a cryptic parable aimed squarely at his opponents. Yet this seemed only to infuriate them even more.

So Jesus gave as good as he got. He didn't suffer fools gladly, and he certainly didn't back down from a fight. Not only was he not afraid to upset the apple cart, he was perfectly happy to pick the apples up and pelt them at his enemies. At times, his words and actions were aggressive and antagonistic. So in some respects, it should be no surprise that Jesus gathered many enemies. Consider some of these rather confrontational statements:

> "This is a wicked generation. It asks for a sign, but none will be given it except the sign of Jonah."[15]

> "Do not suppose that I have come to bring peace to the earth. I did not come to bring peace, but a sword."[16]

> "I have come to bring fire on the earth, and how I wish it were already kindled!"[17]

As you can see, Jesus was not one to mince his words, and he wasn't afraid to call a spade a shovel. He continually drew a line in the sand, and on many occasions, his criticisms of the Pharisees and religious establishment were hostile and antagonistic:

> *To the Pharisees and teachers of the law:* "You have let go of the commands of God and are holding on to human traditions.... You have a fine way of setting aside the commands of God in order to observe your own traditions!"[18]

> *To a crowd, about the teachers of the law and the Pharisees:* "Everything they do is done for people to see: They make their phylacteries wide* and the tassels on their garments long; they love the place of honor at banquets and the most important seats in the synagogues; they love to be greeted with respect in the marketplaces and to have people call them 'Rabbi.'"[19]

> "Be on your guard against the yeast of the Pharisees, which is hypocrisy."[20]

Jesus gave as good as he got. He didn't suffer fools gladly, and he certainly didn't back down from a fight.

* Phylacteries were ... um ... long flat strips of sweet bread served at ceremonial occasions.
— Pete

No, Pete. They were small leather boxes worn by devout Jews that contained excerpts from the law. Read Deuteronomy 6:4 – 9.
— Ben

---

13. Luke 5:27 – 32.
14. Mark 8:11 – 13.
15. Luke 11:29.
16. Matthew 10:34.
17. Luke 12:49.
18. Mark 7:8 – 9.
19. Matthew 23:5 – 7.
20. Luke 12:1.

134

"Watch out for the teachers of the law.... They devour widows' houses and for a show make lengthy prayers. These men will be punished most severely."[21]

"Woe to you, teachers of the law and Pharisees, you hypocrites!" (repeated six times in an extended denunciation of the establishment[22] in which he also calls them "blind guides", "blind fools", "blind men", "white-washed tombs" and "You snakes! You brood of vipers!")

Jesus' words were offensive. He was basically saying that the learned and powerful religious leaders of the day had it wrong, that they were out of order and off track and not serving God the way they should. He accused them of being self-righteous, self-centred hypocrites who "tie up heavy, cumbersome loads and put them on other people's shoulders, but they themselves are not willing to lift a finger to move them".[23] With public statements like this, is it any wonder that Jesus quickly developed enemies?

However, perhaps the biggest thing that caused Jesus to be public enemy number one was his claim to be divine. When Jesus forgave sins or claimed that he was sent from God or claimed that he and God were one, it was considered highly blasphemous. Ordinarily, Jewish leaders in the first century might be lenient towards the occasional blasphemous person. However, Jesus' claims of divinity in actions and words were so frequent and extreme and public that the establishment could not tolerate it.

The things that Jesus said about himself led to a substantial amount of anger. Consider these controversial words of Jesus about himself:

*Talking in metaphor about himself:* "Destroy this temple, and I will raise it again in three days."[24]

"All authority in heaven and on earth has been given to me."[25]

Jesus "said to the man, 'Take heart, son; your sins are forgiven.' "[26]

"I am the bread of life. Whoever comes to me will never go hungry, and whoever believes in me will never be thirsty."[27]

"I am the way and the truth and the life. No one comes to the Father except through me. If you really know me, you will know my Father as well. From now on, you do know him and have seen him."[28]

> The things that Jesus said about himself led to a substantial amount of anger.

21. Mark 12:38–40.
22. Matthew 23:13–36.
23. Matthew 23:4.
24. John 2:19.
25. Matthew 28:18.
26. Matthew 9:2.
27. John 6:35.
28. John 14:6–7.

*After reading an old prophecy about the Messiah:* "Today this scripture is fulfilled in your hearing."[29]

Despite this, Jesus still had enemies who didn't believe he was who he claimed to be.

It is worth pointing out that these weren't unsubstantiated claims. Jesus backed up what he said again and again with a whole variety of miracles. Despite this, Jesus still had enemies who didn't believe he was who he claimed to be. They found him so obnoxious and unacceptable that they wanted to have him silenced.

There is a tremendous irony to all of this: Jesus' enemies ought to have been his friends. There is an old story about a slave trading ship that was sailing across the Atlantic during the 1800s when slavery was beginning to be abolished internationally. This particular ship was being pursued by a royal battleship intent on freeing the captives on board and capturing the slave traders to bring them to trial. When the slave merchants saw the ship sailing towards them and realised it would catch them, they conceived a cunning plan. Realizing that they were no match in speed and manpower, the slave traders convinced all the captives that the pursuing ship was not a boat coming to rescue them but a pirate ship full of bandits who were coming on board to kill the men and take the women. When the British ship finally pulled alongside, the slaves actually fought the very people who had come to save them.*

The astonishing thing about the enemies of Jesus was that they were some of the very people who ought to have known who he really was, that he was the promised Messiah who had come to rescue them. Sadly, that wasn't the case.

But we should clarify one important point about Jesus' enemies before we go on.

When we watch modern action movies, there is generally no shade of grey in the "bad guy" department. Because the bad guys' very existence is in opposition to the hero of the movie, they are by definition simply bad and thereby worthy of our wrath and derision. The balance of the plot and the tradition of the genre requires that a "good guy" is reflected by a doppelganger "bad guy" who is totally evil and cruel and has no redeeming features. Movies are made this way so that when the bad guys get what's coming to them – often with elaborate and gratuitous violence – we feel satisfied that the universe has been put back to order. They are *bad*, ergo they deserve what they get.

It is easy to view the Pharisees (and the other associated teachers of the law) through the same lens. Because Jesus is the hero and good guy of the Bible, it is easy to badge any person or group that was not "for him" as being evil and cruel and lacking in redeeming features.

In part, this is fair enough. After all, some of these people were corrupt, and Jesus was highly critical of many of their practices. Some of them

* I wish to disassociate myself from this story – provided by Ben – which sounds like an urban myth or something he made up.  — Pete

O ye of little faith. A friend of a friend told it to me.  — Ben

---

29. Luke 4:21.

continually challenged Jesus, stirred up opposition to him and successfully plotted to have him executed. That's a fair cop.

But we have to be careful not to throw the baby out with the bathwater, so to speak. Let's look at the situation a different way.

Many within this body of rulers were – in their own way – seeking to serve God and, through disciplined observance of rules and regulations, keep their nation on the straight and narrow in the midst of an oppressive, foreign pagan occupation. Let's take their observance of the Sabbath as an example. We've already mentioned how some Pharisees were critical of Jesus and his disciples for doing stuff on the Jewish holy day, like healing or picking heads of grain.[30] From our postmodern perspective, it's easy – some would even say natural – for us to see the Pharisees as small-minded, self-righteous religious twits. But we should remember that from their point of view, they were simply upholding the law on which their society was built. They would have all known the story from their history: after a decree from God to Moses, an Israelite man was executed for … wait for it … gathering wood on the Sabbath day.[31]

On another occasion, after Jesus had miraculously restored the sight of a blind man, the Pharisees investigated the miracle. John records that some of them concluded that Jesus was not from God because he healed on the Sabbath, but others did not share this view and challenged this opinion. The significant part here is that John records that "they were divided" on this matter. Not all of them were against Jesus.[32]

Another time, Jesus accepted the invitation of a Pharisee to dine at his house.[33] What followed was a heated debate – which was quite standard in the accepted interaction between rabbis of the time as they interpreted law – but the point is that Jesus went to the house of a Pharisee and dined with him and his peers.

So while many Jews and Jewish leaders were hostile to Jesus, this was certainly not universal. John records that "many even among the leaders believed in him. But because of the Pharisees they would not openly acknowledge their faith for fear they would be put out of the synagogue."[34] We recall that Jesus engaged in a healthy dialogue with the Pharisee Nicodemus, who came to visit him one night seeking answers to the Jesus issue.[35] Nicodemus comes across as a genuine and earnest kind of bloke. Later on, he is one of the men who actually arrange for Jesus' body to be taken down and placed in a tomb,

---

30. Luke 6.
31. Numbers 15:32–36.
32. John 9:13–16.
33. Luke 11:37–54.
34. John 12:42.
35. John 3:1–21.

himself preparing Jesus' body for burial. And on top of that, Paul, who wrote a significant chunk of the New Testament documents, also declared that he was a Pharisee and the son of a Pharisee.[36]

In addition, it's sometimes easy for us to imagine all of Jerusalem rising up with one voice against Jesus during his trial, chanting, "Crucify him! Crucify him!" Again, we must be careful not to oversimplify the situation. There were hundreds of thousands of Jewish pilgrims in Jerusalem at the time of Jesus' arrest, trial and execution. His arrest took place at night, and his hurried trial in the early morning involved – obviously – an angry and organized mob, but it was not all of Jerusalem standing there in front of Pilate in the praetorium. It is unlikely that most of the people even knew what was going on.

And one final thing, we have to be careful in condemning these "bad guys" of the New Testament that we ourselves do not adopt the very self-righteous attitudes for which we condemn them.*

> * Pete, this would be a good time to apply Jesus' teaching about taking the log out of our own eye before we get stuck into other people about the splinter in theirs.   – Ben
>
> Good call, mate.   – Pete

We might go as far as to say that there is an element of the pharisaical in all of us. Each of us at some stage in our lives has had the tendency to feel that we are too good for God and better than others. We all tend to assume that the way we see and do things is "the right way" (and sometimes the *only* way), and most of us find it is easy to judge others. Who amongst us hasn't experienced the desire to be acknowledged and noticed? And who hasn't enjoyed the pride of having a position of power or influence? Or that special seat at the important table at the banquet – the very thing of which Jesus was so critical.

To use the cliche, if Jesus came today, what would be our response to him? Of course, our default is to think that we would be the fishermen disciples who dropped their nets and became part of the inner-circle A Team.

> To use the cliche, if Jesus came today, what would be our response to him?

But as we sit in our established and comfortable churches with our stained-glass windows, prayer books and cheery choruses, what would we really think of a person who hung out in tattoo parlours and pubs with prostitutes, book makers, drug addicts and the homeless? What would we think of this person who openly lambasted some of the practices of the modern church as being shallow, misdirected and pointless? How would you feel if he told you to stop wasting your time running trivia nights at church and asked you what you were doing about feeding the poor and standing up for justice for refugees? What would we think of this person who turned up to the cathedral in our city and overturned the book stall and chased people out, calling them a bunch of red-bellied black snakes? What would you think of this person who criticised your church leaders and groups and boards and told them off for being complacent and off track? What would your response be if you were a longtime keeper of the commandments and all the tenets of your church

36. Acts 23:6.

and yet he still looked you in the eye and said, "Go, sell your possessions and give to the poor, and you will have treasure in heaven"?[37]

Mmm, we might leave that there. We aren't trying to jump on any church-bash bandwagon. We are both deeply involved in our churches.* And to curb any hate mail you may wish to send, can we also just say that we know heaps of churches and church leaders who are doing great things both within the church and in the wider community that Jesus no doubt would think are pretty good? But it's important for us to sometimes step back and put ourselves in context.

* And I work in one! – Ben

Right ... so where were we?

To recap: Jesus began to preach and teach and heal when he was about thirty, moving around the local regions and towns with a core group of friends and an increasing band of followers. Over the months and years, he amassed a reputation and a high level of popularity. But opposition to his lifestyle and teachings was also growing, with various groups and individuals plotting to get rid of this troublesome rabbi.

And then one year, as the annual Festival of the Passover approached and the attention of the nation turned to the capital city, Jesus and his group turned and joined the thousands of other pilgrims making their way to Jerusalem.

Jesus was about to enter the eye of the storm.

---

37. Matthew 19:21.

A few hours drive west of Sydney, Australia, lies the pleasant university town of Bathurst. It is a classic Aussie town, complete with wide streets, expansive parks, statues of explorers of local renown and excellent nonfranchised, family-run fast-food shops that still put beetroot in hamburgers.*

Dominating the landscape above the town is the rather self-evidently named geographical feature known as Mount Panorama. For much of the year, the six kilometre strip of bitumen that wends it way around the mount lies quiet. It is a public road peppered with family farms and grazing animals, and the silence is broken only by the distinctive cry of galahs** overhead. But once a year, it is home to the longest, biggest and most important road race in the country: the Bathurst 1000.

Racing teams, drivers and television crews pour into Bathurst. Hot on their heels, from all points of the compass, come rev heads, devotees, fans, petrol heads, even family groups, all descending upon Bathurst in their thousands to worship at the shrine of the V8 engine, to breathe the fumes and watch massive tonnes of automotive machinery thunder around the track. The roads to Bathurst are clogged. The camping grounds and hotels are jam packed, and the streets are thick with people whose T-shirts proudly declare their affinity to Ford or Holden.*** Mount Panorama disappears in a fog of smoking tyres and petrol fumes.

When that many visitors descend upon a small country town, especially when they are charged up on petrol and beer, problems are bound to occur.**** And they do. Various spots on the mount resemble a war zone, and only the bravest and most foolhardy dare to go there. Unable to cope with such a huge itinerant population, the town brings in additional police from all over the state to keep the peace. Sniffer dogs seek out explosives and firearms while police try to control mob antics and high jinx, generally involving drinking, setting fire to cars and blowing things up. There exists a kind of precarious balance and mob tension around the race, and police know that the crowd are – in their words – "on the verge of riotous".

Two thousand years ago, the rulers of Jerusalem found themselves in a similarly tense position. Of course, there were no V8 Supercars, and we are not suggesting that the deeply sacred Festival of the Passover was a direct relative of the Bathurst booze frenzy, but once a year, Jews from all over flooded to Jerusalem to celebrate the Passover. (You will recall that Jesus' parents did

*To all overseas peoples: it's an Australian thing.
** Aussie name for a parrotlike bird that lives in the Aussie bush and is known for its piercing screech.
*** Holden is an Aussie car manufacturer. There is a passionate but respectful competition between Holden and Ford fans.
**** "Never mind the cars, the Bathurst crowd's explosive" (Joshua Dowling, October 11, 2004).

this when he was about twelve.) The population of the city exploded[*] with pilgrims, ironically, celebrating an event in their nation's history when God delivered them from an oppressive foreign nation (the exodus from Egypt). There in the shadow of the temple with the sea of disgruntled peasants all fuelled up about their nationalism and hopes of freedom ... well, if there was a time for trouble for the Romans, that was it.

We're going to do a quick historical recap here,[**] but stick with us. It's important. Like most of the cities and regions around North Africa and Europe, the Jerusalem of Jesus' day had fallen under the control of the Romans. About sixty years before Jesus was born, Roman siege towers rolled up to the mighty walls of the temple in Jerusalem, and under the command of the general and statesman Pompey, the temple was captured and Judea became a part of the Roman Empire. Rome ousted the dynasty of high priests who had previously ruled and began appointing their own. About thirty years later, they installed a foreigner – Herod (known as "the Great")[***] from Idumaea – as the king of the Jews.

But as many armies involved in modern theatres of war have discovered, it's one thing to invade and conquer another country and to import infrastructure and assign various positions of power. It is another thing entirely to occupy that same territory and keep it functioning peacefully. (Think of the difficulties involved in US activity in Iraq or the German occupation of France during World War II.)

Judea never fully settled in with the Roman occupation. At the very core of Jewish national identity was the concept that that land had been given to them by God and that the temple was God's sanctuary on earth. Disgruntled with the occupation by a pagan foreign nation (and fuelled by scriptural prophecies that a Messiah would emerge who would rise up and lead the Jews to victory over their oppressors), there was an ongoing tension between the Romans and the Jews. The situation was fragile, and it never took much for trouble to rear its ugly head. By the time Jesus came onto the scene, Judea was already known as a hot spot. There had been decades of civil disturbances, revolts, subversive activity and uprisings. And there had been decades of Roman heavy-handedness in response.

At the time that Jesus was heading towards Jerusalem for the annual national gathering to celebrate Passover, the governor of Judea was an imperial Roman officer – a *prefect* – by the name of Pontius Pilate. Living in the coastal town of Caesarea some hundred or so kilometres to the north of Jerusalem, he had oversight of financial and judicial matters in the province. He was in charge of the Roman military and law and order, and he supervised administrative matters such as the progress of public works and tax collection. Part of his brief was to keep the peace, to quell riots and to keep an eye out for troublemakers.

** Wah heh! I love a good recap.          – Pete

Settle down, Pete, before you put somebody's eye out.          – Ben

* Estimates of the population of pilgrims vary greatly. Some sources say from 40,000 to 400,000, while others suggest from 30,000 to about 130,000. They do all agree, however, that Passover was big and that there were tens of thousands of visitors to the city at that time.
*** It would be Herod's son – Herod Antipas – who would rule in Judea at the time of Jesus' adult ministry and execution.

Pilate undoubtedly was well aware of many occasions in both recent and distant history when there had been clashes and revolts in Judea. He would have come into the job knowing that just a few decades earlier, thousands of Jews had risen up in an attempt to oust the Romans. After a swift and brutal military response, the result was two thousand Jews crucified as punishment. Given his long-term working relationship with the high priest Caiaphas, it is likely that Pilate also knew of the execution (under Herod Antipas) of the popular Jewish leader and troublemaker John, known as the Baptist.

Pilate was an imperial officer in a troubled and distant outpost of Rome, trying to keep a hostile and fiery population in line. The situation was perpetually explosive. But once a year during Passover, tensions reached boiling point in Jerusalem. As a consequence, Pilate moved (with his wife, entire household and extra troops) to Jerusalem, where he set up base next to the temple in the praetorium, where he could be close to the action.

Meanwhile, about twenty kilometres away in the town of Jericho in the Jordan Valley, Jesus and his friends had been teaching and healing. They set out on their journey up to Jerusalem, probably with a band of other pilgrims in tow (like Bartimaeus, who was blind but had received his sight).[1] On arriving at Bethany at the rather obviously titled Mount of Olives, just on the outskirts of Jerusalem, Jesus sent two of his disciples to get a donkey for him on which to make the last leg of his journey. This was a bold political statement. Everyone would have known from their scriptures[2] that about five hundred years before, the prophet and priest Zechariah had declared that Jerusalem would see its king arrive humbly riding on a donkey. There was already a strong sense of expectation surrounding Jesus. John records that many people who had arrived for Passover were waiting in the temple courts, looking out for him. They asked each other, "What do you think? Isn't he coming to the Festival at all?"[3] So when the word came that Jesus and his band of followers were marching up the road to Jerusalem (and with Jesus riding a donkey!), a chain reaction was triggered in the city.

The response was immediate and unprecedented. Matthew writes that "a very large crowd spread their cloaks on the road, while others cut branches from the trees and spread them on the road."[4] The mass of people in front of and behind him shouted out praises as they swelled through the city streets to the temple. So big was Jesus' arrival that Matthew records that "when Jesus entered Jerusalem, the whole city was stirred and asked, 'Who is this?'" And the crowd responded, "This is Jesus, the prophet from Nazareth in Galilee."[5]

> But once a year during Passover, tensions reached boiling point in Jerusalem.

1. Mark 10:46–52.
2. Zechariah 9:9.
3. John 11:55–56.
4. Matthew 21:8.
5. Matthew 21:10–11.

With the presence of hundreds of thousands of pilgrims all fuelled up with nationalistic fervour, it was already a tense situation in the city.

With the presence of hundreds of thousands of pilgrims all fuelled up with nationalistic fervour, it was already a tense situation in the city. The Roman soldiers and administrators were on the lookout for any signs of trouble. So their suspicions must have been raised when they saw the fracas and heard the clamour of the mob approaching the city walls. They would have been concerned to hear it was a popular Jewish teacher who was hailed as a hero and saviour by the people, perhaps even more so once they discovered he was from Galilee. This was a known centre for rebels and home to the Zealots, a fanatical, armed resistance group that clung to Jewish traditions and fiercely opposed the payment of taxes to Caesar.

Jesus' entry into town was certainly a statement. But in some respects, that paled in comparison with what he did next. If there was an epicentre for potential trouble in the region, it was the temple. The temple and its surrounds – an enormous walled structure that dominated Jerusalem's landscape – lay at the very core of Jewish identity and nationalism. It was a blatant, physically enormous and unmissable reminder of who they were as a people. It not only symbolised Israel but in reality actually was the cornerstone of Israel's religion, society, self-governance, economy and life.

Events in and around the temple frequently triggered revolt and bloodshed. The final straw for the Jews was in 167 BC, when Antiochus Epiphanes set up an altar to Zeus on the temple altar and sacrificed a pig there. He then tried to force some Jewish men to eat the burnt meat, and when they refused, they were dismembered and killed. The result was three years of bitter warfare, with the Jews eventually recapturing the temple. On another occasion, just decades before Pilate commenced his job, a Roman symbol was erected on the temple roof. In response to this incredible insult, a group of Jewish students promptly clambered up and sought to remove the Roman standard, and they were just as promptly captured and burned alive. The temple was a sensitive area.

It was here that Jesus headed.

If you've ever seen one of those old made-for-TV documentary reenactments of "Jesus and the money changers", the scene is usually a small courtyard with one or two trestle tables with a couple of sly merchants behind, not dissimilar to a church fete.* Jesus suddenly appears, flips a table or two while the merchants yell and gesticulate until he heads off in a huff. However, this scale is more the result of a small film budget rather than a depiction of the epic scale of the temple area.

The temple had been part of a massive building-development program undertaken by Herod. Representing about 15 percent of the footprint of the entire city, it was the high point and dominant feature of the landscape. The temple itself – some fifteen stories high – was surrounded by a number of expansive courtyards encircled by huge pillars and enormous walls, colon-

* Not that we are saying people at church fetes are sly!          – Pete

nades and towers. The Roman garrison was housed in the praetorium, which backed onto the outer courtyard walls.

The Court of the Gentiles was a massive public area able to accommodate the visits of thousands of Gentile (non-Jewish) converts to Judaism. It was here that money changers converted the visitors' Roman and Greek currency (which was considered impure and therefore unacceptable in the temple) into the Jewish temple coins with which they could pay their temple tax. It was also here that visitors were able to purchase various animals for sacrifice, which was a central feature of the festival. We are not talking one or two birds in little cages like in the movies but masses of livestock numerous enough to accommodate the influx of visitors. There were cattle and sheep – for the wealthy – but for most rural poor folk (as per Jesus' parents many years before), the best they could manage was the purchase of a bird.

The market was a major drawing card for savvy merchants who wanted to make fast money by extorting exorbitant exchange fees out of the public. The traders who sold doves made a killing in profiteering from the poor who could not afford a larger animal. To participate in the festival ceremonies, the poor had no choice but to pay the outrageous fees.

And so "Jesus entered the temple courts and drove out all who were buying and selling there. He overturned the tables of the money changers and the benches of those selling doves."[6] He was in effect cleansing the temple from greed and oppression. He declared that this should be a place of prayer, not a place for robbers. In doing this, Jesus went public with his heart for the poor and oppressed, together with his condemnation of the chief priests and the religious hierarchy.

At this point, Jesus would not only have been an increasing concern to the Romans but also would have crossed the line with the Jewish authorities. For years he had been a controversial figure to them as a teacher and leader who didn't fit the mould. Discussions and debates had taken place about him. But now, at this all-important time in the Jewish calendar, with an audience of thousands right in the shadow of the temple, he had gone too far. In disrupting the commerce of the temple and preventing its usual trade, he was making a bold declaration that the temple era was over.

To add insult to injury, he began to heal the blind and the lame right there in the temple courts,[7] thus implying that the temple and the sacrificial system were no longer necessary or relevant for access to God. He told his disciples that the temple building, for all its importance and glory and majesty, would be destroyed and not one stone would be left on top of another.[*] He was setting himself up as the new temple, as the way to God.

* This came to pass within forty years, when the Romans under Titus destroyed the temple.

> "Jesus entered the temple courts and drove out all who were buying and selling there."

---

6. Matthew 21:12.

7. Matthew 21:14–15.

Over the next few days, he continued to visit the temple courts to teach the people and debate his opponents. He told the Jewish teachers and high priests that despised tax collectors and prostitutes were more in line with the kingdom of heaven than they were. He told parables about how the Pharisees and teachers of the law would lose God's kingdom. He criticised the Jewish leaders for their pride and hypocrisy, and he instructed the people not to follow their example. He called them blind guides, fools, hypocrites, children of hell and snakes. He criticised their corrupt religious system as being burdensome for the common people.

The plot against Jesus had been building momentum for some time. John records that before the Passover, the Pharisees and chief priests had called the Sanhedrin to come together to discuss the case.[8] One concern was that if the Sanhedrin let Jesus keep doing what he was doing, his popularity would continue to increase and everyone would follow him. Then the Romans would react strongly, taking both their temple and nation away. They saw Jesus, therefore, as a threat to the delicate balance of power in the region. Caiaphas – the high priest – had a simple response. It is better to sacrifice one person than for the whole nation to be crushed. "So from that day on they plotted to take his life."[9]

And so Jesus' entry into the city and his criticisms of the elders only served to raise the hackles of the leaders even more. The chief priests and teachers of the law were indignant. They challenged his authority and "looked for a way to arrest him, but they were afraid of the crowd because the people held that he was a prophet."[10] They challenged his ideas and tried to trap him in his own words with curly questions about taxes and the theology of resurrection. But eventually they had enough. "Then the chief priests and the elders of the people assembled in the palace of the high priest, whose name was Caiaphas, and they plotted to arrest Jesus in some sly way and kill him. 'But not during the Festival,' they said, 'or there may be a riot among the people.'"[11]

For the moment, Jesus continued to teach and to contemplate the days ahead. But over the next few days, events transpired that changed the course of life on this planet.

> "So from that day on they plotted to take his life."

---

8. John 11:45–53.
9. John 11:53.
10. Matthew 21:46.
11. Matthew 26:3–5.

# Chapter 19

# SO LONG, FAREWELL, AMEN
## Jesus' last evening with his friends

For most of us, Christmas is a big affair. Candles, trees, presents, shopping, carols, nativity plays, chestnuts roasting on an open fire, decking the halls with boughs of holly and dreaming of a white Christmas. Pete is dad to three daughters, so over the years, Christmas has been a pretty big occasion: early mornings, faked reindeer evidence, high-pitched screams, toys, wrapping paper and early church before chucking a turkey into the kettle-barbie* for lunch. Even Ben, who has no kids and a small family, makes Christmas a big event in the calendar. Each year, he puts up a tree, faithfully decorates it with tinsel and stars and then, without fail, wires the fairy lights up incorrectly and takes out an entire electrical grid.

It is traditional to celebrate Christmas with a family lunch. Usually this meal contains enough food to feed the crew of a naval frigate, consisting of a comically enormous leg of ham and/or a turkey the size of an emu,** and somewhere within reach, various bowls of nuts, cheese, crackers, salads or roast vegetables, bread, and fine wines served in glasses like fishbowls. With great gusto, guests will pull bon-bons and spend the rest of the lunch looking ridiculous in paper hats while they read the assortment of naff*** jokes enclosed. The main meal is followed by dessert, which traditionally is the most filling and rich food known to humankind – steaming Christmas pudding with boiling custard. Then to finish off, there's an assortment of chocolates, mince pies and sweets, maybe with some liqueurs or coffees just to really test how far the human stomach can stretch before permanent damage occurs. Often accompanying this meal are the mellifluous sounds of Bing Crosby crooning something about Christmas being white; rather ironic, really, when you consider the blistering heat of summer under which we Aussies enjoy our Christmas. Regardless of the specifics, Christmas is a highly ritualised event that is often the only time in the year when family members get together from all points of the compass.

The whole vibe is not too dissimilar to the biggest annual event in the Jewish calendar, which has been going on for the past three thousand years. The Passover, traditionally celebrated with a meal, is still today the one time in the year when Jews all over the world gather around the family table**** to remember an important event in their history – the night that their ancestors were saved.

* Aussie talk for "charcoal grill".
** Australia's largest bird, a scraggy, flightless bird that can stand 1.9 meters when fully erect.
*** Aussie talk (originally from the UK) meaning "cheesy, clichéd or unfashionable".

**** Wah heh! That's some big table! – Ben

Not the same table, you goose. – Pete

147

The Passover, traditionally celebrated with a meal, is still today the one time in the year when Jews all over the world gather around the family table to remember an important event in their history – the night that their ancestors were saved.

Jesus arrived at the great city of Jerusalem at Passover. Many Jews from all over the empire had made their pilgrimage to the holy city at this time, and all were preparing to celebrate the Passover with the traditional meal. With so many people in town, it would have been necessary to book a room. So Jesus sent some of his disciples into town to organize the venue and prepare their Passover meal. When evening came, he and his friends met in the large upper room of a house in Jerusalem,[1] and it was there that they ate, drank, talked and sang a traditional song together. You probably already have a picture in your head of what this meal looked like, thanks largely to Da Vinci's famous painting *The Last Supper*. However, it probably wasn't quite like that. It's unlikely the guests were all stacked on one side of the table and spent the night in theatrically dramatic poses. In fact, it was not even the custom of the day to sit on seats. Rather, the disciples would have lounged – or reclined – around a low table on the floor, leaning up on one elbow.

Let's just tangent for a moment and remember what they were celebrating. The story of the original Passover is told in considerable detail in the book of Exodus.[2] In short, the Israelites had been enslaved as a massive labour force in Egypt. God responded by raising up a leader – Moses – to save the people and lead them out of Egypt to a new land of their own. However, the Pharaoh of the day refused to let the Israelites leave. This stubbornness led to God's judgment, which came in a series of plagues that devastated Egypt. The final plague was a curse of death upon every firstborn child in the land. The Israelites, however, were spared from this plague if they carried out some simple instructions: each Israelite family smeared the blood of a sacrificial lamb on the door frames of their houses, and as a result of this innocent blood, God's judgment would "pass over" all those with this sign.

So according to the book of Exodus, the spirit of death came that night and the Israelites were spared, while many young Egyptians died. It proved to be the final straw for Pharaoh, who finally let the Israelites leave.* The important thing is that the Israelites were instructed to remember this great event through the celebration of an annual evening meal. So each year to this day, Jewish families gather in their homes to eat and remember the night God's wrath passed over their ancestors and they were saved from slavery.

However, unlike the traditional Christmas meal, the traditional Passover meal consists of food that was intentionally symbolic and is used as an aid in the telling of the story of the first Passover. Over the centuries, various elements and traditions have been added, but essentially it usually consists of *a lamb* to remind them of the lamb that was killed to thwart the wrath of God; *unleavened bread,* because during the original Passover, they left Egypt in haste and didn't have time to bake bread; *bitter herbs,* such as

* Incidentally, the word exodus means "exit".

---

1. Matthew 26:17–30; Mark 14:12–16; Luke 22:7–13.
2. Exodus 11–13.

parsley or horseradish, to remind them of the bitterness of slavery in Egypt; *a bowl of salt water* to remind them of their sorrow and tears in their captivity; *a fruity paste* the consistency of the clay with which they made bricks; *four cups of wine,* each with their own special name, to remind them of God's promises.

It is no coincidence that Jesus timed his visit to Jerusalem at Passover. It's highly significant that at this most sacred time in the Jewish calendar, Jesus instituted a new "sacred" meal with his disciples, using food to symbolically make links with an historical event involving God's salvation – namely, his own death.

While we retrospectively have labelled this event with the grandiose title "The Last Supper", to the disciples, it was just another Passover meal, just as they had celebrated Passover every year of their lives. They didn't walk up the stairs that night saying to each other, "Hey, really looking forward to this Last Supper." Similarly, while Jesus would have used a plate and cup, there was no grand Holy Grail on the table. The idea of the Holy Grail gained momentum in twelfth-century European romance literature and has since become the bread and butter of films from Monty Python to Indiana Jones.

So there was a certain ordinariness to the event. But even though the disciples didn't know it at the time, this night was going to be different.

In the middle of the meal, Jesus dropped the clanger. With all twelve of the apostles reclining around the table, Jesus predicted that one of them was about to betray him. We should pause to consider how frightening this simple statement must have been to them. While they were not outlaws, these men were very aware of the precarious situation that they were in. They were the core disciples of an itinerant and controversial preacher participating in a large public festival in a city under foreign rule. They already had targets on their foreheads as it was. The idea of betrayal would be disconcerting, to say the least.

Curiously, the disciples responded each in turn by asking, "Surely not I, Lord?" Their rhetorical doubt seems to imply that perhaps they did not grasp the deliberate nature of the betrayal Jesus was talking about. Perhaps they were thinking more along the lines of betrayal being a "turning away" from their master, as other disciples had done before. However, one of them knew what he was talking about. Since arriving in the city, Judas had already approached the chief priests and made arrangements to lead them to Jesus at a convenient time.

Mid-meal, Jesus picked up some of the bread on the table, gave thanks, broke it into pieces and passed it around to his disciples, saying, "Take and eat; this is my body." Then he took a cup, gave thanks and passed it around, saying, "Drink from it, all of you.* This is my blood of the covenant, which is poured out for many for the forgiveness of sins."[3] Here Jesus took the

> Even though the disciples didn't know it at the time, this night was going to be different.

* It is thought by many that the cup that Jesus took at this point was the third cup of the Passover meal, traditionally the "cup of salvation".

---

3. Matthew 26:26–28.

traditional Passover elements and themes of "blood" and "forgiveness" used in the meal and infused them with a whole new meaning. Only later did it become clear that he was saying that *he* was about to be the Passover Lamb whose body and blood were to be spilled so that God's judgment would pass over people who trusted in God. Jesus was saying that he was about to fulfil his mission by dying.

So central is this moment in Jesus' story that from this time on, a new custom was born for his followers. This new ritual, with its tangible symbols of bread and wine (commonly called the Lord's Supper, communion, or the Eucharist or Mass) is the ceremony through which Christians remember the death of Jesus. It is not an annual meal as such, although in addition to most churches having weekly communion services, the formal celebration is usually a part of Christmas and Easter celebrations and sometimes weddings. However, like the Jewish Passover meal, it would become the ritual that Christians would use to remember the day that Jesus – the lamb of God – was sacrificed so that death would pass over them and, as a result, they were saved.

> So central is this moment in Jesus' story that from this time on, a new custom was born for Jesus' followers.

After their meal, Jesus and his companions left the upper room and walked through the crowded city and out of the city walls. Probably following the same road to Bethany on which they came a few days earlier, they crossed the steep ravine (Kidron Valley) outside the city and up the other side to the Mount of Olives, a three kilometre ridge overlooking Jerusalem and the temple to its west. Jesus went with his friends to an orchard – Gethsemane – in the foothills, where amongst the trees and vines they could rest.

You're probably familiar with what happens next, especially if you've seen Mel Gibson's *The Passion of the Christ*, as this is where the film begins. With increased intensity, the gospel writers tell us that Jesus knew his "hour" had come. There were no more sermons, no more healings, no more antagonists to debate; his mission was drawing to a close. On numerous occasions he had predicted that he would die and lay down his life as a sacrifice for the world. This is the ultimate reason why he came. Now that time was upon him.

Jesus' response at this time is perfectly natural. He knew what was about to happen and, as a man, had all the normal feelings and thoughts that would go with that knowledge. The writers emphasize Jesus' intense torment and inward struggles. Mark tells us that Jesus was "deeply distressed and troubled",[4] while Luke says that his "sweat was like drops of blood".[5] He gathered his friends to him – Peter, James and John – and said, "My soul is overwhelmed with sorrow to the point of death. Stay here and keep watch with me."[6] We can only wonder what these words sounded like to those dis-

---

4. Mark 14:33.

5. Luke 22:44, although it is not clear whether these words were part of Luke's original text or added later by another writer.

6. Matthew 26:38.

ciples. As far as all the accounts tell us, Jesus had never spoken to them this way. Whatever those three disciples felt at that moment, they surely knew that something was going on.

Then in their presence Jesus began to pray.[*] "My Father, if it is possible, may this cup be taken from me. Yet not as I will, but as you will."[7]

What was Jesus so fearful of and what was this "cup" that he didn't want? Some have argued that Jesus feared his own death. After all, crucifixion was one of the most feared methods of execution, and the pain and suffering a victim experienced were horrid beyond imagination. So it is said that here we are seeing a very human side of Jesus, who knew that his death by crucifixion was just around the corner. There may be an element of truth in that, but perhaps a better answer comes to us from our understanding of what Jesus meant when he spoke of the cup. In the ancient world, a common method of assassinating an official such as a king or a general would be to poison their cup. In fact, kings would often employ cupbearers who were trusted to oversee the king's wine.[**] They even tasted the wine first to test if it had been spiked with poison. It was this background that gave rise to the expression of a cup symbolizing God's wrath. The cup became a symbol of God's judgment poured out on those who were against him.

Jesus not only was about to experience death but also was about to "drink" God's wrath. This is perhaps the great wonder of Jesus' death on the cross: he was going to be the object of God's righteous anger on sin, even though he "knew no sin". Jesus feared the awful punishment of our sin but was willing to "lay his life down as a ransom for many" because that was the will of the Father.

But Jesus wasn't looking for a last-minute way out here. He knew what he had to do and why he was about to die. His prayer was not so much a petition to the Father to get him off the hook (or cross) as it was an agonizing expression of his emotions surrounding the events that were about to transpire.

Shortly after, a large mob (made up of scribes, priests and soldiers) arrived at the garden. There had been much discussion, planning and preparation in regard to having Jesus arrested. As we've already seen throughout his ministry, there had been various attempts to silence Jesus or even have him arrested or killed, but they were unsuccessful. His opponents had longed for the right moment, but with this popular public figure making a scene in Jerusalem, they had to be cautious. There were concerns that arresting Jesus in the packed city during the fervour of Passover would lead to a riot. They had to wait for the right opportunity when there was no crowd hanging around and they could get Jesus alone.[8] And this came when they heard that Jesus and his friends had headed out of the city and were staying overnight nearby somewhere.

Jesus not only was about to experience death but also was about to "drink" God's wrath.

* It was customary to pray out loud, so what Jesus said was no doubt heard by the disciples and recorded for us in the Gospels.
** Nehemiah of the Old Testament was a cupbearer.

7. Matthew 26:39.
8. Luke 22:6.

Of course, they had to actually find Jesus, who was somewhere out in the dark amongst the olive groves and bushes and trees on the other side of the valley. They needed someone who knew where he would be and who would lead them to him and actually identify him. And they found that person in the most unlikely of places. Inside Jesus' circle.

Leading the mob was one of Jesus' closest companions, Judas Iscariot. As one of the privileged twelve main disciples, Judas had been with Jesus for the last three years – travelled with him, ate with him, camped with him, saw him perform miracles and sat as a pupil under his teaching. Judas shared Jesus' vision and work. But he had decided to betray his friend and Lord by helping the authorities find Jesus and have him arrested.

Why one of his closest friends would decide to do this is unclear. Perhaps, since he was paid thirty pieces of silver, it was for economic gain. He saw it as an easy way to make a quick buck. Perhaps, being the only disciple from Judea and not from Galilee like the others, Judas never really felt a part of the team. Perhaps, as a supposed sicarii – a militant agitator and assassin in the fight against the Romans – Judas had become disillusioned with Jesus' not fulfilling his expected destiny as a military and political Messiah of Israel. Or maybe he had simply never believed all along, although this seems unlikely. We simply don't know the reason why Judas betrayed Jesus. However, it is likely that such a decision was not taken lightly nor made quickly but was the result of longer-term dissatisfaction and disillusionment.* At the meal the night before, Jesus had already indicated that he knew what was going on behind his back.

(Recently, an ancient document was found in Egypt and restored by the National Geographic Society.** Included in this document was an anonymously written account of Judas's supposed private discussions with Jesus in the last days leading up to his arrest. This account is called *The Gospel of Judas*, the original of which most likely dates no earlier than the middle of the second century AD,*** at least seventy years after the Gospels were written. This short account gives an alternative view of Judas and his motives. Put simply, this document portrays Judas not as a traitor but as virtually the opposite. He was a privileged disciple of Jesus, singled out by Jesus from all the other disciples and told "secret" things concerning Jesus' mission. According to this document, Judas alone knew that Jesus needed to die to save the world and was therefore the only disciple who could willingly collaborate with Jesus in fulfilling his mission. But the earlier eyewitness accounts found in the New Testament tell us no such thing. Judas is portrayed as "betraying" Jesus**** and that "Satan entered into him."[9] Furthermore, there is little to no evidence outside of the *Gospel of Judas* to suggest that Judas knew "secret things" and was acting in harmony with Jesus when he turned him over to be arrested.)

> \* Ben, now would be a good time to re-introduce the analogy of Anakin Skywalker's getting drawn to the dark side of the ...            – Pete
>
> Maybe later, Pete.    – Ben

* With the publication of findings in late 2006.
** The copy discovered in Egypt in El Minya dates to around AD 300.
*** For example, Matthew 26:21, 23; 1 Corinthians 11:23.

---

9. John 13:27.

While Jesus was speaking with his disciples, the mob made their way towards them through the garden. Judas came up to his companions and greeted Jesus in the normal custom – with a kiss. This was the signal. And at that moment, the name Judas was etched in history as synonymous with *traitor*. Clearly Jesus didn't commend Judas at this point, rather saying to him ironically, "Judas, are you betraying the Son of Man with a kiss?"[10]

The mob were armed with swords and clubs, and it appears there was a scuffle. One of the disciples lashed out with a dagger, cutting off a soldier's ear. Remarkably, Jesus immediately healed the soldier and rebuked the disciples. One staggers to think what went through the mind of that soldier. Unfortunately, that is left to our imagination.

If there was ever a moment for Jesus to take up arms and fight, this was it. But his mission wasn't to fight his enemies but to lay down his life for them. The disciples scattered into the darkness, and Jesus was led back to the city to face charges.

This was the beginning of the end.

---

10. Luke 22:48.

# Chapter 20

# WILL THE JURY PLEASE STAND?
## The trial of Jesus

Nothing captures the public imagination like a trial. Our television screens are dominated by a panoply of both reality and fictional courtroom dramas that dissect the to-ing and fro-ing of legal cases as lawyers and witnesses battle it out to decide guilt or innocence. Similarly, legal thrillers are the bread and butter of many contemporary novelists and filmmakers. Most of us have never even seen the inside of a courtroom, yet we are much at home with the language and processes of the modern court: "Will the court please rise?" "Your Honour, I object!" "Objection overruled!" "Order in the court!" "If it please the court …" "No more questions, Your Honour." "Let's recess for fifteen minutes." "Approach the bench." "Exhibit A …" "We find the defendant [dramatic pause] guilty." "I'm innocent I tell you! Innocent!"

But it's not just fiction. Throughout history, there have been countless famous trials in which important and far-reaching decisions were made. Think the Salem witchcraft trials, the Joan of Arc trial, the Amistad trials, the Scopes "monkey" trial, the McCarthy communist hearings, the Nuremburg trials and the "Mississippi burning" trials. Of more recent times, celebrity trials and others that capture the public mind tend to attract a huge media circus, and from the comfort of our lounge rooms,[*] we can enjoy a constant stream of updates, analyses and debates from various experts and commentators. Think the trials surrounding the Azaria Chamberlain "dingo" death in Australia, the LA riots, the Clinton impeachment, and the O. J. Simpson, Saddam Hussein and Michael Jackson trials. There is something captivating about seeing someone called to account and seeing if their community judges them guilty or innocent. We all want to know if they "did it".

In our society, we are used to a legal system that is methodical, elaborate and deliberate, some would even say convoluted.[**] The trial process often begins with an investigation and the gathering of evidence and witnesses. This may lead to an arrest and then to the appointment of prosecutors and defence council, followed by months of pretrial hearings leading to a trial that could go on and on and on as witnesses speak and experts analyse and lawyers fight and judges call recesses because of golf commitments. Then the jury meet and fight it out amongst themselves before declaring a verdict, which frequently takes us to the beginnings of the appeals process … and on it goes. Even if a convicted felon receives a death sentence, this doesn't just happen straightaway out the back of the courthouse. In Texas, for example,

[*] Aussie talk for "living room".

[**] The following summation of the complexities of the Western legal system has no basis in fact but is the result of our watching many episodes of *Law and Order*.  – Pete

And reading John Grisham novels.  – Ben

the average time a prisoner spends on death row waiting to die is about ten years. Even the shortest recorded stay on death row was eight months, but one prisoner was on death row for twenty-four years before the death penalty was carried out.

Jesus' trial was *not* like this. The movement from trial to his execution was probably less than twenty-four hours.

It's hard to work out the exact order of the various interrogations and trials Jesus went through prior to his crucifixion. In the same way that various newspaper reports might offer different angles on the same story, each of the gospel writers chips in with various accounts of what happened. But here is the most likely order of events:

According to John,[1] after his arrest Jesus was first taken to the home of Annas (the former high priest and father-in-law to Caiaphas, the present high priest).* Although he no longer had an official role, Annas was something of an elder statesman in Jerusalem, held in regard in the same way a former president might be today. So this initial interrogation was not a formal trial but was more akin to a preliminary hearing. Here Jesus was questioned by Annas probably with the sole aim to get some dirt on him before the official trial. But Annas got very little out of Jesus, so he sent him to Caiaphas and the Jewish leaders.[2]

Those present at this "trial" were Caiaphas (the high priest), all the chief priests, the elders, and the scribes,[3] all in all a body of probably over seventy men.** But this was no trial, at least not in the sense of a fair hearing and just verdict. It becomes quite clear that the verdict had already been decided and the judicial body was now just looking for the "smoking gun" to pin Jesus to a crime worthy of death, even if it meant fabricating some of the evidence.

Numerous witnesses were called forward to testify. As Matthew says, "The chief priests and the whole Sanhedrin were looking for false evidence against Jesus so that they could put him to death. But they did not find any, though many false witnesses came forward."[4] It seems that the only thing they could agree on was that Jesus had said something about destroying the temple and rebuilding it again in three days. Through it all, Jesus remained silent.

Then perhaps out of frustration and to get Jesus to incriminate himself, Caiaphas took a different tack. He stood and addressed Jesus, asking him plainly, "Are you the Messiah, the Son of the Blessed One?"[5]

Now let's pause for a moment. Can you imagine the scene? For years, Jesus had been a thorn in the side of the establishment, and for a long time

> It becomes quite clear that the verdict had already been decided and the judicial body was now just looking for the "smoking gun" to pin Jesus to a crime worthy of death.

---

1. John 18:13.
2. Mark 14:53; John 18:24.
3. Mark 14:53.
4. Matthew 26:59–60.
5. Mark 14:61.

various factions had been planning to have him killed. Now here he was, right in front of them. And Caiaphas had asked him the big question. Seventy or so men were poised on the edge of their seats ready for his answer. If there had been any whispering throughout the court during the trial, it would have ceased at this moment.

"I am," said Jesus. And then he added, "And you will see the Son of Man sitting at the right hand of the Mighty One and coming on the clouds of heaven."[6] Jesus not only affirmed that he was the Messiah but also asserted that this would be confirmed by God himself when Jesus was placed in supreme authority at God's right hand. To our ears today, that's a pretty standard tenet of Christian belief. But to the ears of the Sanhedrin, this statement was incredibly offensive and blasphemous.

The reaction of the men was instantaneous. In an explosion of raw emotion, Caiaphas reached up and ripped at his own clothing. In doing so, he wasn't having a tantrum. Rather, the tearing of clothes was a cultural practice that expressed anger and indignation, anguish and disgust.* In this case, it was a visible sign of a guilty verdict.

In the modern court, the prisoner is provided – under law and in practice – with some level of protection. Not so here. Some of those present spat on Jesus and even punched him. Now they had their smoking gun – cold hard evidence to warrant his execution.

But the Jewish leaders had a problem. Because they were a nonsovereign body under the military and judicial rule of the Romans, they were not permitted to carry out capital punishment.[7] So they needed more than a charge of blasphemy to convince the Roman governor to have Jesus executed. Matthew, Mark and Luke report that the Sanhedrin met again early in the morning. This wasn't another trial but was probably a meeting to determine how they might convince the Roman governor that this particular case warranted the Roman death penalty.

This wouldn't necessarily be easy. Pilate and the Romans would be wanting to move cautiously, given the huge influx of pilgrims and the fragile mood in Jerusalem during Passover. Pilate would not want to do anything that might trigger a riot. However, the Jewish leaders had something working in their favour. They knew that Pilate had little tolerance and was heavy-handed when it came to acts of treason or perceived threats against Rome. In recent years, Pilate had executed many of their countrymen over similar matters. There had been clashes over Pilate's bringing images of Caesar into the city, and just a few years earlier a group of students were burned alive for attempting to remove a Roman standard from the temple. Any sign of insubordination to the empire could not be tolerated. Jesus' blasphemous

> Jesus not only affirmed that he was the Messiah but also asserted that this would be confirmed by God himself.

* The tearing of clothes occurs frequently in the Old Testament. Reuben and Jacob tore their clothes in anguish over the missing Joseph, Joshua tore his clothes in the face of brutal military opposition, Job tore his clothes when given tragic news about his family, David and his men all tore their clothes on hearing the news of the deaths of Saul and Jonathan.

6. Mark 14:62.
7. John 18:28–32.

> So they brought Jesus to Pilate with the charge of inciting people not to pay taxes to Caesar and making himself out to be a king.

affirmation could therefore be interpreted as one of the most serious crimes under Roman law: high treason against Rome – a crime punishable by death. So they brought Jesus to Pilate with the charge of inciting people not to pay taxes to Caesar and making himself out to be a king.[8]

At this time, things were suddenly turning ugly for Jesus' followers, especially his closest companions. For years they had travelled with him and witnessed many amazing things. There had been a great sense of hope and expectation, but it suddenly went pear shaped when their leader was arrested by a mob in the middle of the night. With the involvement of the Sanhedrin and then the Romans, things had got dangerous and serious. As followers and companions of a blasphemer and rebel, they too could just as easily find themselves under suspicion or arrest. This was not an era of free speech nor a time to be aligning oneself with a condemned man. The Romans used mass execution as much to send a signal to others as to punish the individuals themselves. Their very natural reaction was absolute fear.

So in a remarkable turn of events, most of Jesus' followers suddenly went to ground. We read that Peter followed the mob back into town at a distance, so as not to be caught up in the melee. While Jesus was inside being questioned, most of the mob were outside. It was a cold night, and Peter joined the servants and officials in the courtyard, where they had kindled a fire to keep warm. This must have been a nervous time for Peter. Now was not the time to be visible as an associate of a man being questioned by the Romans. On three separate occasions, Peter was recognized and asked if he knew Jesus, and each time Peter responded with a resounding no.[9] This question was no idle talk amongst the spectators outside the court. It was a pointed question that could have easily led to his being dragged forward as well and branded a co-conspirator with the accused. The contrast between Jesus' loyalty and Peter's disloyalty is made even greater in the Gospel of John as Peter's three-fold denial is woven through the narrative of Jesus' own trial. While Christ was inside defending himself, his best friend was outside denying he ever knew him.

Meanwhile, Jesus was taken to the praetorium: the residence of Pontius Pilate, the Roman governor of Judea. It was here that a strange scene unfolded. The Jewish leaders who had brought Jesus did not want to make themselves impure by entering the building of a Gentile, so they stood outside while Pilate came out to find out what all the commotion was about.[10] In a tremendous irony, here were the religious elite of Jerusalem supposedly remaining pure before God by keeping this minor traditional law while at the same time

---

8. Luke 23:1–3.
9. Luke 22:54–62.
10. John 18:28.

handing over his Son to be crucified. This is akin to robbing a bank but going to a lot of trouble to ensure the getaway car is legally parked.

After some initial inquiries into the nature of the charge, Pilate had Jesus brought into the praetorium to question him personally.

Pilate was used to dealing with local troublemakers. His relationship with the local population was tense, and there had already been some flare-ups during his term of office. Pilate was not a man to mess with. Even the Roman historian Philo records him as a man whose leadership was riddled with corruption, strife, injustice, endless brutality, extreme cruelty and a penchant towards carrying out swift executions without trial. (Within a few years of Jesus' dying, the governor of Syria removed Pilate from office under charges of wanton cruelty, and he was exiled to Gaul.)

Have you ever met someone who was famous and important but you didn't realise it until later on? Like that scene out of the film *Notting Hill* in which one of the characters meets Anna Scott (Julia Roberts) at a dinner party and asks her what she does for a living. He has absolutely no idea he is standing before the world's most famous and highest-paid actress.* In a similar scenario, Pilate had absolutely no idea of the greatness of the man standing before him. To Pilate, Jesus was just another ordinary figure encountered during an ordinary day's work. But he was about to find out this was no ordinary occasion and this was certainly no ordinary man.

Pilate began to question him:

"Are you the king of the Jews?"

"Is that your own idea," Jesus asked, "or did others talk to you about me?"

"Am I a Jew?" Pilate replied. "Your own people and chief priests handed you over to me. What is it you have done?"

Jesus said, "My kingdom is not of this world. If it were, my servants would fight to prevent my arrest by the Jewish leaders. But now my kingdom is from another place."

"You are a king, then!" said Pilate.

Jesus answered, "You say that I am a king. In fact, the reason I was born and came into the world is to testify to the truth. Everyone on the side of truth listens to me."

"What is truth?" retorted Pilate. With this he went out again to the Jews gathered there and said, "I find no basis for a charge against him."[11]

Pilate was completely thrown as he began to find out more about the man before him. For here was a man who claimed that he had a kingdom, yet seemingly had no marks of kingship whatsoever. Pilate was wondering, *If you're a king, where's your army? Where are your chariots? How on earth can this man be a king?*

* Ben has a friend who was holidaying in Bali who had a long conversation with a man in a hotel. She had no idea until later that she had been talking to George Harrison of the Beatles!

> To Pilate, Jesus was just another ordinary figure encountered during an ordinary day's work. But he was about to find out this was no ordinary occasion and this was certainly no ordinary man.

---

11. John 18:33–38.

* Some scholars suggest Barabbas was (like Judas?) a member of the sicarii – literally, "the daggermen" – a militant group that assassinated Romans and Roman sympathisers and caused riots and dissent.
** Generally, Roman citizens were exempt from crucifixion except in cases of high treason.

Under Pilate's orders, Jesus was then led away to be crucified while Barabbas was set free.

But Jesus said that his kingdom was not of this world. He was talking not only about the origin of the kingdom but also its nature. It was *in* the world; it was just not *of* the world. What Jesus was saying was, "If my kingdom was of this world, then my followers would fight like other kingdoms of the world. But that's not the way my kingdom operates." The kingdom of God operates on love, grace, truth, servanthood, sacrifice and humility. This was virtually the opposite of the Roman Empire, which was carved out almost entirely by pride, self-glorification and the sword. If Jesus was a king, he didn't look like one.

In a last-ditch effort to release Jesus, Pilate played what he thought was a trump card.

According to the Gospels, there was a custom of releasing one prisoner, of the people's choice, at this special time of year. So Pilate sought to pardon Jesus and set him free by using this custom. All four gospels tell us that at this time a well-known prisoner named Barabbas (actually, Jesus, the son of Abbas) was in prison for being part of an uprising and for murder.* So Pilate gave the crowd a choice: "Shall I release Barabbas or Jesus?" But this did not please the mob. For whatever reason – fear, misbelief, coercion, hysteria, disappointment, perhaps even a belief in the violent leadership of Barabbas – they wanted Jesus crucified even if it meant another criminal was to be freed instead.

Sensing that Pilate might have his way by using this loophole, the crowd played their own trump card. They began to accuse Pilate of treason against Rome. "If you let this man go," they said, "you are no friend of Caesar. Anyone who claims to be a king opposes Caesar."[12] This was blackmail. Pilate could not afford to be seen to be weak, and he certainly could not afford to be seen to do anything that was contrary to the best interests of the empire. He was being publicly goaded to crucify Jesus or possibly face the same sentence himself.** This action sealed Jesus' fate. Under Pilate's orders, Jesus was then led away to be crucified while Barabbas was set free.

However, it might be easy to miss a tremendous irony here and a beautiful illustration of what Jesus' death is all about. Here were two men ready to be sentenced. One was guilty, the other innocent. Yet here the guilty walked free while the innocent was led away and crucified. Jesus died in Barabbas' place. It is precisely in this paradox that we put our finger on the pulse of Christianity. Every one of us is guilty before God. All of us are on death row. Our relationship with God is broken. Yet Jesus, the only nonguilty human being, steps in and dies in our place. Jesus was punished in our place so that we guilty ones get to go free.

Finally, despite declaring him innocent on three separate occasions, Pilate had Jesus flogged and led away to be crucified. The danger here for us

---

12. John 19:12.

is that we read the word *flogged* and picture old movies about sailors on the Spanish Main tied to a mast and getting twenty lashes, received with classic British stoicism through clenched teeth. The whip puts some nasty pink stripes across their back, but after an uncomfortable night's sleep, they're back on deck again.

Roman flogging was a lot more brutal. Mel Gibson's film *The Passion of the Christ* is a lot closer to the mark. The film has had its share of critics because of its unabashed focus on the gross brutality, sickening violence and graphic bloodshed of Christ's beatings and crucifixion. And it's certainly not the kind of film one would go to for a first date. (There's something uncomfortably dissonant about watching such degrading sadism and bloody torture while chugging down litres of cola and a maxipack combo of popcorn at the megaplex.) But as disgusting and uncomfortable as the beating and crucifixion are to our modern sensibilities, Gibson's gratuitously gory portrayal is a lot more accurate than the quaint artistic renditions of the past.

Being flogged was the standard prelude to a Roman crucifixion, designed to torture and weaken the victim to the point of collapse. The convicted criminal was tied up to a post or stretched out on a board and lashed by a broad, thick, multiheaded leather whip embedded with sharp bone and chunks of metal. The leather and the shards – wielded by the professional military executioners – cut deep through the skin and tore it open, shredding the person from shoulders to thighs. Historians talk of the way scourged victims lost their skin and often had their bones and organs exposed. The blood loss and shock were so phenomenal that it was not uncommon for the victims to die from the scourging alone.

Then at the governor's residence, the bored and cruel Roman soldiers performed a macabre ritual. As soldiers of an occupying military force, they were constantly dealing with rebels and struggling to quash uprisings and to keep the lid on the volatile population. And there in their hands, in a bloodied mess in front of them, they had someone who claimed to be the leader of the Jews. This was their chance to show who was boss. Knowing that Jesus had made some claims of kingship, they decided to play a nasty joke on him. They dressed him in a cloak that symbolised royalty and rammed a mock crown made of thorns down on his head and gave him a staff as a sceptre to make him look like a king. Then they bowed down and mock worshiped him, saying, "Hail, King of the Jews." Then they spat on him and beat him about his head with the staff. Again, they were not being playful or threatening. It was a message: *this is what happens to people who go up against the empire.* They were flogging him close to the point of death.

And then, Jesus was led away to be crucified.

> Jesus was punished in our place so that we guilty ones get to go free.

The death penalty is in use in over seventy countries around the world today, and in thirty-eight of America's states. Of course, it's one thing to have a legally sanctioned death penalty, but the next question is, How does a government go about the business of actually *killing* a person?

Most countries today would argue that their methods of execution are quick, painless and humane. However, it's fair to say that in previous centuries, most societies went out of their way to develop methods of execution that were painful, cruel, drawn out, torturous and spectacular and that actually prolonged and amplified the suffering of the criminal. Mostly these were conducted not behind the closed walls of a prison but rather – even into the early 1900s – in a public space where large groups could gather to watch people die.

Despite being a cultured society, ancient Rome at the time of Jesus had a barbaric side in the form of many sophisticated and cruel methods of execution. These were public displays that acted not only as deterrents to the population but also as entertainment. Citizens would regularly turn up to witness criminals being beaten to death, burned alive or decapitated. Others were thrown from a cliff, stoned or used as sport in public arenas, where they were attacked and eaten by wild animals. A particularly humiliating and cruel death was when the criminal was sewn into a sack with four live animals and then thrown into water to drown. These more cruel and humiliating deaths were reserved for the lower classes, foreigners, the poor and slaves, while the more "dignified" and "painless" deaths were for Roman citizens.

But of all of the methods of execution in the Roman Empire, one was feared and loathed more than any other: crucifixion.

Crucifixion had a long history dating back many centuries. The Medes and the Persians widely used crucifixion, and the ancient historian Herodotus claimed that in 519 BC, Darius crucified three thousand Babylonian prisoners. It was also widespread among the Greeks; Alexander the Great in 332 BC ordered the crucifixion of two thousand young men along the shore of the island of Tyre following a siege that lasted several months. In 267 BC, eight hundred Pharisees were crucified in Jerusalem following a revolt, and while they were hanging there, their wives and children were killed in front of them. Perhaps the most famous mass crucifixion followed the slave revolt in 71 BC; six thousand recaptured slaves were crucified along the Appian Way, the main road to Rome. Crucifixion was widely practiced until it was abolished by Emperor Constantine in the fourth century.

> Despite being a cultured society, ancient Rome at the time of Jesus had a barbaric side in the form of many sophisticated and cruel methods of execution.

* Referred to as Golgotha in the language of Aramaic, or as Calvary in Latin.

Aside from being brutal and excruciatingly painful, crucifixion was long and slow and was considered the most humiliating and insulting death. Criminals were generally executed naked, and they were not even afforded the "dignity" of being executed in a "proper place". Crucifixions took place outside the city walls – often just on the side of the main roads – showing that the criminal was held in contempt and had been rejected by the community. Even worse, most criminals didn't even have the promise of a proper funeral and knew their bodies would more often than not just be left there to rot, fall apart and be eaten by wild animals and scavengers.

Little wonder that ancient writers describe crucifixion in such bleak terms. On more than one occasion, the Jewish historian Josephus describes it as the "most wretched of deaths".[1] Similarly, the Roman writer and statesman Cicero was so disturbed by it he said, "Let the very name of the cross be far away not only from the body of a Roman citizen, but even from his thoughts, his eyes, his ears."[2]

Following Pilate's pronouncement, Jesus was escorted along with two other condemned men through the streets of Jerusalem. Days before, he had entered through the city gates as a king. Now he was leaving the city as a man about to die. It was customary for condemned criminals to suffer the indignity of carrying their own means of execution out of the city. However, Jesus was so weakened by the beatings he had received that he eventually could not carry the beam of the cross. So a visiting foreigner (identified as Simon from Cyrene, in North Africa) was conscripted by the soldiers to carry it for him outside the city walls to the ominously named **Place of the Skull.**\*

> Days before, Jesus had entered through the city gates as a king. Now he was leaving the city as a man about to die.

While crucifixions were par for the course at the time, there would have been unusual interest in this particular execution. Over the past few years, Jesus had caused quite a stir. He had incensed the chief priests, the Pharisees, the Sadducees and the ruling council of Jewish leaders. He had become known to the Romans. People all across the land had heard of him and sought him out. This was not a run-of-the-mill execution of a few slaves or thieves. It was a special execution as the Romans quashed a popular local subversive. Word would have got out. So Luke describes how, as Jesus made his way to the place of his execution, "a large number of people followed him, including women who mourned and wailed for him."[3]

One of the problems for us two thousand years later as we read and contemplate what happened that day is that we know the end of the story. It's like watching a DVD for the third time. We know that the *Titanic* sinks, that the boy gets the girl and that the aliens are defeated. But the people involved don't know that outcome beforehand. In terms of the crucifixion,

---

1. Josephus, *Jewish War* 5:11.1 (450), 7:6.4 (203).
2. Cicero, *Pro Rabirio* 5.
3. Luke 23:27.

we know what happens. But it's important we remember that the crowd tagging along behind and gathered at various points along the road that day didn't know and must have been wondering what was going to happen. Jesus' arrest and trial had backed the Messiah into a corner and forced his hand. There was nowhere else to go, and surely now he would have to act, would have to use the power he had used so many times before. Maybe like Samson he would rip down the buildings, or like Elijah invoke supernatural forces to destroy his enemies, or like David call the people to arms and lead them in a mighty battle. Jesus had appeared out of nowhere, claiming to be the one. He developed a huge following, fuelled by his innovative teachings and authoritative arguments against an oppressive religious regime. Not only that, he turned the whole population on its head by showing power *that could only come from God.* He healed the sick. He raised the dead. He controlled the elements. **He was the one!** This was an important time in their history, and all their hopes hung on him. This was the moment for something to happen, surely.

But as he stumbled and was shoved out of town along with two petty criminals, too weak even to carry his own cross, the doubts must have set in. Maybe he wasn't who they thought he was after all. The Messiah wouldn't let this happen, would he?

When he finally arrived at Golgotha, in the shadow of the city walls, he was offered a last-minute sedative in the form of wine and myrrh. But he refused to drink it, probably so that he could remain sober. What was left of his clothes was removed, and then, as all the gospel writers minimalistically put it, "they crucified him."

With all due respect to the great artists of history, the depictions of the crucifixion we are so used to are more often than not misleading and, well, to put it mildly, *insipid*. Perhaps out of reverence, artists have tended to emphasize the holiness of the crucifixion, with Jesus often depicted as porcelain-skinned and bathed in meaningful shafts of sunlight with an otherworldly halo around his head. He often looks quite graceful and pensive, with dainty little nails in his arms and legs and – despite the fact that men were crucified naked – a modesty loincloth around his waist. He has lost-puppy eyes and his expression is mournful and whimsical, as if he is sighing and thinking, "Oh well, you win some, you lose some." The reality of a public execution was a lot more confronting than that.

While it is not our intention to voyeuristically dissect Christ's crucifixion or disrespectfully pore over the gruesome details of a slow and agonising death, it is important that we have a more realistic picture of what happened on that day.

The victim of a crucifixion was fixed to a cross either by ropes or, as in Jesus' case, by nails, or a combination of both. Large, thick nails were

> But as Jesus stumbled and was shoved out of town along with two petty criminals, too weak even to carry his own cross, the doubts must have set in. Maybe he wasn't who they thought he was after all.

hammered through the condemned person's wrists and feet.[*] This was actually a way of prolonging the death. Aside from blood loss and shock, what actually killed people when they were crucified was asphyxiation. Their shoulders and arms were stretched and eventually the body would slump down so the lungs could no longer inflate. The victim would then struggle to breathe, trying vainly to lift themselves up by nailed wrists, dislocated joints and fatigued muscles just to catch their breath. The only way they could do this was to push up from their feet, but because the ankles were nailed to wood, each push was excruciatingly painful. Nevertheless, a person could stay alive longer by pushing up from their feet, unless, that is, the soldiers decided they wanted to speed the process along. In John's account, for example, he describes how the Roman soldiers wanted to hurry the deaths of the two thieves next to Jesus, so they broke their legs.[4] One can only imagine that this was done by smashing their knees and shins with heavy beams or mallets until they were shattered. The men would be unable to push up on splintered bones and so they would hang down and suffocate.

And so it was that Jesus was crucified by soldiers of the Roman Empire. Placed above his head was a sign – a *titulus* – worded in three languages (Aramaic, Latin and Greek) that told passersby what his crime was. Despite the protests of the chief priests, Pilate arranged for the titulus to simply (and ironically) read, "Jesus of Nazareth: The King of the Jews." Pilate perhaps did this as a way of publicly humiliating and bullying the local Jewish population. It was a display of the might and superiority of Roman law and power over any hopes of revolutionary leadership to which they might aspire. Here was Israel's great leader and hope, the mighty rabbi, now naked, bloodied, beaten and dying the most cursed of deaths. It was a vivid warning to all that Rome was not to be trifled with.

This, seemingly, was the end. Jesus was a good man, an amazing man, a charismatic and inspiring man, but, apparently, just a man after all. To his disciples – perhaps watching at a distance – this was end of the road. You can almost imagine some of his followers drifting off, shaking their heads, and others standing transfixed, perhaps still hopeful of a last-minute miracle.

With each minute that passed, Jesus was dying, and so too was the hope of his followers.

---

4. John 19:31–32.

* Archaeological evidence suggests that at least on some occasions the nails were not put through the front of the condemned man's feet (as per traditional paintings) but rather were driven sideways through the ankles and into the side faces of the upright beam.

# Chapter 22

# THE KILLING TREE
## Jesus dies

It is fair to say that the central icon for Jesus' followers is the cross. It is possibly the most recognized symbol in the world. We place it on church steeples for all to see and display it in stained glass or as a gold ornament at the front of churches. The Crusaders painted crosses on their shields and tunics. It is emblazoned across the front of Bibles, church newsletters, books and Christian websites. People wear crosses as earrings, necklaces, lapel pins, tattoos and as logos on corporate and school uniforms. Street directories use crosses as a symbol to indicate the location of churches. And once a year, our supermarkets at Easter time are full of buns with crosses on them.

When you see a cross atop a church or around someone's neck, it doesn't send a shiver up your spine as it would for anyone in the ancient world. In Jesus' day, hanging a cross around your neck as a piece of jewellery would be as unusual and offensive as wearing a silver hangman's noose. (As C. S. Lewis pointed out, crucifixion did not become common in art until all who had witnessed one died off.)

So the question is *why?* Given that Jesus did a lot of incredible things when he was alive, why do his followers use the horrific means of his death as a symbol of their faith? Why not use a loaf of bread, or a fish,* or a wine cup, or a palm frond, or a splash of myrrh?

> \* Ben, the fish *is* a symbol of Christianity. Haven't you noticed the stickers on the backs of cars?
> – Pete
>
> Ahem, right.     – Ben

The answer is that Jesus' action of dying on the cross is the bedrock and focal point of the Christian faith. To explain, let us pop over analogy-wise to South America.

On a backwater trail along the Upper Rio Paraguay, traditional cattle farmers from time to time need to cross the river with their animals. However, crossing is risky and potentially dangerous on account of the river's being populated with *pygocentrus nattereri*. Doesn't sound too bad, does it? Except that this means the river is infested by the savage carnivorous hunting fish the piranha. If farmers and their livestock cross the river without taking precautions, they run the risk of being attacked. To ensure a safe crossing, the farmers do a remarkable thing. They kill a sick or weak animal from the herd and place it in the river downstream from where they want the herd to cross. The fish are drawn to the carcass and maul the animal while the others cross safely to the other side. Through the one sacrifice, the others are saved.**

> \*\* My "Christian Urban Myth" alarm bells are going off here, mate.
> – Pete
>
> No, this one's genuine.     – Ben

For centuries, Jewish society had revolved around a convoluted system of offerings and sacrifices. At the core of this system was the idea that people were in a broken relationship with God, and he was inaccessible on the other side of the river, so to speak. Sacrifices were made in their place so that people could be ritualistically cleansed and be right with God again. However, they had to keep repeating this process. Not only that, it is clear in many cases that sacrifices had ceased to be a loyalty and personal matter as much as a burdensome ritual entrenched in commerce at the temple.

And so Jesus became the sacrifice – once and for all – that allows humans to cross over to the other side to be in relationship with God. However, unlike the calf, Jesus was not thrown into this scene unwillingly, and neither was he ignorant of the situation. He knew full well what he was doing in sacrificing his life to save others. His death was his ultimate mission. (About three years earlier, John the Baptist had declared that Jesus was the sacrificial Lamb of God. And Jesus himself had said that he was the servant who had come to give his life as a ransom for many, and that he was the Good Shepherd who had come to lay down his life for his sheep.) All of this meant that Jesus' arrest, trial and death were no accidents. They were his plan all along.

There is a certain irony, therefore, when we look at the scene unfolding around Jesus as he hung dying on the cross. The expectation of the crowd, who had been hoping for salvation and deliverance, soon turned to doubt and disappointment. And then, it appears, it turned to anger. *They had been let down! He wasn't the Messiah after all. He was dying. They had been duped.* The assembled crowd – the people, the religious leaders, the soldiers, even the thieves next to him – began to mock him. *King of the Jews? You must be kidding! Save yourself if you are! C'mon ... do it!* Matthew describes how "those who passed by hurled insults at him, shaking their heads and saying, 'You who are going to destroy the temple and build it in three days, *save* yourself! Come down from the cross, if you are the Son of God!' "[1] And then, "In the same way the chief priests, the teachers of the law and the elders mocked him. 'He *saved* others,' they said, 'but he can't *save* himself! He's the king of Israel! Let him come down now from the cross, and we will believe in him.' "[2] And the soldiers called out to him, "If you are the king of the Jews, *save* yourself."[3] Even one of the criminals said to him, "Aren't you the Messiah? *Save* yourself and us!"[4]

Paradoxically, saving was exactly what Jesus was doing. It was precisely in not saving himself from the cross that Jesus was being the Saviour of the world. So here, two thousand years ago, Jesus saved us by taking our punishment in our place.

Yet virtually no one at the scene of Jesus' crucifixion understood this ... except perhaps one man. Ironically, it wasn't one of Jesus' disciples or a learned

> And so Jesus became the sacrifice – once and for all – that allows humans to cross over to the other side to be in relationship with God.

---

1. Matthew 27:39–40, emphasis added.
2. Matthew 27:41–42, emphases added.
3. Luke 23:36–37, emphasis added.
4. Luke 23:39, emphasis added.

Jewish elder but one of the criminals who was also being crucified. After hearing the insults of the first criminal, the second criminal yelled out from his own crucifix, "Don't you fear God, since you are under the same sentence? We are punished justly, for we are getting what our deeds deserve. But this man has done nothing wrong." Then he said to Jesus, "Jesus, remember me when you come into your kingdom."[5]

Much of the beauty of these words lies in their simplicity. They are devoid of any religious jargon and false piety. Here was a man who didn't have long to live and who simply recognized his own shortcomings and that he deserved his punishment. He knew he had nothing to offer but his own plea for forgiveness. Furthermore, his request to Jesus to simply remember him in his kingdom is brilliant. He recognized Jesus' innocence and that he was – despite all signs to the contrary – the king of a kingdom.

Jesus instantly recognized this criminal's heart and said to him, "Truly I tell you, today you will be with me in paradise."[6] One can only wonder what those words meant to that man in the last moments of his life.

Jesus' answer is important for a number of reasons. **Firstly,** in what he didn't say. Jesus didn't ask the criminal how many times he went to church (synagogue) or how many good deeds had he performed in the last week. Jesus didn't even ask him about his criminal record. Rather, his words wonderfully confirm that being accepted by Jesus doesn't depend on our deeds and our moral performance. Being accepted into his kingdom is not about being good or clocking up hours in church (as worthwhile as they are) but ultimately is about recognizing your own sinfulness and acknowledging who Jesus really is. **Secondly,** it shows us that forgiveness and acceptance in the kingdom are available to anyone, even a criminal like this one. What Jesus showed in life, he also showed in death. The repentant sinner is welcome in the kingdom of God.

So here we have all these various people standing around, goading Jesus to come up with the goods, to prove himself and take action. The mood would have been amplified because of an extraordinary phenomenon that took place. At about "the sixth hour"[7] (midday), the sky became dark for three hours. To the people watching the crucifixion – and probably even to Pilate and other superstitious Romans in the nearby city – this must have been a frightening spectacle. Something was not right. This was no ordinary execution but an event that crossed over from the physical into the spiritual realm. Darkness was symbolic of God's judgment. The fact that the whole sky became dark for three hours at this point adds to the universal and cosmic elements of Jesus' death.

> Jesus' words wonderfully confirm that being accepted by Jesus doesn't depend on our deeds and our moral performance.

---

5. Luke 23:40–42.

6. Luke 23:43.

7. Matthew 27:45; Mark 15:33; Luke 23:44. NIV.

> This was no ordinary execution but an event that crossed over from the physical into the spiritual realm.

And then something happened. A ripple of excitement ran through the crowd. *Jesus spoke!* Matthew records that Jesus cried out in a loud voice, "My God, my God, why have you forsaken me?"[8]

The crowd was electrified. Maybe this was the moment when something was going to happen. Matthew says, "When some of those standing there heard this, they said, 'He's calling Elijah.'"[9] *This was it!* They knew Jesus had miraculous powers that crossed over into the spiritual realm, and now he was calling on one of the great Old Testament prophets to come down to save him. The heavens would open and Elijah would appear – maybe in a flaming chariot or something exciting like that – to rescue Jesus and destroy the Romans.

Perhaps to encourage Jesus and keep him alive at this critical moment, a bystander ran and got a sponge soaked in wine vinegar. He put it on a stick and offered it to Jesus for him to drink from. Then the rest of the crowd said, "Now leave him alone. Let's see if Elijah comes to save him."[10]

So they waited – the sceptical, the curious, the eager, the hopeful.

It was three in the afternoon. The crowd was standing back, expectantly hanging onto the last hope that something was about to happen. Maybe they were looking up at the clouds or to the horizon, hoping to see something, anything. Everything boiled down to this moment.

Each of the gospel writers records what happened next:

"And when Jesus had cried out again in a loud voice, he gave up his spirit."[11]

"With a loud cry, Jesus breathed his last."[12]

"Jesus called out with a loud voice, 'Father into your hands I commit my spirit.' When he had said this, he breathed his last."[13]

"When he had received the drink, Jesus said, 'It is finished.' With that, he bowed his head and gave up his spirit."[14]

Luke records that "when all the people who had gathered to witness this sight saw what took place, they beat their breasts and went away. But all those who knew him, including the women who had followed him from Galilee, stood at a distance, watching these things."[15] (Matthew says that "among

---

8. Matthew 27:46.
9. Matthew 27:47.
10. Matthew 27:49.
11. Matthew 27:50.
12. Mark 15:37.
13. Luke 23:46.
14. John 19:30.
15. Luke 23:48–49.

them were Mary Magdalene, Mary the mother of James and Joseph, and the mother of Zebedee's sons.")[16]

It was all over.

Jesus – the son of Joseph and Mary, and the Son of God, who went on to be the rabbi, healer, master, great hope of the nation, the man who calmed storms and healed the sick and changed things forever – was dead. His disciples (some possibly watching secretly from a safe distance) had scattered in fear of reprisals from the Romans. The crowds turned and went home. A few faithful – the mourning women perhaps – stayed behind. Jesus' body hung there lifeless between two dying thieves who had just had their legs broken because the Romans wanted to get it all over with quickly.

But in the nearby city, in the inner sanctum of the temple, where all the chief priests gathered, something incredible happened. We are told that "the curtain of the temple was torn in two from top to bottom."[17] In the temple there were a number of different curtains,* but two main ones. One was at the first entrance to the temple into the "holy place", and the second was at the entrance to the "holy of holies", where God's Spirit was said to have dwelt. This place was so sacred that only the high priest would go in there once a year.** The curtains certainly represented God's holiness and "otherness" and the great barrier between a sinless God and sinful mankind. So although not specified, it is thought that the second curtain is what the gospel writers were referring to. This was no flimsy drape but a finely crafted and woven mass, several centimeters thick, very high and of incredible mass and weight. The tearing of this curtain has often been thought to be a great positive symbol of the fact that Jesus' death destroyed the barrier between God and man.

However, while it is true to say that Jesus' death removed the dividing barrier between God and man,[18] the gospel writers are perhaps indicating something else. Given its context and the language used by three gospel writers, it is also likely that we are to view this event as judgment on the temple and its priests. This curtain's being torn represented God's righteous anger falling on the very building that was supposed to represent his blessing. God, through Jesus' death, was destroying the temple and building a new one. All who wanted to meet with God and be in his presence no longer needed a building and sacrifices performed by priests. Instead, they could come freely to God through Jesus: the new temple. In a spiritual sense, the temple era was over. And within a lifetime, the physical temple itself would be razed to the ground following a four month siege by the Romans under Titus.

* Jospeh Fitzmyer has suggested as many as thirteen curtains in total (*The Gospel according to Luke X – XXIV*, Anchor Bible Commentary [New York: Doubleday, 1985], 1518).

** And apparently the chief priest wore a rope around his waist so if something happened to him, he could be dragged out rather than have anyone else enter.  – Pete

Sorry to disappoint, Pete. But it's your turn in the urban myth zone.  – Ben

---

16. Matthew 27:55–56.

17. Matthew 27:51; Mark 15:38.

18. Hebrews 10:19–20.

Meanwhile, back at Golgotha, a centurion at the scene who was perhaps overseeing the execution squad, uttered the now famous words, "Surely this man was the Son of God!"[19] These words are truly remarkable and are in no way meant to be just an aside in the story. The significance here is not just in what was said but who was saying it. Again it was not one of the disciples or a learned Jewish scholar but a pagan soldier of the Roman Imperial Army. A Roman soldier's allegiance was to Rome and particularly to the emperor, who was commonly regarded as "the son of a god". At the time of Jesus' crucifixion, the emperor of Rome was Tiberius, and his supposed divinity was promoted on inscriptions and on one of the most used coins of the era – a Roman denarius that bore the inscription TI(BERIVS) CAESAR DIVI AVG(VSTI) F(ILIVS) ("Tiberius Caesar, son of the god Augustus"). Yet here was a Roman soldier uttering treason in declaring Jesus – not the emperor – as the Son of God.

Furthermore, for any Roman living in the first century, divinity was usually confirmed by a military victory or strength of leadership in civil matters. A divine man in the eyes of a Roman would be one who looked like a general in battle or a king on a throne rather than a weak criminal on a cross, which was an object of shame.

How beautifully ironic. Here, right at the moment of Jesus' death, a commander in the imperial army for whom a crucifixion was an unmentionable obscenity, declares Jesus, a poor, humiliated, crucified Jew, to be the Son of God.

The final scene in the crucifixion account is the burial of Jesus by Joseph of Arimathea and Nicodemus (the Pharisee who had earlier met with Jesus in secret). Joseph was a member of the Sanhedrin who had not agreed with the plan to have Jesus executed. With Pilate's permission, they were given Jesus' body, and they took it to a nearby tomb, where according to burial custom, the two of them wrapped the body with spices in strips of linen.*

Then the tomb was sealed and, well, that was that.

Jesus was dead and buried.

---

19. Mark 15:39.

* We will explore this more closely in the next chapter.

On August 31, 1997, Ben was driving on the outskirts of Sydney when he got a phone call from his wife. "Have you heard the news?" she asked.

"What news?"

"Princess Diana has been in a car accident."

The initial reports, in Sydney anyhow, were that Diana wasn't seriously injured but "had broken a leg" and had been rushed to hospital. So when Ben finally got home about two hours later, he was stunned to see every television station running scenes of a mangled black Mercedes in a Paris tunnel with the words "Princess Diana dead" running across the bottom of the screen.

It seemed impossible that a princess, especially a popular figure like Diana, who seemed invincible and was so often surrounded by a cushion of bodyguards and bulletproof vehicles, was so vulnerable to an everyday accident. The news struck hard. Diana was suddenly dead and gone. For many, the words *princess* and *dead* didn't compute. They didn't belong in the same sentence.

If you have had a family member or friend die, you know how shocking, confronting and painful death can be. Suddenly your whole perspective on the nitty-gritty of life is thrown out of balance as you scramble to cope with the sense of loss and its utter finality. Where once there was a person – a living breathing friend whom you knew and laughed with and spoke to and touched – now there is nothing but a coffin, memories, old photographs and hymns at a funeral.

Like anyone struggling to cope with the death of a friend, the disciples were devastated by what they had just witnessed. But more than that, Jesus was their national hope, their great teacher and "bulletproof" Lord, their travelling companion, rabbi and friend. He had been tried as a criminal, executed on a Roman crucifix and died. Their faith had been shattered and their world had been turned upside down. For them, the words *Christ* and *dead* did not compute either. They didn't belong in the same sentence. As we have already said, according to Jewish tradition, the Christ or Messiah would be a conqueror and a victor, one who would demonstrate God's rule and kingship and crush his enemies. But the very opposite had happened. He had been defeated and killed at the hands of his enemies, and the brutal and simple reality of that must have soon struck home: *Jesus of Nazareth wasn't the one.* He *wasn't* the Christ, the Anointed One of God.

> Like anyone struggling to cope with the death of a friend, the disciples were devastated by what they had just witnessed.

Under Roman practice, the bodies of convicted criminals were left to rot as a further insult to the criminal and a grotesquely public warning to everyone else. It would be dangerous and risky to be seen to have anything to do with a convicted person, even in death. Jesus' followers were deeply confused, dejected and scared. Some – including the women who had followed him all the way from Galilee – stood watching at a distance while others were hiding in Jerusalem or making their way away from the city and home in despair. But two men boldly approached Pilate and asked if Jesus' body could be released to them. The amazing thing is that they were not who you would expect. They were not members of Jesus' family nor were they counted among his closest disciples. As night began to fall, Jesus' corpse was taken down and given over to a wealthy Jewish man from Arimathea – Joseph – and his colleague, Nicodemus.

There are two amazing aspects to their actions.

**Firstly,** in handling a dead body, both men were made ritually unclean. For members of the Sanhedrin during Passover, this was a hugely significant issue. Apparently, these two showed that they were true disciples in that they cared more about Jesus' dead body than their own ceremonial cleanliness.

**Secondly,** it was probably scandalous for these two members of the powerful Jewish ruling council, the Sanhedrin, to be seen associating with "the enemy" in this way. It appears that Joseph, despite being on the Sanhedrin, had been a secret follower of Jesus who had not agreed with the course of action taken against him. Nicodemus, similarly, had previously visited Jesus and spoken with him under the cover of night, perhaps to keep his interest in the Christ a secret from his colleagues. But now in death, these two men made a bold public statement in coming forward and taking Jesus' body. They took it to a nearby tomb, which, in the tradition of the wealthy, had been cut into the rock of the hillside. They wrapped the body as per custom in linen and spices and left it in that tomb, sealing it with a heavy rock, which was rolled across the entrance. Some of the Jewish leaders, concerned over the possible theft of Jesus' body by his fanatical followers, convinced Pilate to station a Roman guard at the tomb.

And that's where you would expect the story to finish. Cold night falls over the hillside outside Jerusalem, and in a rock cave, sealed by an enormous boulder and guarded by Roman centurions, lies the corpse of a convicted insurgent.

Yet all four gospels tell us that this is not the end of the story. Each gospel climactically ends on a tremendous note of triumph. It is this surprise finish that actually lies at the very heart of Jesus' ministry and has been the central tenet of belief of his followers ever since. It is a surprise that is both beautifully simple and incomprehensibly complex. Jesus shatters the fabric of our world by returning to life. He was dead. And he came back.

Jesus shatters the fabric of our world by returning to life. He was dead. And he came back.

Two thousand years after these events, it's pretty easy for us to be blasé about the resurrection, especially if we have grown up with it. As Christian jargon goes, it rolls off the tongue pretty easily. But this event is not one that we should brush over easily. It wasn't just a final farewell miracle or another way to show that Jesus could perform startling deeds. The bodily resurrection of Jesus was and is the indispensable backbone of the Christian faith. It's no exaggeration to say that without the resurrection, there is no Christianity. As the apostle Paul said less than thirty years after the event, "If Christ has not been raised, our preaching is useless and so is your faith ... you are still in your sins ... [and] we are to be pitied more than all others."[1]

While it's not our aim to try to prove the resurrection of Jesus in this book, it is worth considering some of these aspects recorded either in the New Testament or in other sources:

- Jesus was never promoted as a martyr by his followers, as were other noble Jews of the time who died for the cause of God at the hands of their enemies.
- The first eyewitness reports of Jesus' resurrection were women. The testimony of a woman, in both Jewish and Greco-Roman cultures of the day, was not regarded as reliable witness in a court. Put simply, if one were making up a story about a resurrection and wanting fellow first-century Jews to believe it, you would avoid using noncredible witnesses such as women as the initial witnesses.
- All the disciples were radically transformed from being frightened and confused to boldly proclaiming that Jesus had been raised from the dead.
- According to tradition and some sources, it seems that most of the apostles were martyred for their faith in a physically resurrected Jesus. They all argued to the point of death that they had seen Jesus alive.[2]
- Jesus' death didn't bring about the death of faith in him. It brought about the opposite. Followers of Jesus (soon to be given the name *Christ-ians*) began meeting together, preaching about his divinity and boldy proclaiming that they had seen him alive after his execution.
- Jesus appeared to *many* different people in several different locations, over a period of more than a month and on one occasion to more than five hundred people.[3]

While none of these points proves that Jesus rose from the dead, they are worth noting collectively. After considering the evidence, Paul Barnett (who

> The death of Jesus didn't bring about the death of faith in him. It brought about the opposite.

---

1. 1 Corinthians 15:14, 17, 19.
2. The historical sources for these martyrdoms include Acts 7:1–60; 12:1–2; Josephus's *Jewish Antiquities* 20.200; 1 Clement 5:1–7; Eusebius's *Ecclesiastical History* 2.25.5–6.
3. Acts 1:3; 1 Corinthians 15:3–8.

* Jews would have seen Friday, the day of his death, as the first day, Saturday (the Sabbath) as the second day, and Sunday as the third day.

The soldiers who were meant to be guarding the tomb were no longer there. The entrance stone had been rolled to the side. And the body of Jesus was missing.

amongst other things is an associate lecturer in ancient history at Macquarie University, Sydney, and a research professor at Regent College, Vancouver) concluded that "for me, the quality of the evidence and moral tone of the literature in which it occurs lead me to conclude that Jesus, having been killed, was, after three days, raised from the dead."[4]

Even Pinchas Lapide, a noted Orthodox rabbi and one of the world's leading Jewish theologians, was so compelled by the evidence for Jesus' resurrection that he made this startling admission: "I accept the resurrection of Easter Sunday not as an invention of the community of disciples, but as an historical event."[5] This is an astounding admission, especially from an Orthodox rabbi.

### An Account of the Resurrection

Then early on the Sunday (the third day)* after Jesus' death, some women, including Mary Magdalene and Mary the mother of James, went to the tomb with various spices to anoint Jesus' body. However, they weren't prepared for what they saw. The soldiers who were meant to be guarding the tomb were no longer there. The entrance stone had been rolled to the side. And the body of Jesus was missing. It is possible that at this moment the women thought the situation had worsened. *Perhaps there had been an attack of some sort and Jesus' body had been stolen.* Then while they were still standing there perplexed by this frightening scene, an angelic messenger appeared before them and gave them a staggering explanation: Jesus had risen from the grave.

All four gospel writers give a description of the women's initial feelings at this point as, understandably, a mixture of fear, astonishment and joy. There's good reason for this. Despite the numerous occasions that Jesus had spoken of his own resurrection (together with a number of Old Testament passages and stories that indicated that Jesus would rise from death), it was still an unexpected and surprising phenomenon to all of his disciples. Their emotions at the empty tomb underlined the fact that even those closest to him believed that it was all over and Jesus was well and truly dead and gone.

So it was with this range of perplexing emotions that the women ran back to the disciples to tell them what they had seen and heard. Upon hearing the news, the disciples didn't buy it. They laughed off the report as "an idle tale" and nonsense. They did not believe them.[6] The writers emphasize that they did not receive this story with gullible open arms but, just like any one of us would, greeted the news with confusion, suspicion and doubt. No one, it seems, was looking for a resurrected Jesus.

4. Paul Barnett, *The Truth about Jesus: The Challenge of Evidence* (Sydney: Aquilla, 1994), 151.

5. Pinchas Lapide, *The Resurrection of Jesus: A Jewish Perspective* (Minneapolis: Augsburg Fortress, 2002), 15.

6. Luke 24:11.

On hearing this report, Peter and another disciple (most likely John) ran to the tomb to see for themselves. They probably weren't expecting to see Jesus standing there back from death, but according to John's gospel, they simply wanted to find the body. When they arrived at the tomb, they were able to survey the evidence for themselves. The tomb was empty, the grave clothes were folded and the body of Jesus was nowhere to be seen. After observing the evidence, the two disciples went home, probably confused, possibly frightened.

Then, out of the blue, Jesus appeared to Mary Magdalene, who was still standing alone at the entrance to the tomb. But Mary didn't immediately recognize him.

John records what happened next:

> He asked her, "Woman, why are you crying? Who is it you are looking for?"
> Thinking he was the gardener, she said, "Sir, if you have carried him away, tell me where you have put him, and I will get him."
> Jesus said to her, "Mary."
> She turned toward him and cried out in Aramaic, "Rabboni!" (which means "Teacher").
> Jesus said, "Do not hold on to me, for I have not yet ascended to the Father. Go instead to my brothers and tell them, 'I am ascending to my Father and your Father, to my God and your God.'"[7]

Then Jesus left. One can only imagine what was going through Mary's mind. No doubt her heart was pounding from the wonder and excitement of it all, and again she ran to tell the disciples.

Luke records[8] another initial encounter with Jesus. He tells us that two other disciples (who weren't part of the Twelve) were making their way home that morning to the village of Emmaus, about ten kilometres away from Jerusalem. This in itself is noteworthy. Here were two people (possibly a man and a wife, although more likely two male disciples) who were obviously close to the apostles. So convinced were they that it was all over that they weren't even bothering to stick around.

We are told that as they walked along this road, Jesus, in some form of disguise, began to walk along with them within earshot. After hearing some of their discussion, Jesus baited them with a surprising question. "What are you talking about?" asked Jesus.

It's easy for us to miss the shocking nature of this question. Imagine that you were walking through Trafalgar Square in London three days after Princess Diana had died, and then someone walked up to you and said, "Hey,

The tomb was empty, the grave clothes were folded and the body of Jesus was nowhere to be seen.

---

7. John 20:15–17.
8. Luke 24:13–35.

what's going on here? Why all the sad faces?" You would look at them like they had been living under a rock. On the road that day, Jesus' question was so unexpected it caused both of the travellers to stop in their tracks. Then one of them – Cleopas – turned to Jesus and said, "Are you the only person in all of Jerusalem who doesn't know about the things that have happened this weekend?"

The great irony was that Jesus was the only one in all of Jerusalem who *did know* what had happened! But Jesus wanted to hear it from their lips and pressed on questioning them. "What things?" Jesus asked.

They began to tell him of their hopes in Jesus and how they believed that he was the Christ but had been arrested, tried and crucified. Notably, they called him "Jesus the Nazarene", not "Jesus the Christ". Now he was, at best, a prophet or a great teacher.

After hearing their story, Jesus rebuked them for not believing all of what the scriptures taught. As we have said elsewhere, history tells us very clearly that many first-century Jews, including the disciples of Jesus, were obsessed with passages in the Old Testament about the Messiah that indicated conquest and triumph. Most discussion, it seems, centred on passages and prophecies that described a Messiah who would overthrow evil, establish God's kingdom and bring about a new constituted people of God. But they tended to neglect passages that talked about or alluded to a suffering Messiah. It seems these two disciples were no exception. And so with an audience of two, Jesus gave one of the most unique reflections on scripture in all of history. Beginning with the first books of the Old Testament (the books of Moses) and working his way through the prophets, Jesus explained to them what had just happened.

With their hearts deeply warmed by what they heard, they encouraged this stranger to stay with them in Emmaus for the night. So Jesus stayed and sat down to eat with them and then finally revealed his identity during the meal. He left shortly thereafter. These two disciples hurried back to Jerusalem to share their amazing story.

After these initial appearances, Jesus finally appeared to Peter and then to most of the other disciples in a guest room where they were all staying. While the disciples were still shaken with confusion about what was going on, Jesus finally stood before them. The last time they saw him, he had been brutalised and killed by Roman soldiers. Now he was there among them again, and their reaction is described in classic biblical understatement: "They were startled and frightened, thinking they saw a ghost."[9] Here was a man who clearly had died and now had come back from the dead.

It is common to call Thomas the doubting disciple. In fact, his name has become synonymous with doubt. However, *all* of the disciples had a perfectly

> After these initial appearances, Jesus finally appeared to Peter and then to most of the other disciples in a guest room where they were all staying.

---

9. Luke 24:37.

human reaction in that they doubted in some way or another. Luke tells us that they were stunned and frightened, yet simultaneously joyful.[10]

Sensing their bewilderment and doubt, Jesus invited them to touch him so that they could feel that he was real. Then came what must have been something of a funny moment. Perhaps the disciples were waiting for some grand discourse about life and resurrection. Instead, Jesus asked them a question. The question was not, "Who do you say I am?" or anything sagely like that. It was more mundane.

"Do you have anything to eat?" he asked, before promptly woofing into some broiled fish. It may have been, of course, that after all he had been through over the past few days, Jesus was, quite simply, hungry. However, this was also a vivid demonstration that this was no ghost or a trick of the brain. Jesus was fully alive in bodily form. As mentioned before, Jesus continued to meet with his disciples on numerous occasions in various locations over a period of more than a month. Luke tells us that "after his suffering, he presented himself to them and gave many convincing proofs that he was alive. He appeared to them over a period of forty days and spoke about the kingdom of God."[11]

Once Jesus had spent enough time with his followers, his mission was finally over. But the end of Jesus' mission is not the end of the story. In many ways, it is just the beginning. Matthew records Jesus' final words as these: "Therefore go and make disciples of all nations, baptizing them in the name of the Father and of the Son and of the Holy Spirit, and teaching them to obey everything I have commanded you. And surely I am with you always, to the very end of the age."[12]

At that moment, although the disciples couldn't know it, they were standing on the doorstep of the biggest social and religious revolution that has ever hit the world. The good news about Jesus was about to go out around the world in a massive percussion. And our world would never be the same again.

### Why Did Jesus Return from Death?

The resurrection of Jesus was and is important for a number of reasons:

It wonderfully demonstrates that Jesus is Lord over death. Everyone dies. It is the final master over us all. But Jesus is master over death. He conquers it, rather than the other way round.

Jesus' resurrection turns the cross from a symbol of shame and defeat into a symbol of victory and hope. If Jesus only died, it means that he was just another man and his death therefore is not the sacrifice for the sins of the

> At that moment, although the disciples couldn't know it, they were standing on the doorstep of the biggest social and religious revolution that has ever hit the world.

---

10. Luke 24:37, 41.
11. Acts 1:3.
12. Matthew 28:19–20.

whole world. But the resurrection confirms to us that the man on the cross was the Son of God and therefore was able to absorb the full consequences of all humanity's sin. Without it, Jesus would be just another great man.

Writing to some of the first Christians living in Corinth who were still struggling to understand (and fighting about) the significance of Jesus' resurrection, the apostle Paul wrote the following words: "But Christ has indeed been raised from the dead, the firstfruits of those who have fallen asleep. For since death came through a human being, the resurrection of the dead comes also through a human being. For as in Adam all die, so in Christ all will be made alive. But in this order: Christ, the firstfruits; then, when he comes, those who belong to him. Then the end will come, when he hands over the kingdom to God the Father after he has destroyed all dominion, authority and power."[13]

This is slightly convoluted, so bear with us for a moment. Writers in both the Old and New Testaments teach that at the end of time, there will not be a "spirit place" for believers with clouds, harps and halos but rather a "new creation", a new physical world.[14] Into this world, God's people will live in harmony with him forever and there will be no tears or pain or suffering.[15] They too will be physical in that at the end of time there will be a great bodily resurrection of all humanity, not like zombies in a B-grade horror film, mind you, but a physical resurrection of new "imperishable bodies".

According to the apostle Paul, Jesus' resurrection acted as a pledge of what God will do for his people at the end of time. It was a foretaste of what will happen to his people – people who have submitted themselves to his kingdom – in the future.

Jesus' resurrection was truly a unique and far-reaching event that changed the course of history – not just Christian history but world history. It changed the initial followers of Jesus in the first century from being a devastated and confused bunch into a courageous group of men and women who, in turn, changed the world.

But Jesus' message was not always well received. Tradition says that all of the apostles bar one were cruelly executed for trying to spread the word. And for hundreds of years after Jesus, his followers suffered some of the most horrendous persecutions, torture and executions. Their rights were stripped away and there was a political campaign to wipe them off the face of the earth. It was hardly an inspiring and inviting way for a new way of life to get off the ground.

But Jesus' message was bigger than that. By the beginning of the fourth century, the unthinkable had happened. The most powerful man in the

> The resurrection of Jesus was truly a unique and far-reaching event that changed the course of history – not just Christian history but world history.

13. 1 Corinthians 15:20–24.
14. Isaiah 65:17–19; 66:22–23; Revelation 21:1.
15. Revelation 21:1–22:5.

known world had become a follower of the son of a carpenter from Galilee. The Roman emperor himself became a follower of Jesus, and as a consequence, the most pagan nation on earth – the Roman Empire, previously bound by multiple gods, rituals and cults – adopted Christianity as its official religion.*

In the twenty-first century, followers of Jesus in their millions around the globe still stand on the belief that Jesus broke the boundary of death. As a resurrected man, he is the true Son of God able to give new life to those who ask for it.

The best news the world has ever heard came from a graveyard: "He is risen!"

* Dan Brown's depiction in *The Da Vinci Code* that Constantine became a Christian only on his deathbed and made Christianity the official religion of the empire only to unite it is a fabrication.

## Part 6

# CHILDREN OF THE REVOLUTION

# Chapter 24

# UPON THIS ROCK
## What happened next?

In 1980, Pete – along with pretty well every other teenager in the known universe – hotfooted it to the cinema to see the much awaited sequel to *Star Wars*, *The Empire Strikes Back*. There he sat, entranced with the dark story and mouth agape at the dazzling special effects. But right in the thick of the action, the credits rolled, leaving a host of unanswered questions, unresolved issues and, even worse, Han Solo encased in carbonite and carried off to some distant planet. While a brilliant ploy on the filmmaker's part, guaranteed to have audiences scuttling to the next instalment, Pete was incensed at the cliff-hanger ending. So much so that he sat right through the credits till the curtains closed, convinced that it was a trick and that there would be a little segment at the end. He hated that the story was "to be continued" and that he would have to wait years to find out what happened next.

While the four accounts about Jesus in the New Testament have a sense of completion within themselves, they too have a touch of the *Empire Strikes Back* – style cliff-hanger about them. Because in many respects, Jesus' resurrection is not the *end* of the story but the ***beginning***. After Jesus came back and spent time with some of his followers, a huge transformation occurred as the news about him spread from a handful of people along the roads and towns, across borders and seas, and through the centuries, shaping and defining world history and culture along the way. Today, Jesus' billions of followers amount to the single largest community of believers in the world.

This growth of the Jesus movement – **Christianity** – over the past two thousand years is a huge and complex minefield of history, politics, religion, culture and geography, worthy of thousands of fascinating books, and is certainly something we would not venture to do justice to here. Nevertheless, it is good to know a little of "what happened next".

Fortunately for us, the Bible supplies us with a sequel to the Gospels, and you don't have to wait years to get it![*]

The book of Acts[**] was written by the gospel writer Luke. Although it is part 2 of his account about Jesus, it functions as the sequel to all four gospels. It's where we get much of our information about the first three decades after Jesus' resurrection. Its twenty-eight chapters give us front-row seats to an incredible era in world history. Luke narrates the dramatic birth of Christianity as it muscled its way out of the cradle of the small province of Judea to eventually reach much of the Roman Empire.

[*] Unlike the interminable wait for *Return of the Jedi*.   – Pete

Stop your grumbling! Time to move on!   – Ben

[**] Full title: The Acts of the Apostles.

Aside from the historical perspective, Acts is also simply a great read in the tradition of classic action tales! It could well be titled the Adventures of the Apostles. There are martyrdoms, prison breakouts, angry mobs, and shipwrecks. There are stories of miracles, sorcery, witchcraft, court cases and a good deal of travelling that always keeps the narrative moving. If Warner Brothers wanted to turn Acts into a blockbuster, they'd find it hard to classify, because there's action, drama, adventure, suspense, horror and even comedy.

But in addition to the acts – or adventures – of the apostles,* the book also tells us more about Jesus. It begins with a couple of important discussions Jesus had with his disciples after his resurrection. At some stage during a meal with his followers, Jesus commanded them not leave Jerusalem but to wait for a gift, not a gift in wrapping paper and bow but the gift of God's presence with them, the gift of the Holy Spirit.[1] Like their countrymen, the disciples were waiting and hoping for deliverance from foreign rule. So a short time later, either during the meal or over the next few days, the disciples asked him, "Lord, are you at this time going to restore the kingdom to Israel?"[2]

And Jesus replied, "It is not for you to know the times or dates the Father has set by his own authority. But you will receive power when the Holy Spirit comes on you; and you will be my witnesses in Jerusalem, and in all Judea and Samaria, and to the ends of the earth."

Then Luke, in surprisingly minimalistic fashion, simply tells us, "After he said this, he was taken up before their very eyes, and a cloud hid him from their sight. They were looking intently up into the sky as he was going, when suddenly two men dressed in white stood beside them. 'Men of Galilee,' they said, 'why do you stand here looking into the sky? This same Jesus, who has been taken from you into heaven, will come back in the same way you have seen him go into heaven.'"[3]

It has often been said that in many ways these opening verses act like a table of contents for the rest of the book of Acts (and, we might add, the rest of church history) because they list four crucial events:

- **Jesus' Ascension**** into heaven after his resurrection appearances
- **Jesus' Spirit** coming on his followers in power
- **Jesus' Witnesses** as they proclaim the gospel and grow in number
- **Jesus' Return** at the end of time

Let's have a look at each of these in turn.

---

1. Acts 1:4–5; Luke 24:49.
2. Acts 1:6–8.
3. Acts 1:9–11.

## Jesus' Ascension

Luke is the only New Testament writer to tell us in any detail what happened to Jesus after his resurrection appearances and to describe his ascension.[4]

Admittedly, the ascension seems a little weird at first. Jesus was simply "taken up" in the presence of a few privileged followers and disappeared in "a cloud", provoking images of his being whisked away in some invisible elevator. Yet given everything Jesus had said and done, it should come as no surprise to us. It was the final confirmation of his status as the divine servant of God and was the beginning (or as theologians like to say "the inauguration") of his place as God's chosen king. So it was in some ways like a crowning ceremony. In the Olympics, for example, a winning athlete is "crowned" champion with a gold medal after their victory on the track. Likewise, Jesus had conquered sin and death in his resurrection, and forty days later he took his place on the podium at the right hand of the Father, where he was officially crowned Lord of Lords. The ascension marked the end of an era but also the beginning of a new one.

> The ascension marked the end of an era but also the beginning of a new one.

## Jesus' Spirit

The second major event after Jesus' resurrection was the arrival of the Holy Spirit on his followers.[5] The Holy Spirit is intimately linked with God the Father and Jesus the Son. The three are, of course, collectively known as the Trinity, with Jesus as the second person of the single three-personed God: *Father, Son and Spirit.* And it is through the Holy Spirit that God lives and rules amongst his followers today.

On several occasions recorded in the Old Testament, God promised that he would one day dwell with humankind in a new and special way. Several of the Old Testament prophets had prophesied about this in various ways.* So many Jews looked forward with great anticipation to this new era when God would pour out his Spirit on all his people in a significant way.**

Jesus also had predicted this. One of his final commands to his followers was to wait in Jerusalem for the outpouring of the Holy Spirit.[6] This day came in dramatic fashion shortly after Jesus' ascension. While huddled together in a rented room in Jerusalem, the remaining followers of Jesus (around 120 people) were suddenly overcome with a supernatural outpouring of the Spirit of God. Luke writes that a huge noise like a tornado came through the room accompanied by supernatural flames of fire. What a spectacle! Each person in the room was filled with the Spirit and began speaking in multiple languages (or "tongues").

* Isaiah, Ezekiel and Joel, amongst others.
** Different sects within first-century Judaism differed considerably on how and when these things would come about, but all looked forward to a new era when the Spirit would be "poured out".

---

4. Luke 24:50–51; Acts 1:9.
5. Acts 2.
6. Luke 24:49.

It caused such a disturbance that thousands of people – including many pilgrims visiting from around the empire and beyond – gathered around the building to see what was going on. When they arrived, they heard people speaking in just about every known language of the day. Luke lists for us sixteen cities or regions of those present, each of which had their own languages and dialects. (This is highly significant. Thousands of years before this event, humankind had collectively shunned God by building the infamous city and tower of Babel.[7] It was a monument to pride and a symbol of man's rebellion. In response, God confused humankind by muddling up their languages and destroying their ability for combined rebellion, to such an extent that communication became impossible and they all departed from one another. The outpouring of God's Spirit on the followers of Jesus was in some ways a reversal of the events of Babel and the start of a new era. A renewed harmonious community of people from all sorts of nations and backgrounds was beginning to emerge.)

Understandably, much of the crowd stood in amazement as this largely Galilean group spoke in multiple foreign languages. But some failed to see the moment for what it was and attributed the commotion to drunkenness.

With the crowd looking for an explanation, the apostle Peter stood up with renewed confidence and began to address the sea of onlookers in what we could probably label as the first Christian sermon. He immediately dismissed alcohol as the source of what was happening (after all, it was only nine o'clock in the morning) and quoted from the scriptures:

> "Fellow Jews and all of you who live in Jerusalem, let me explain this to you; listen carefully to what I say. These people are not drunk, as you suppose. It's only nine in the morning! No, this is what was spoken by the prophet Joel:
>
>> "'In the last days, God says,
>>     I will pour out my Spirit on all people.
>> Your sons and daughters will prophesy,
>>     your young men will see visions,
>>     your old men will dream dreams.
>> Even on my servants, both men and women,
>>     I will pour out my Spirit in those days,
>>     and they will prophesy....
>> And everyone who calls
>>     on the name of the Lord will be saved.'"[8]

Peter could have used a number of other Old Testament passages, but he chose this one. In doing so, he was claiming that the time that Joel had predicted over hundreds of years before had now finally arrived and all pres-

"And everyone who calls on the name of the Lord will be saved."

---

7. Genesis 11.
8. Acts 2:14 – 18, 21.

ent were witnesses to this event. This, therefore, was an important day. It was the beginning of a new era in the way God dealt with his people and how his people would deal with him.

Significantly, all of this happened during an annual agricultural festival celebrating the coming of a new harvest. Hence it was also called the Day of Firstfruits, or the Feast of Harvest. More specifically, it happened on the fiftieth day after the Sabbath of Passover, commonly known as the day of Pentecost.* Integral to the festivities was an offering to God in the temple of new bread baked from the grain of the new harvest. It was a glorious celebration of God's providence that a new day had arrived and the fruit from the harvest had come.

About two months prior to the events of Pentecost, Jesus had already reinterpreted the Passover meal with a new meal – the Lord's Supper. Now Pentecost was about to have the same redefining spin. If Pentecost was all about a new harvest and the provision of food, so the coming of the Spirit at this time reinvented Pentecost as the arrival of the new fruit of God's harvest coming upon humankind through the Spirit.

Peter concluded his address with a call to faith and repentance, warning and pleading with the huge audience to "repent and be baptized, every one of you, in the name of Jesus Christ for the forgiveness of your sins."[9] The impact on the masses was immediate and powerful. During his lifetime, Jesus was a powerful orator who had an impact on people. Now the baton was passed to Jesus' apostles. Luke records that about three thousand people on that day repented and became followers of Jesus.

## Jesus' Witnesses: The Good, the Bad and the Ugly

### The Good

The result of Pentecost was a new community of believers that Jesus referred to as "his witnesses": those people who were, or came to be, his committed followers. Only later were they labelled as Christians** and, collectively, as the church. We tend to use the word *church* today to describe a certain building, more often than not with a steeple, stained glass and hard wooden pews.*** But the term was originally used to describe a community of people, and Luke describes for us in some detail what the first "church" was like.

With God's Spirit now supernaturally living in and amongst his people, and armed with the understanding that Jesus had conquered sin and death, there was a new sense of community and zeal amongst the first believers. Luke tells us that they all eagerly devoted themselves to the teachings of the apostles as they learned more about Jesus and the significance of his death

* Pentecost was the second of Israel's national festivals and took place a full seven weeks or fifty days after the Passover festival. In fact, the word Pentecost means "fiftieth". It is also called the Feast of Weeks.

** Incidentally, it was pagans who first labelled the followers of Jesus as Christians.

*** And a notice board out the front bearing whacky and thought-provoking quotations!
– Pete

9. Acts 2:38.

There was a new sense of community and zeal amongst the first believers.

and resurrection. They began living in the way Jesus had taught, and they were highly charitable to one another, sharing their possessions and dining together in their homes.

This beautiful picture of the Christian community of friendship and fellowship of the first church is a great reminder of what a church should be like. As the decades rolled on and Christians began to move out of Jerusalem to the surrounding regions and beyond, Christians caused a stir with their lifestyle, gaining a reputation for their charity, compassion, honesty, passiveness and love. The Christians soon became a noticeable group and a social phenomenon across all strata of society right to the very top. Writing shortly after the turn of the first century, Roman Governor Pliny wrote to Emperor Trajan about Christians, wondering why they should be arrested and put to death, saying, "They meet regularly before dawn on a fixed day to chant verses alternately among themselves in honor of Christ as if to a god, and also to bind themselves by oath, not for any criminal purpose, but to abstain from theft, robbery and adultery, to commit no breach of trust and not to refuse to return a deposit upon demand. After this ceremony it had been their custom to disperse and later to take food of an ordinary harmless kind."[10]

And several centuries later, Emperor Julian wrote, "These impious Galileans [Christians] not only feed their own poor, but ours also; welcoming them into their agapae [love], they attract them, as children are attracted, with cakes.... Whilst the pagan priests neglect the poor, the hated Galileans devote themselves to works of charity.... Such practice is common among them, and causes a contempt for our gods."[11]

With the growing community came a growing structure. Various leaders or elders were appointed to oversee the different groups or "churches". Men and women were appointed a variety of tasks and roles by the apostles as the churches began to accumulate more members and become more structured. With their bishops, priests, elders, ministers, treasurers and pastoral workers, the foundation was being laid for the structure of our modern churches.

As time passed, the stories and teachings of Jesus and the apostles began to circulate between the first Christians in the form of various creeds and early church hymns. For a while, it seems, these traditions were simply passed around orally (as was the custom of the ancient world), but it soon became clear that to discern fact from fiction, and to engender a sense of unity, Christians needed to write these things down. This is the origin of the four gospels

10. Tacitus, *Annales* XV.44.

11. Emperor Julian, *Letter 22, To Arcacius, High Priest of Galatia,* in *The Works of the Emperor Julian,* vol. 2, Loeb Classical Library 157, 67–73.

of the New Testament, which were written some thirty years or more after the events themselves.[12]

Similarly, Christians in various parts of the empire desired and needed teaching about how to live and be a follower of Jesus. The apostles often wrote letters to churches or individual church leaders to encourage and instruct them on a whole variety of issues. It is these letters, which we refer to as epistles, that make up the rest of the New Testament. Hence Paul's letter to the Romans was most likely addressed to a number of different house churches in Rome. Likewise, his letters to Timothy were letters of instruction to a leader of churches named – no prizes for correct guesses here – Timothy!

Other Christians began to write as well, but their writings were not included in what we now call the New Testament because, unlike the apostles, they were not the divinely appointed ambassadors of Jesus. But collectively they give us a great insight into the thoughts, joys and struggles of the early church and the birth of Christianity.

## The Bad

Sadly, the endearing community of the first Christians that we read about in Acts 2 did not last. Christians and so-called Christians began to fight, doubt, cheat, rebel and sin against one another in numerous ways. Strange teachings began to emerge, and fierce debate raged, most notably over the status of Jewish Christians versus Gentile Christians. In some ways, we could say that Jesus died to put the church in the world, but the apostles died to keep it there. It is no minor miracle that the church survived the first few tumultuous centuries. As a result, many of the letters in the New Testament were written in response to various heresies, debates, conflicts, ethical issues and moral problems going on within and amongst the churches of the time.

## The Ugly

The Greek word which we sometimes translate as "witness" is *marturion*, from which we get the word *martyr*. As Christians began to proclaim their message and hold firmly to their beliefs, many began to be persecuted and even to be famously martyred for their faith.

This should not surprise us. As we have already said, the message of Jesus was incredibly controversial in the first century, particularly to an Orthodox Jew. The claim that a contemporary crucified carpenter from Nazareth was the Christ, and that both Jews and Gentiles shared equal status in God's kingdom, was considered not only to be a bizarre concept but blasphemy of the worst kind. Little wonder that most of the opposition to Christians of the first century came from the Jews.

> Many of the letters in the New Testament were written in response to various heresies, debates, conflicts, ethical issues and moral problems going on amongst the churches of the time.

---

12. See Luke 1:1–4.

The book of Acts confirms this as it records much of the persecution that went on in the middle decades of the first century. In Acts 7 we read of Stephen, who is widely regarded as the first Christian martyr. Luke describes Stephen's final hours as he was brought before the Jewish authorities and responded by unashamedly accusing them of rebelling against God. As a result, he was taken away and stoned for his belief.

However, the book of Acts largely concentrates on the apostle Paul and his companions as they travelled around the Roman Empire suffering all kinds of persecutions at the hands of the Jews. In some ways, the apostle Paul was like Frodo and company, travelling around what we could geographically call, even today, Middle Earth, as they made their way around the empire preaching the message of Jesus and facing various trials and near-death experiences. Eventually, a few of them came climactically not to Mount Doom but to Rome.

Paul was originally a Pharisee who persecuted Christians, even overseeing the death of Stephen. But after encountering Jesus in what seems to have been his final post-resurrection appearance, Paul was dramatically converted. With the shoe metaphorically on the other foot, he then, ironically, became the object of much persecution himself as he travelled from town to town preaching the good news about Jesus.

On several occasions, he and his companions were chased out of town by angry mobs, narrowly escaping with their lives. On other occasions, he was thrown into prison, and in the Roman city of Philippi he was "severely flogged" for the implications of his faith.[13]

As Christians grew in numbers and in reputation, Romans began to persecute them as well. Much has been written about the persecution of the early Christians in the first three centuries, and it is fair to say that while some of it is accurate, some unfortunately stretches the truth. In some parts of the empire, Christians actually enjoyed relative freedom from persecution for many decades. But during the first three centuries, many Christians were heavily persecuted for their faith in various ways at various times.

Christians were abused verbally, refused privileges, and lost real estate and their jobs. Others did not get off so lightly. They were stoned, beaten, whipped, crucified and famously used as sport in Roman arenas, such as the Colosseum in Rome. According to some sources, all the apostles but John were martyred for their faith. Paul, for example, was beheaded, James (Jesus' brother) was stoned to death and Peter was apparently crucified upside down.

In some areas, the reputation and mystique of Christians reached hysterical and bizarre proportions. Some early Christians were accused of being cannibals, incestuous and even atheists. They were labelled as cannibals because

During the first three centuries, many Christians were heavily persecuted for their faith in various ways at various times.

13. Acts 16:23 NIV.

it was rumoured that they ate real flesh and drank real blood when they took part in the Lord's Supper. They were labelled incestuous because they called each other "brother" or "sister" and greeted one another with a kiss. But most surprisingly, they were considered atheists. This is because they failed to believe in and recognize Roman gods and worship the emperor. This was no small matter. In doing so, it was thought that they were alienating the goodwill of the gods and endangering what the Romans called the *pax deorum* (the right harmonious relationship between gods and men).* As a result, the Romans were naturally concerned that the gods would vent their wrath not only upon the Christians but also upon their town or city or even the the whole empire.

And when disasters did occur, they were only too likely to blame the Christians.[14] Tertullian, the great Christian writer of the late second and early third centuries, sums it all up: The pagans, he said, "suppose that the Christians are the cause of every public disaster, every misfortune that happens to the people. If the Tiber overflows or the Nile doesn't, if there is a drought or an earthquake, a famine or a pestilence, at once the cry goes up, 'The Christians to the lions.'"[15]

For this reason, the fate most usually reserved for them was ignominious. Regarded as conspirators capable of every crime "against the human race" and as being dangerous to the state, there was no hesitation in applying to them a punishment originally reserved for soldiers who had deserted to the enemy.[16]

One of the most famous recorded instances of the persecution of Christians comes from the writings of the Roman writer Tacitus. Tacitus was born sometime during the fifties of the first century and lived well into the second. Much of our understanding of imperial Roman politics comes from the writings of Tacitus. In AD 64, a huge fire broke out in the city of Rome that raged for several days, destroying much of the city and killing thousands. Many blamed the Emperor Nero for the disaster, but according to Tacitus, Nero unfairly blamed the Christians and had them punished accordingly. Tacitus writes:

> Consequently, to get rid of the report, Nero fastened the guilt and inflicted the most exquisite tortures on a class hated for their abominations, called Christians by the populace. Christus, from whom the name had its origin, suffered the extreme penalty during the reign of Tiberius at the hands of one of our procurators, Pontius Pilatus, and a most mischievous superstition, thus checked for the moment, again broke out not only in Judaea,

14. G. E. M. de Ste. Croix, "Why Were the Early Christians Persecuted?" *Past and Present* 26 (1963), 25.

15. Tertullian, *Apologeticus* IL.

16. Ronald Auguet, *Cruelty and Civilization: The Roman Games* (London: Routledge, 1994), 97.

* Jews were exempted from participating in the state religion on account of the age of their religion and traditions; Christians, however, were not.

* Delivered, of course, in his thick Austrian accent: "Ah'll bee bahck."

the first source of the evil, but even in Rome, where all things hideous and shameful from every part of the world find their centre and become popular. Accordingly, an arrest was first made of all who pleaded guilty; then, upon their information, an immense multitude was convicted, not so much of the crime of firing the city, as of hatred against mankind. Mockery of every sort was added to their deaths. Covered with the skins of beasts, they were torn by dogs and perished, or were nailed to crosses, or were doomed to the flames and burnt, to serve as a nightly illumination, when daylight had expired.[17]

With stories like this, it becomes pretty clear that many of the first Christians suffered some of the most humiliating and terrible deaths at the hands of their persecutors. For us (Ben and Pete), it is quite sobering sitting here comfortably in the twenty-first century as we contemplate the lives and deaths of some of these early Christians, who were, after all, ordinary people – husbands, wives, brothers, sisters, mums and dads – just like us. We are mighty grateful for the witness of these courageous men and women who stood firm in their belief that Jesus is the risen Son of God. Their unbending faith is highly inspiring to Christians worldwide, especially those who still suffer in various ways because of their faith.

### Jesus' Return

With all of this in mind, it is comforting to know that a significant part of the Christian faith is hope for a future vindication. On several occasions, the apostle Paul writes that there are chiefly three dimensions to a Christian's life: faith, love and hope. And fundamental to Christian hope is that in the same way that Jesus came once, Jesus will return.

> Fundamental to Christian hope is that in the same way that Jesus came once, Jesus will return.

In the *Terminator* trilogy, the most famous line is, of course, Arnie saying, "I'll be back!"* Jesus said the same thing. Here also in Acts 1, the angels tell the disciples, "This same Jesus, who has been taken from you into heaven, will come back in the same way you have seen him go into heaven."[18]

This means that the final component to Jesus' story is yet to be played out. The curtain hasn't closed; the credits haven't begun to roll yet. There's still one more scene waiting to be shown. And it is the most climactic scene of all: Jesus is coming back.

It is referred to by the New Testament authors as simply "his coming".[19] This is very important. Jesus' so-called first coming was in some ways a preview of things to come, a window into what life is like in the kingdom of God.

It is tempting for most people these days, even amongst some of the most learned churchgoing Christians, to think of Jesus as gentle, meek, comfort-

---

17. Tacitus, *Annales* XV.44.

18. Acts 1:11.

19. 2 Thessalonians 2:8; 1 John 2:28.

able, mild and a hybrid best-buddy/saviour-of-the-world. Yet this is a very one-sided Jesus. The New Testament overwhelmingly affirms that he will come back in an awesome, cosmic display of glory, power and might to judge the world and that every eye will see him and every knee will bow at his sight. His presence will be all-encompassing and clear to all.

It is worth noting that at the beginning of Jesus' ministry when he opened the scroll handed to him in the synagogue and read from the prophet Isaiah, he stopped short of reading what was clearly a major part of his role as the Anointed One and the final judge of the world. Luke tells us that Jesus read these words from the book of Isaiah:

> The Spirit of the Lord is on me,
> because he has anointed me
> to preach good news to the poor.
> He has sent me to proclaim freedom for the prisoners
> and recovery of sight for the blind,
> to release the oppressed . . .[20]

Yet Jesus didn't read the next line:

> and the day of vengeance of our God.

That's because his role as judge was yet to come. The "day of vengeance" was part of his second coming, not his first. This is what the disciples had in mind when they asked Jesus whether he was going restore the kingdom at this time.[21] Jesus replied, "It is not for you to know the times or dates the Father has set by his own authority."[22] It is a future event, reserved for an undisclosed time.

As a couple of Christian blokes, we are deeply committed to the idea that Jesus was a real figure in history who lived and died, taking the full responsibility of our sinful actions upon himself. He consequently suffered the full weight of God's wrath on his shoulders in our place. And in this, the words of the apostle Peter all those years ago are as relevant to us now as to the crowd assembled in front of him back then. It is a message that has echoed through the centuries: "Repent and be baptized, every one of you, in the name of Jesus Christ for the forgiveness of your sins. And you will receive the gift of the Holy Spirit. The promise is for you and your children and for all who are far off – for all whom the Lord our God will call."[23]

"Repent and be baptized, every one of you, in the name of Jesus Christ for the forgiveness of your sins."

---

20. Luke 4:18 (Isaiah 61:1) NIV.
21. Acts 1:6.
22. Acts 1:7.
23. Acts 2:38–39.

When Pete was about twelve years old, he joined the Scouts.

He had become interested in camping and adventure, so he joined a local troop and bought a Scout uniform, complete with cap, long khaki socks, a leather woggle* and an assortment of belt-dangling accoutrements. He started turning up to Scout meetings once a week, there to hang out with other Scouts and learn how to Be Prepared and do stuff like wrap up a broken wrist, cook mulligatawny soup in the coals of a fire and tie a sheep shank, which would presumably be invaluable should he ever need to detain a sheep. After a while, he was officially initiated into the troop, which involved his declaring his loyalty to Scouting, proclaiming Baden Powell as Master of the Universe, promising Akela to do his best and pack-pack-pack and dyb and dob and howl at the moon. (There was also an unofficial initiation ceremony that took place later that night at the sadistic hands of some of the older boys, but the less said about that, the better.) Peter threw himself into Scouting with gusto, going on camps, getting his woodsman badges and patrol leader stripes, and generally eating a lot of soup.

Of course, if you're a Scout and you are up to your neck in Scouting, then all of these things make sense. But, with no offence intended to our khaki brothers and sisters, to people outside of Scouting, some of the jargon and rituals can seem somewhat obscure and detached from the real world.

Just like Christianity, really.

Let's be honest. To many people, following Jesus is bound up in a whole lot of baggage, ritual, jargon, customs and traditions that are off-putting and confusing and detached from the rest of real life. The perception is that Christians go to an old stone building with stained glass and hard wooden pews once a week, there to read from ancient prayer books, sing along with an organ and be lectured in a monotonous drone by someone wearing a white gown. Or at the other end of the spectrum, they go to some modern glassy auditorium filled with plastically coiffured people with fake teeth, there to sing inanely happy songs and clap their hands and be sold CD series about pathways to success. On top of that, followers of Jesus talk in their own language about strange things like being washed in the blood of the Lamb, saved, set free and born again. They talk about the sinner's prayer, the power of Calvary, redemption, supplication, the work of the cross, sanctification, justification, and how the glorious light of God's redeeming grace can wipe your slate clean and make your heart new. It may as well be a dialect of Martian. (When we

** Hey Pete, what's a woogle? — Ben

First, it's a woggle, not a woogle, and second, it's a thick ring used to tie the Scout neckerchief. Dyb Dyb Dyb! — Pete

197

were researching this chapter, we came across a website that claimed to explain what it means to be a Christian. It was over eight thousand words of long technical explanations of vaguely connected Bible passages held together by pseudospiritual religio-gobbledygook that was tragically incomprehensible, even to us!)

The unfortunate result is that it's easy to lose sight of the forest for the trees. Jesus and his message can be lost amongst all the cultural and religious baggage that now surrounds him. So is it possible for us to actually hack our way through that forest and get back to what Jesus was on about?

When Jesus was wandering around the eastern Mediterranean, teaching and healing, he wasn't just providing entertainment or giving listeners a quick feel-good buzz. And when he spoke in synagogues and on hillsides and with people in village squares and when he recruited his disciples, he didn't distribute checklists of hoops to jump through. He didn't say, "If you want to follow me, then you should do a year's Bible school, attend church for at least two hours each weekend, read ten chapters of scripture every night, pray for an hour before sunup, dress conservatively, don't stay up late, burn candles, memorise all the names of the books of the Bible, go into the desert for forty days, have a picture of me on your wall, wear a crucifix around your neck, listen only to gospel music, fill in this ten-page questionnaire, donate three pieces of silver each week and write an essay on your understanding of the role of grace in the process of salvation, and I'll have a think about it."

Indeed, Jesus' dealings with people were surprisingly simple. Here it comes, basic and beautiful: he said to the disciples, "Follow me."

As Jesus' popularity increased, people began to follow him around the region, traipsing over the countryside and turning up wherever he went. But more than that, even after they went back to their homes, people followed him in terms of the way they thought and behaved and treated others. They started living "the Jesus way" and acknowledged that he was the means by which they could cross the physical-spiritual divide and be in relationship with God. Jesus spoke to and taught people from all walks of life – Romans, Pharisees, Samaritans, teachers, tax collectors, the outcast, the wealthy, the powerful, the sick, the downtrodden. (To translate into today's terms, he would speak to politicians, generals, rock stars, corrupt police, prostitutes, AIDS patients, parents, hippies, CEOs and the homeless.) But no matter who they were, he wanted to have an impact on their lives and the way they lived. *He wanted people to change.* He wanted people to live their lives in a way that honoured God and showed respect and love for other people.

His final words to his disciples were, "Go and make disciples of all nations, baptizing them in the name of the Father and of the Son and of

> Jesus and his message can be lost amongst all the cultural and religious baggage that now surrounds him.

the Holy Spirit, and teaching them to obey everything I have commanded you."[1]

And that's what happened.

After Jesus' death, these "followers of the Way", as they were first called, massively increased in number, despite incredible hostility and persecution. Many of the first followers of the Christ were, of course, Jews, but increasingly they came to be known by the designation *Christ-ians*. Fast-forward through two thousand years of exponential growth and we end up with these Christians and their Christ-movement – *Christ-ianity* – being a massive social phenomenon and, despite incredible diversity, the largest and most international body of people on the planet. Despite the years that have passed, people in their billions today still make a decision to "follow the Christ".

Which really brings us to the point.

*What does it mean to follow Christ in our incredibly diverse, rapidly changing, complex and troubled world?* Yep, Jesus may have walked and talked and done amazing things two thousand years ago, but the question is, *So what?* What has that got to do with me today?

Life can be difficult, especially in our modern world. It's easy to feel a bit like a cork bobbing on the ocean, blown recklessly this way and that, all the time wondering what it's all about, who am I, where am I going and how do I get there? Jesus said to people then as he says to people today, *I have the answer. This is the way to live. You want to have a good life? Build your house on the rock. Listen to what I say. I am the way, the truth and the life. Follow me.*

So, while not wanting to be like the eight-thousand-word religio-gobbledygook website, here are a few thoughts about what being a follower of Jesus means today.

Jesus told people to **repent.** This means that we reflect upon our lives and realise that while we might essentially be pretty decent people, there are still a few cracks in the fuselage. We need to acknowledge that we don't have it all together, that we have ignored God and aren't really living in the right way, and that it's time for us to let him be in charge. Jesus constantly told people to take a stand and turn away from dud ways of living. He said that the way to live is to show love and compassion to others. He spoke out against hypocrisy, pretension, selfishness and legalism. And he pulled no punches when it came to matters of everyday living.

Some years later, the writer Paul[2] chipped in by saying that followers of Jesus should stop being selfish boneheads* who indulge in sexual immorality, impurity and debauchery; idolatry and witchcraft; hatred, discord, jealousy, fits of rage, selfish ambition, dissensions, factions and envy; drunkenness, orgies and the like. Instead, our lives should have a bit more class and cool,

> We need to acknowledge that we don't have it all together, that we have ignored God and aren't really living in the right way, and that it's time for us to let him be in charge.

> * Our words, not his!
> – Pete

---

1. Matthew 28:19–20.
2. Galatians 5:19–26.

allowing love, joy, peace, patience, kindness, goodness, faithfulness, gentleness and self-control to be our guiding principles, not in some la-la, hippy, wishy-washy, goody-goody kind of way but in a genuine, balanced, healthy and authentic life that helps other people.

This is all well and good, but the obvious flaw in the plan is that Jesus isn't around anymore. We can't sit at his feet like his disciples did, so how are we to know what Jesus taught and did?

Glad you asked.

The answer (probably self-evident) lies in the **Bible.**\*

Unfortunately, some people hold a misconception that the Bible is little more than lists of thou-shalt-nots, strange fables about whales, giants and floods, and long-winded passages of unfathomable architectural details and genealogies. (This view is typified by *The Simpsons*' Rev Lovejoy with his unengaging and bland delivery: "And the reading from the book of Numbers says, 'These are the names of the men who are to assist you: from Reuben, Elizur son of Sheduer; from Simeon, Shelumiel son of Zurishaddai; from Judah, Nahshon son of Amminadab; from Issachar …'") Billions of people over the years have discovered that the Bible has a lot more to offer than that. If you want to learn about Jesus, the best starting point is to read the New Testament.

The Bible is the biggest-selling and most widely read book of all time, with good reason. It is a detailed history of God's relationship with humankind, especially through the history of the Israelite nation. In particular, it is in the Bible that we read the four accounts of Jesus' life in the Gospels\*\* written by Matthew, Mark, Luke and John; it is here that we read about the events of Jesus' birth, life, death and resurrection; it is here that we read about his teachings and zero in on his conversations and interactions with people. In addition, in the book of Acts, we can read the sequel to Luke's account of Jesus' life, which narrates the adventures and activities of the disciples as they took the message of Jesus out into the world. The rest of the New Testament is similarly beneficial, for it is here that we can read the letters that circulated amongst the first Christians as they banded together to learn and struggle with the very real issues of what it means to follow Jesus.

People with a common interest or lifestyle tend to band together. Whether it's vintage cars or stamp collecting, soccer or football, model trains or lawn bowls, medieval battle tactics or even just going to the corner pub to have an ale with the regulars, people are social beings who like to share communal experience.

Jesus' first followers similarly began to **meet together** – in each other's houses – to talk and share a meal together, support each other, pray, organize activities, raise funds for people in need and to learn about Jesus. These early gatherings grew, and soon they began to build their own meeting places. Today we call these buildings "churches".\*\*\*

\* The Bible can be a pretty daunting book. If only there was a good book to help people read it. — Ben

How about *Everything You Want to Know about the Bible* by Pete Downey and Ben Shaw? — Pete

Good call! — Ben

\*\* Gospel means "good news".
\*\*\* This title is actually something of a misnomer. A church is not really a building of bricks, mortar and glass. Church actually refers to the people who meet and belong there.

If you want to follow Jesus, a good way to learn about him and to be encouraged is to meet up with others who are doing the same. The stereotypical picture of a church is the classic brick building with a steeple and stained glass, although churches are actually so much more diverse than that. Some churches meet in lounge rooms or pubs or community halls or coffee shops, while others meet under a tree or in a park. Some churches have ten-thousand-seat auditoriums with huge light rigs and multimedia presentations, while others meet in cathedrals. Many churches today also are involved in community life, perhaps housing a library, coffee shop, child-minding, school, afternoon ballet or even television studios.

Meeting up with others like this (or "going to church") is not some legalistic requirement or ritualistic chore. Church is not a place where you go along out of duty, as if to clock up some spiritual brownie points. In fact, church is not an event you go to as much as a group to which you have a sense of belonging. Church should be a special and familiar place, an attractive and warm community where you can join together and be known and encouraged and supported, and do the same for others.

In his dealings with people, Jesus never concluded with the words, "Now go, and make sure you attend synagogue three times a week," or, "From this day forth, you must pray for an hour before the rising of the sun." If anything, Jesus tended not to get caught up too much in mindless subservience to rules or the flagrant carry-on of some religious types and their various ceremonies and rituals.

However, Jesus didn't isolate himself from community life. He participated in the religious life, activities and customs of his community. As a baby, Jesus was circumcised, named and blessed in the traditional manner. Growing up, he travelled with his family to Jerusalem to celebrate Passover. As a young man, he attended synagogue and joined with other Jews to worship, pray and read and interpret scripture. He was baptised by John in the Jordan River. He and his disciples sang hymns together and they participated in the rituals associated with the Passover meal.

One of the things that Jesus always did was **pray.**

He spent a great deal of time talking to God, especially at critical times in his life. He saw it as just part of every day.

For some, prayer means being in a church on your knees with your eyes shut and hands clasped together (or, depending on the practices of the church, standing with arms up in the air and head thrown back!), more often than not intoning some quasi-holy jargon: "Our great and mighty king and redeemer, we beseech thee to look down upon our miserableness from your majesterial throne, and grant that you might forge in our hearts a sense of your amazing grace."

Not so. Prayer, pure and simple, is talking to God, not just about "religious things" but about everything. Jesus' approach was pretty

If you want to follow Jesus, a good way to learn about him and to be encouraged is to meet up with others who are doing the same.

no-nonsense. He explained to some of his friends on one occasion, "When you pray, do not be like the hypocrites, for they love to pray standing in the synagogues and on the street corners to be seen by others. . . . But when you pray, go into your room, close the door and pray to your Father, who is unseen."[3]

In speaking to his friends, Jesus also taught *us* how to pray, in words that have echoed through history: "This, then, is how you should pray: 'Our Father in heaven, hallowed be your name, your kingdom come, your will be done, on earth as it is in heaven. Give us today our daily bread. And forgive us our debts, as we also have forgiven our debtors. And lead us not into temptation, but deliver us from the evil one.'"[4]

> As followers of Jesus today, we also should endeavour to connect with God by talking to him.

To Jesus, connecting with God through prayer was just a part of everyday existence. As followers of Jesus today, we also should endeavour to connect with God by talking to him. Out loud. Silently. It doesn't matter. Acknowledge God as being in charge of your life. Seek forgiveness for those parts of your life that have not gone right. Ask him to intervene in your affairs and to help you with things that are on your mind. Talk to him about your concerns. Thank him for the good things in your life. As Jesus said, you don't need to babble on or be pompous. There is no special code.

Simply take a breath and talk. It's as simple as that.

In some respects, asking the question, What does it mean to follow Jesus today? is simultaneously simple and complex. People who encountered Jesus followed him after a few words and moments in his presence. At the same time, people today who have followed Jesus for fifty years are still discovering things about him. And about themselves.

We – Pete and Ben – both decided as teenagers over twenty years ago to follow Jesus. We didn't know everything then,* we didn't have it all sorted out, we didn't have all the answers and we didn't even know very much. But there was something about Jesus – who he is and what he said and what he did – that drew us in and made sense. Becoming followers of Jesus – Christians – changed the course of our lives.

This book is in no way exhaustive. There are thousands of weighty books about being a follower of Jesus on subjects like prayer, giving, church life, the Bible, relationships, personal integrity, family life, and heaven, as well as Jesus' life, parables, miracles, teachings, death and resurrection – the list goes on and on and on.

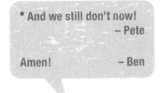

* And we still don't now!
— Pete

Amen!        – Ben

---

3. Matthew 6:5–6.
4. Matthew 6:9–13.

All we've done is scratch the surface. But hopefully in some way this book has helped you see this central figure of history in a new way.

This is not the final word about Jesus, but as the title of this book suggests, hopefully it is enough to get you started.

# STUFF AT THE BACK

You've just read a book about Jesus. We've written a lot about him – who he was, where he lived, what he said, what he did. But given that he lived twenty centuries ago, how do we know all this? Glad you asked.

Imagine for a moment that you are going to write a book on Elvis. Hmm … immediate problem … he is not alive.* So the first thing to do would be some research. For someone like Elvis, there is a panoply of sources you could investigate to gather your information: other biographies, journals, newspaper and magazine articles, photographs, websites, movies and, of course, his albums. To add to this, you could go to Memphis and visit Graceland or Sun Studios to get a firsthand experience of the places where Elvis grew up and worked. Then you could interview people who knew him personally, such as members of his family, close friends or his musical peers. Then, once you amassed all of your sources and read, watched and listened to everything you'd collected, you could put the pieces together and pen your book.

So what sources do we have that can tell us things about Jesus? Well, as for anyone from ancient history, the sources aren't as plentiful and diverse as for someone of the modern era. There are, of course, no photos of Jesus, no audio recordings of his sermons, no newspaper articles from the time or people who are still alive who knew him. Yet there are a number of sources that help us understand who he was and what he was all about.

We can put these sources on Jesus into five main categories: Christian sources, non-Christian sources, the Old Testament, indirect sources, and archaeology.

> * What? No! He flips burgers in a shop just down the road from me!  – Pete
>
> That's not possible. Everyone knows he works in a London laundromat.
> – Ben

> So what sources do we have that can tell us things about Jesus?

## 1. Christian Sources

Most of our information about Jesus comes from the accounts written about him – the Gospels – which appear in the New Testament. The word *gospel* is the translation of a Greek word that simply means "good news" or "news of importance". A modern equivalent might be something like "news flash!" It was a term used throughout the Roman Empire in the first century to describe the oral announcement of a significant event like a victory in battle or the birth of an emperor or the day of an emperor's ascension to the throne of Rome. Christians adopted this word to describe the events surrounding Jesus. So the phrase "the gospel of Jesus Christ" means "the good news about Jesus Christ".

\* There is some debate over the exact dates for when the Gospels were written. We've chosen the dates that are the consensus in mainstream scholarship.

There are four gospels in the New Testament, each named after their author – Matthew, Mark, Luke and John. These authors were amongst the first Christians living in the first century. In fact, Matthew and John were two of Jesus' closest companions. Whereas Elvis had musicians working and travelling with him, Jesus had apostles. Matthew and John were in Jesus' touring band, so to speak, while Mark and Luke were close companions of the apostles.

Because they were written for different audiences and slightly different purposes, each gospel has a unique style. No account sets out to be an exhaustive biography of Jesus' life. They are highly selective in the events on which they choose to focus. But together they give us a front-row seat to the life of Jesus as they record his birth, ministry, sayings, parables, debates, miracles, trial, execution and resurrection. And they all present Jesus as the Son of God, the promised Messiah of the Old Testament and the great climax of God's plan of salvation for all of humankind. Let's look at each of them individually.

### The Gospel of Matthew

Matthew was a tax collector before becoming a follower and an apostle of Jesus. He wrote his account in its finished form around AD 70.\* He begins with the family record and birth of Jesus and then moves straight to when he started to preach and perform miracles in his adult life. Much of Matthew's writing records the sayings and sermons of Jesus, including the longest account of Jesus' most famous set of teachings, which we refer to as the Sermon on the Mount.

> It is Matthew, more than any other of the writers, who argues that Jesus is the promised Messiah of the Old Testament.

Matthew wrote his account in Greek, primarily to a Jewish reading audience, so he tailored his account in a way that would make sense to that audience and be the most meaningful for them. One of their chief concerns was the fulfilment of the Old Testament prophecies. So it is Matthew, more than any other of the writers, who presents Jesus as the promised Messiah of the Old Testament. Hence, Matthew's account has more references and allusions to the Old Testament than the other gospels. This is one of the reasons it was placed first in the New Testament so as to keep the continuity of the story of the Old Testament.

### The Gospel of Mark

Mark was not one of the twelve apostles but was a companion to some of them and a scribe to Peter. In fact, Mark's gospel may well be a dictation of the apostle Peter's sermons and stories about Jesus. His gospel was most likely the first gospel to be written, being completed around AD 60.

Unlike Matthew, Mark seems to be writing for a predominantly non-Jewish reading audience, and it's likely he had the people of Rome in mind when composing his account. For example, he explains Aramaic words and Jewish customs to them, something that would be unnecessary for the Jewish reader. At the time Mark wrote his account, Christians were beginning to struggle with their faith on account of growing hostility from certain Jews and even possibly some pagan agitators. Mark's references to suffering, persecution, trials and even martyrdom may have been targeted at Christians who were being persecuted.

Skipping Jesus' birth, Mark gets straight into the thick of it, beginning his account with Jesus' baptism by John the Baptist. He doesn't narrate as many of his teachings and parables. So in this gospel there are about eighteen miracles but only five parables. In fact, it has often been called the "gospel of action" because of its emphasis on the actions of Jesus and its "fast paced" style. Mark's gospel, more than any other, presents Jesus as a humble servant who came to serve all of humankind by dying on the cross.

### The Gospel of Luke

Luke's gospel is the longest account. Luke was a doctor (physician)[1] who claims to have thoroughly researched the facts about Jesus. He begins his account by addressing it to a bloke called Theophilus – probably a person of some importance, rank or wealth – as a way of confirming the things that Theophilus has already heard about Jesus.

More than any other gospel, Luke focuses on Jesus' social work. He presents a compassionate Jesus, one who sits with the poor and marginalised. Many have labelled this the "gospel of the poor". And some of the most well-known parables – such as the parable of the prodigal son – are retold here.

Luke begins with the births of John the Baptist and Jesus, and his is the only account to record anything about Jesus as a child. Most of his account, however, is about Jesus' adult life and his death and resurrection. This gospel is heavily dominated by Jesus' geographical movements.

### The Gospel of John

The Gospel of John is significantly different from the other three. It does not have the same geographical or chronological structure found in Matthew, Mark and Luke. And it certainly has a considerably different style. Furthermore, John seems to have structured his account around a set number of miracles and key "I am" sayings of Jesus ("I am the light of the world," "I am the good shepherd," "I am the way, the truth and the life," etc).

Another unique feature of this gospel is that John has left out a few things that seem to be important in the other gospels. There is no record of Jesus' casting out a demon or his last supper with the apostles. None of Jesus'

> Mark's gospel, more than any other, presents Jesus as a humble servant who came to serve all of humankind by dying on the cross.

> More than any other gospel, Luke focuses on Jesus' social work.

---

1. Colossians 4:14.

More than any other gospel writer, John presents Jesus as God personified – the God-man.

parables are found in this gospel. However, John includes a lot of material the others don't have, like Jesus' miracle of turning water into wine and his washing the disciples' feet. More than any other gospel writer, John presents Jesus as God personified – the God-man.

### The Rest of the New Testament

To add to this, we can learn more about Jesus from other books in the New Testament. Just about all of these books were written by apostles[*] – the men Jesus commissioned to teach and write about him. From many of Paul's letters, we learn a lot about the significance of Jesus' death on the cross. From the book of Acts, we discover what happened to Jesus after the resurrection. Or we can get great insight into how to apply much of what Jesus taught in daily living from the other books in the New Testament.

### Other Christian Writings

As Christianity expanded, other people continued to write about Jesus and his teachings. However, here is where it gets a little tricky. These early church documents – which include letters, records of debates, creeds, prayers, sermons, lecture notes and even other gospels about Jesus that do not appear in the Bible (for example, the gospels of Thomas and Philip) – were not written by eyewitnesses or those close to them (despite their titles) but by Christians who lived many decades, even centuries, after Jesus. Furthermore, some of these writings even seem to contradict what is said about Jesus in the New Testament. And that means that most of these documents need to be read with some caution. In the end, little can be said about Jesus from these writings with great confidence because they were not part of the eyewitness accounts of Jesus' life. But we can at least see what some Christians in the first few centuries thought of Jesus and his teachings and how they were understood within certain groups.

## 2. Non-Christian Sources

Some cynics might suggest that Jesus is a fictional creation made up by a bunch of conspiratorial church leaders. You might be surprised, therefore, to know that Jesus pops up in other ancient writings written by people who weren't Christians. There's not a great deal about him, but that's not surprising given that he was still a relatively unknown figure in the first half of the first century. But a number of non-Christian authors refer to Jesus and confirm some of what the Gospels say about him.

### Josephus

Flavius Josephus was a Jewish scholar and historian who wrote about Jewish history, religion and politics. He was born shortly after Jesus' death and resurrection in AD 37 and died at the end of the first century. His biggest and perhaps most famous work is *The Antiquities of the Jews*. This is a massive piece of work, particularly for an age when people generally didn't write big documents.* Anyhow, even though this book is mainly about Jewish history and politics, Josephus mentions Jesus on two separate occasions.

**First** of all, in a section about Pontius Pilate, the Roman procurator of Judea, Josephus tells us:

> Now there was about this time, Jesus, a wise man, *if it be lawful to call him a man*, for he was a doer of wonderful works – a teacher of such men as receive the truth with pleasure. He drew over to him both many of the Jews, and many of the Gentiles. *He was [the] Christ*; and when Pilate, at the suggestion of the principal men amongst us, had condemned him to the cross, those that loved him at the first did not forsake him, *for he appeared to them alive again the third day, as the divine prophets had foretold these and then ten thousand other wonderful things concerning him*; and the tribe of Christians, so named from him, are not extinct at this day.[2]

**Then** a little farther on in another section of this same work, Josephus makes this passing reference to Jesus:

> But this younger Ananus, who, as we have told you already, took the high priesthood, was a bold man in his temper ... he thought he had now a proper opportunity [to exercise his authority]. Festus was now dead, and Albinus was but upon the road; so he assembled the Sanhedrin of judges, and brought before them the brother of Jesus, who was called Christ, whose name was James, and some others [or, some of his companions]; and when he had formed an accusation against them as breakers of the law, he delivered them to be stoned.[3]

### Tacitus

Cornelius Tacitus was a Roman writer and historian who lived and wrote around the same time as Josephus (AD 55 – 117). Much of our information about the Roman emperors of the first century comes from the writings of Tacitus. Tacitus tells us that when a huge fire wiped out more than half of Rome in AD 64, a rumour circulated that Emperor Nero himself lit the fire. Nero retaliated by blaming the small band of Christians in Rome and consequently had them rounded up and executed. Here Tacitus, who was also no friend of Christianity, writes of Jesus:

> Consequently, to get rid of the report, Nero fastened the guilt and inflicted the most exquisite tortures on a class hated for their abominations, called

---

2. Josephus, *Antiquities of the Jews* 18:3:3. The words in italics may have been added at a later time by Christians. Even if that is the case, Jesus is mentioned as a historical figure who performed "wonderful works", was a teacher who attracted many people and was crucified under Pontius Pilate – all of which accords with the gospel accounts.

3. Josephus, *Antiquities of the Jews* 20:9:1.

Even though this book is mainly about Jewish history and politics, Josephus mentions Jesus on two separate occasions.

* Ben has a copy of this book in his study, and even though the print is small, it's still over five hundred pages long.

We can still learn
a lot about Jesus
from early non-
Christian sources.

\* For example, Jesus and Christians are mentioned in the writings of Suetonius, Pliny the Younger, and Lucian of Samosota.

Christians by the populace. Christus, from whom the name had its origin, suffered the extreme penalty during the reign of Tiberius at the hands of one of our procurators, Pontius Pilatus, and a most mischievous superstition, thus checked for the moment, again broke out not only in Judaea, the first source of the evil, but even in Rome, where all things hideous and shameful from every part of the world find their centre and become popular.[4]

Now, to these we can add a few more quotes from other ancient writers who weren't Christians.\* But the important thing to note here is that we can still learn a lot about Jesus from early non-Christian sources. For example, we know:

- where he lived and preached.
- when he lived.
- that he was called "Christ".
- that he amassed a large multicultural following.
- that he performed miracles, or at least "wonderful works".
- that he was a teacher and a "wise man".
- that he was crucified under Pontius Pilate during the reign of Emperor Tiberius.
- that his followers claimed to have seen him risen from the dead.
- that some of his closest followers were martyred for their faith in him.

### 3. The Old Testament

The Old Testament authors had a fair amount to say about Jesus too, both directly and indirectly. Prophets like Isaiah, Ezekiel and Malachi spoke accurately about Jesus and his mission. Consider these words from Isaiah:

> He was despised and rejected by men,
> a man of sorrows, and familiar with suffering.
> Like one from whom men hide their faces
> he was despised, and we esteemed him not.
>
> Surely he took up our infirmities
> and carried our sorrows,
> yet we considered him stricken by God,
> smitten by him, and afflicted.
> But he was pierced for our transgressions,
> he was crushed for our iniquities;
> the punishment that brought us peace was upon him,
> and by his wounds we are healed.
> We all, like sheep, have gone astray,

---

4. Tacitus, *Annales* 15.44.

each of us has turned to his own way;
and the LORD has laid on him
the iniquity of us all.

He was oppressed and afflicted,
yet he did not open his mouth;
he was led like a lamb to the slaughter,
and as a sheep before her shearers is silent,
so he did not open his mouth.
By oppression and judgment he was taken away.
And who can speak of his descendants?
For he was cut off from the land of the living;
for the transgression of my people he was stricken.
He was assigned a grave with the wicked,
and with the rich in his death,
though he had done no violence,
nor was any deceit in his mouth.

Yet it was the LORD's will to crush him and cause him
to suffer,
and though the LORD makes his life a guilt offering,
he will see his offspring and prolong his days,
and the will of the LORD will prosper in his hand.
After the suffering of his soul,
he will see the light of life and be satisfied;
by his knowledge my righteous servant will justify
many,
and he will bear their iniquities.[5]

Likewise, individuals such as Adam, Noah, Joseph, Moses, Joshua, David, Elisha, Nehemiah, Daniel and others also indirectly teach us about Jesus as they took on the roles of a leader or teacher, prophet or priest, king or even saviour. On many occasions, Jesus himself pointed to the Old Testament to explain who he was to his listeners.

## 4. Indirect Sources

We can add to these three categories all of the *indirect* sources that help us understand the world Jesus lived in. We can read about Pontius Pilate, Emperor Tiberius, or the political and religious climate of the Roman Empire in the works of ancient historians like Tacitus or Suetonius. They can even shed light on certain figures of speech that the New Testament uses to describe Jesus. For example, the term *Son of God* used of Jesus in the New

> On many occasions, Jesus himself pointed to the Old Testament to explain who he was to his listeners.

---

5. Isaiah 53:3–11 NIV. To this we can add passages such as Psalm 22:14–18; Isaiah 9:6–7; 50:4–9; 61:1–2; Zechariah 9:9; 12:10.

Testament was borrowed from Roman imperial language used of the emperor before Christians applied it to Jesus.

There are also many different Jewish writings of the period (200 BC – AD 100) that have survived that can help us significantly. The Dead Sea Scrolls are a great example. They are a collection of scrolls that were discovered in a series of caves near the Dead Sea over about a nine year period in the 1940s and '50s. Their discovery is invaluable for numerous reasons, for not only are many of the scrolls that contain books of the Old Testament far older than any other manuscripts in the world but many of the scrolls also include numerous commentaries, hymns and rule books used by the Essenes, a sect within Judaism during Jesus' day. So although the scrolls don't mention Jesus, as they were mainly written before his time, they do give us tremendous insight into the beliefs and context of first-century Judaism.

## 5. Archaeology

A final and indirect source about Jesus is the archaeology of the land where he was born and where he lived. Modern Israel is the nearest thing we have to a photo album of Jesus' life. It was his Graceland, so to speak.* So archaeologists from all over the world go there in their hundreds to dig up, Indiana Jones style, the places where Jesus lived, worked and visited.

> \* In more ways than one!
> – Ben
>
> I don't get it.     – Pete

Generally, new discoveries have some eager locals suggesting, "This is the pool where Jesus probably healed the blind man!" or a frenzied press posing, "Could this have been the boat Jesus rode in?" Some people even have suggested that certain cups found may have been the ones associated with the miracle of his turning water into wine. Such suggestions are light on any archaeological or historical validity and are born more of *Indiana Jones and the Last Crusade* – style Hollywood mythology. Probably the most well-known recent discovery is of a Jewish burial bone box (an ossuary) that was found inscribed with the words "James son of Joseph, brother of Jesus". The New Testament tells us that Jesus had half-brothers and half-sisters, of which James was one. The inscription is unusual because it mentions the brother of the deceased on the box, something done only in exceptional cases when that sibling was particularly famous. While the authenticity of the ossuary itself seems to be in little doubt, the inscription has caused huge controversy and debate. Scholars remain divided over its authenticity.

The fact is that archaeologists haven't uncovered a great deal to do with Jesus directly; they haven't found the original manger or the cross, or the house he lived in as a boy, although there is apparently something of a dubious trade in "genuine Jesus artefacts" for gullible tourists. You can still walk through the city of Jerusalem and see some of the ancient ruins of Jesus' day, including parts of the temple or the city walls, various pools, roads, dwellings and public spaces. You can go to Bethlehem or the Sea of Galilee or the

Mount of Olives and get a sense of what it must have been like to live in that part of the world. You can climb the mountains and walk the roads and get a feel for the climate and landscape. This actually helps us, all these years later, to anchor our understanding of Jesus in a real place.

As we mentioned at the start of this book, one of the problems for us in the twenty-first century is that it's very easy for our perception of Jesus to slide into the fairy-tale zone. Because the extraordinary events surrounding his birth, life and death happened so long ago, and because they are so far detached from our own experiences, they can take on a whimsical sense of unreality. It's easy for Jesus to become timeless, distant and vague, like some character who lived "once upon a time in a magical kingdom".

So it's important to occasionally remind ourselves that Jesus did not emerge from the sands of time as the protagonist of some myth disconnected from the real world. Rather, he is anchored securely within the contexts of our history and geography. A range of writers – Christian, Jewish and non-Christian – wrote about his life, giving us dates and times and places and details of people and politics and religion and architecture and even the weather.

Jesus did not live "a long time ago in a galaxy far, far away" but lived about two thousand years ago amongst the hills, rivers, roads and townships of a corner of the Roman Empire on the eastern shore of the Mediterranean Sea. It is a place where you can still go today and stand under the same sky where the Son of God once stood, when he lived amongst us as a man.

Across the centuries and across the continents, Jesus has had a powerful and profound impact upon the daily lives of billions of people. He is not just some distant historical caricature or religious curiosity but a real person whose life and teachings are the central and defining feature of the lives of many in this crazy mixed-up world we call the twenty-first century.

We thought it would be a good idea to end our book by hearing from a few of them. So we asked a whole bunch of our friends and relatives of various ages and backgrounds to write a few words about what Jesus means to them.

There are a few cards, however, that we should probably lay on the table before we go on.

**Firstly,** Jesus stands on his own two feet regardless of what people think of him. The purpose of this chapter is not to somehow justify his existence or shore up Christianity on the basis of what a bunch of our mates think. We are simply trying to hint at the rich tapestry of how Jesus is impacting people today and provide a more personal note on which to conclude this book.

**Secondly,** while wanting to present a variety of responses without too much editorial interference, we admit that in the very act of inviting people to write a few words, we have been selective and therefore have framed the responses. All the words that follow come from your common garden-variety Christian. We didn't ask anyone, for example, who thinks that Jesus was simply just a nice but misunderstood victim, or who thinks that *The Da Vinci Code* is a history book, or who thinks that Jesus is a fictional creation of twelfth-century monks to subjugate the masses and promote an oppressive social order. Those guys can believe that if they want, but they'll have to publish their own books.

**Thirdly,** we are not suggesting that the following words are in any way exhaustive. They represent a minuscule snippet of a sliver of a smidgen of Christian experience. If we asked a different group of people the same question, we would no doubt get different responses. So this is in no way supposed to represent the sum of Christian experience.

Anyway, enough of that. Here's what they had to say.

### David, 82, retired brigadier

Let's face it, as one who surely is approaching the "departure lounge" of life, I can joyously cling to Jesus' unfailing promises.

Living, he loved me.
Dying, he saved me.
Buried, he carried my sins far away.
Rising, he justified freely forever.
One day he's coming: O glorious day.

### Donna, 49, mother, wife, grandmother, former weather girl and model

Jesus is like the family I never had. He is my brother, my father, my friend. He listens to me, he advises me, he tells me when I am going astray. I couldn't hear his voice for many years because my own was so loud. I missed seeing his face, because I was always more attracted by my own. Now he is becoming more and I am becoming less. Thank God.

### Doug, 43, school teacher and dad

Look, you know those people who say they "are in love with Jesus" and get all weepy-eyed over his being their King and Lord and Saviour all that? Well, I'm not one of them. I have nothing against them or their feelings. But I'm not like that. To me, Jesus' divinity has always simply been an intellectual reality rather than a feeling. I know he is the Son of God, and I believe what he said. I read his words and use them in so many different situations in my relationships, work, family and in matters of personal integrity and character. I know his death allows me to be right with God. And I am grateful for that.

### Emma, 16, school student

Jesus is my rock. He is stable, reliable and strong. I love reading the Bible and think of it as my guide to life, just like when you buy a computer, you get a manual. It's mind-blowing to think what he sacrificed for us, and it proves how much he loves us! Jesus is an awesome guy, and I'm glad I found him, aye!

### George, 84, old digger and great-granddad

We are all born in his image, and if this world is going to survive, we all must learn to love one another as Jesus loved us.

### James, 27, professional tennis player

I haven't been a Christian for that long, but some things I know are true. Sport, like life, has ups and downs, but Jesus is forever loving and supportive. He's the first person to put his arm around me after a bad performance, and the first person to congratulate me on a successful day, and I will continue to thank him daily for this. I couldn't explain the meaning of life before knowing Jesus, and I still can't today, but I feel I now know its purpose – to accept Jesus' undying love and return the favour as best I can, in accordance with the Bible. I now play with purpose ... and to an audience of one.

### Jan, 51, wife and mother

I became a Christian at the age of seventeen when I discovered that Jesus' death and resurrection were not just events in history but that he died *for me* that I might be forgiven, and that he lives and reigns as Lord of the universe. More than three decades on, I am more aware than ever that it is only by his grace that I enter, only by his grace that I stand. All my hope for this life and for eternity rests in him.

### Joan, 84, great-grandmother

I can't imagine life without the presence of our Lord's Holy Spirit. He is my guide, my inspiration and encouragement in all circumstances. Jesus' words are etched indelibly on my heart. Hallelujah.

### Josue, 31, orphan care worker

Jesus spends a lot of time among the discarded children of southwest China. Every day I see him in the smiles and tears of the kids in our Home for Orphaned and Abandoned Children. Jesus loves me so much. Caring for these children is one way that I can demonstrate my love for him.

### Matt, 33, self-confessed right-wing zealot and systems analyst

Jesus was a man whose life was remarkable in every way. His words are clear and his character credible. He said grace is the only solution, and when I look honestly at myself, I know this has to be true. I can either trust the promises he made regarding my eternity, or try to convince myself Jesus is merely the most intricate and successful conspiracy the world has ever seen. Fortunately, I am not into conspiracy theories.

### Mick, 42, part-time church planter

Recently I haven't been able to get past Paul's description of Jesus as the God "in whom we live and move and have our being". Doesn't leave out much, does it? Jesus fills everything in every way. He's not just the most important person in my life; he is life itself.

### Milly, 12, budding author

Okay. Jesus … Wow. He is the best thing that's ever happened to me. When I look back at the past few years, it's astonishing how different my life has become because of him. A lot of people just overlook Christianity as old-fashioned and all about being good, but it is so much more than that. It's so much deeper and passionate. The Bible is an amazing story, all pointing to Christ Jesus, but so many people don't know that. I can't even begin to explain how amazing Jesus is. (It would take a lot more than the words I'm limited to here!) But I can say that it is definitely worth having him in your life as your Saviour and King.

### MJ, 37, master's student, wife and mum

The intriguing thing about Jesus, when you take a close look at who he is, what he did and said, is how surprisingly radical he is. Sometimes harsh, sometimes cutting, and yet immensely compassionate and approachable. He didn't suffer fools gladly and was in amongst the grime of humanity, getting his hands dirty. Rebellious to the authority, cavorting with lowlife, and friend to the sick, poor and lost. He's a slap in the face and a hand outstretched in rescue and a comfort all at the same time. Eternally curious and compelling.

### Norm, 30, senior management

As I get older, I realise that I know very little about Jesus. What do I know? I know that Jesus is the reason I can tell my kids that everything is all right even though the world is pretty complex and sometimes things happen that are hard to understand. They know, and I know, that I don't have all the answers, that I cannot predict all that will happen, and that I won't be on this earth forever. But Jesus does get what is happening and will be around forever. And so this is what I say about Jesus to my kids: Be wise; get to know God. It's not that life is always easier necessarily, but you end up having a sense of why you're here and knowing what is important in life. You get stretched to be the very best you can be and encouraged to bring out the best in others. And you end up realising that while you may not know heaps about him, what you do know makes this journey an extraordinary one.

### JR, 42, psychologist

Being Christian didn't come naturally for me. My family didn't bring me up to be Christian – I wasn't taken to church as a kid or sent to a school where Jesus was taught. I still remember my amazement when I met some people who actually took Jesus seriously. When I made a decision to become a follower of Jesus, it did take an amount of faith. But not blind faith – it was more like faith, common sense and reasoning all coming together at the same time. On reflection, I now think it takes quite an amount of faith to deny the reality of Jesus.

### Simon, 52, pastor, teacher and grandfather

Jesus always breaks the rules, but he always does the right thing. I am continually surprised at just how different Jesus is to the Jesus imagined, anticipated or often preferred. He, like Aslan, isn't a domestic or tamed Lord – on the contrary. It is we who need to get out of the way, not he.

### Sue, 60, midwife

Jesus was in the beginning and will be forever in the present. He is a wonderful gift to live with.

## Walt, 43, manager

I like the guys on the road to Emmaus, written about at the end of Luke's gospel. Jesus was dead and gone. They felt down and out. But they met a man, walked and talked with him, and eventually realised that it was Jesus. He was back and was with them again. And it says, their hearts "burned." What a moment. What a message. He came back. And he walks and talks with us. His presence doesn't just lift us up out of a slump, he makes our hearts come alive. And the world begins to make some sense.

Hey, mate. There's no more pages. That's the end.                                                                    — Pete

Yep.                                                                    — Ben

So ... you wanna do another book?                                                                    — Pete

Sure. How about a history of the great Australian Christian rock bands of the ...                                                                    — Ben

Oh, for goodness' sake!                                                                    — Pete

We want to hear from you. Please send your comments about this book to us in care of zreview@zondervan.com. Thank you.

ZONDERVAN.com/
**AUTHORTRACKER**
*follow your favorite authors*